The Ghetto

The Ghetto

LOUIS WIRTH

WOODCUT ILLUSTRATIONS
BY TODROS GELLER

THE UNIVERSITY OF CHICAGO PRESS
CHICAGO AND LONDON

The University of Chicago Press, Chicago 60637
The University of Chicago Press, Ltd., London

ISBN: 0-226-90252-8
LCN: 56-14116

TO MARY

FOREWORD

The ghetto seems to have been originally a place in Venice, a quarter of the city in which the first Jewish settlement was located. It became, in the course of time, an institution recognized in custom and defined in law. It became, in short, not merely the place in which Jews lived, but the place in which they were compelled to live. The walls of that ghetto have long since crumbled, but the ghost of the ancient institution lingers. It is still a place of refuge for the masses of the Jewish people and still imposes upon them, for good and for ill, something of the ancient isolation.

Meanwhile other alien peoples have come among us who have sought, or had imposed upon them, the same sort of isolation. Our great cities turn out, upon examination, to be a mosaic of segregated peoples—differing in race, in culture, or merely in cult—each seeking to preserve its peculiar cultural forms and to maintain its individual and unique conceptions of life. Every one of these segregated groups inevitably seeks, in order to maintain the integrity of its own group life, to impose upon its member some kind of moral isolation. So far as segregation becomes for them a means to that end, every people and every cultural group may be said to create and maintain its own ghetto. In this way the ghetto becomes the physical symbol for that sort of moral isolation which the "assimilationists," so called, are seeking to break down.

It is in this sense that the word is used in this volume. "Ghetto," as it is here conceived, is no longer a term that is limited in its application to the Jewish people. It has come into use in recent times as a common noun—a term which applies to any segregated racial or cultural group. The ghetto, as it is here conceived, owes its existence, not to legal enactment, but to the fact that it meets a need and performs a social function. The ghetto is, in short, one of the so-called "natural areas" of the city.

The casual observer, looking over this vast complex, the modern metropolitan city, is likely to see it as a mere congeries of physical structures, institutions, and peoples contiguous in space, bound together in some sort of mechanical fashion, but in no sense a whole consisting of organically related parts. This impression finds an indirect expression in the familiar statement "God made the country, but man made the town." Nowhere else, in fact, is the order which exists so manifestly the order imposed by man's intelligence and design; nowhere else has man shown himself more completely the master of the world in which he lives.

On the other hand, nothing is more certain, as recent studies of the urban community have shown, than the fact that the city as it exists is very largely the product of tendencies of which we have as yet little knowledge and less control. Under the influence of these forces, and within the limitation which geography and historical accident impose, the city is steadily assuming a form that is not conventional merely, but typical. In short, the city is not merely an artefact, but an organism. Its growth is, fundamentally and as a whole, natural, i.e., uncontrolled and undesigned. The forms it tends to assume are those which represent and correspond to the functions that it is called upon to perform.

What have been called the "natural areas of the city" are simply those regions whose locations, character, and functions have been determined by the same forces which have determined the character and functions of the city as a whole. The ghetto is one of those natural areas. The historical ghetto, with which this study is mainly concerned, is merely the one most striking example of a type. It is in the history of the Jews, in the Diaspora, that we have access to a body of facts which exhibit in convincing detail the moral and cultural consequences of that isolation which the ghetto enforced; consequences that touch both those who live within and those who live without the pale. The history of the ghetto is, in large measure, the history, since the dispersion, of the Jewish people.

The ghetto has been the center of all that may be described as sectarian and provincial of Jewish life. It has put its imprint, not only upon the manners of the Jew, but upon his character. It is the interaction of this culture of the ghetto and that of the larger gentile community outside, involving the more or less complete participation of Jews in both worlds, that is the source of most that is problematic and enigmatic in the situation of the Jew of today, as of yesterday. And so it has turned out that this attempt to investigate, in its more fundamental and permanent aspects, one of the typical local areas of the Chicago urban community has led to the exploration of one of the most fundamental problems in sociology, and in doing this it has thrown a new light upon one of the puzzling and tragic situations in history.

ROBERT E. PARK

PREFACE

This study was made possible through a research fellowship granted by the Laura Spelman Rockefeller Memorial Fund and administered by the Local Community Research Committee of the University of Chicago. It originated in an investigation of the ghetto district of Chicago. The attempt to understand the life in that area, however, soon led to a redefinition of the subject into the form in which it is now presented. Having started with the study of a geographical area, I found myself, quite unwittingly, examining the natural history of an institution and the psychology of a people.

Much of what I have written is probably traceable to sources which I have forgotten, or is the echo of what I have read and read into the writings of others. There are numerous obligations, however, of which I am keenly conscious. My debt to such writers as David Philipson, Israel Abrahams, and Israel Cohen is greater than the numerous citations from their writings indicate. To Professor Ernest W. Burgess, at whose suggestion the study was begun, to Professor Ellsworth Faris, and to Professor Robert E. Park, my teachers and former colleagues in the Department of Sociology of the University of Chicago, I wish to express my gratitude for their aid, encouragement, and guidance. Without the constant interest and inspiration of Professor Park this work would not have been the pleasant adventure which it was.

LOUIS WIRTH

CONTENTS

CHAPTER I

This study is an attempt to understand some of the details of the cultural life of a group that has a long history. The history of the Jews for the past one thousand years furnishes an opportunity to study the ways in which the culture of a group reacts upon the character of a people, and conversely, the mutations that take place in a culture as a result of the changing experiences of a people. The story of the Jews for this period is the story of the ghetto.

THE CONCEPT "GHETTO"

The word "ghetto" applies to the Jewish quarter of a city. The origin of the word is not clear, although it has been in common usage for at least five hundred years. It is fairly certain, however, that ghettos existed long before they were designated by a specific name. What is known about the origin of the word may nevertheless be of some value in determining the original character if not the approximate beginning of the historical phenomenon to which it refers.

It seems to have been first in use in Italy, and its form points to Italian origin. The Italian Jews, however, derived the word which they spelled *gueto* from the Hebrew word *get*, meaning bill of divorce, "finding the idea of divorce expressed by the one term, and that of exclusion in the other, sufficiently analogous to point to a common origin."[1] The word "ghetto," according to another explanation, has been connected with the German word *gitter*. While this is suggestive, since, as we shall show later, the ghetto did bear

[1] David Philipson, *Old European Jewries* (Philadelphia, 1894), p. 24.

I

some resemblance to the bars of a cage, it seems to be, on the whole, a rather far-fetched and ill-founded explanation. The word might also be derived from the Italian *borghetto* or "little quarter." The evidence for this is scant, however. It is more probable that the word is derived from the Italian *gietto*, the cannon foundry at Venice near which the first Jewish settlement was located.[1] The Jewish historians H. Graetz and A. Berliner[2] lean toward the derivation from the Venetian *gheta*, or cannon foundry. It is not unusual that a local place name should come into general use to designate similar phenomena. Berliner mentions the illustration of the word "catacombs," derived from the first subterranean burial vaults at Rome, which were situated *ad Catacombas*.[3]

Historically, then, the modern ghetto traces its ancestry

[1] The *Jewish Encyclopedia*, one of the most authoritative works on such matters, says: " 'Ghetto' is probably of Italian origin, although no Italian dictionary gives any clue to its etymology. In documents dating back to 1090 the streets in Venice and Salerno assigned to the Jews are called *Judaca* or *Judacaria*. At Capua there was a place called "San Nicolo ad Judaicam," according to documents of the year 1375; and as late as the eighteenth century another place was called "San Martino ad Judaicam." Hence it is assumed that *Judaicam* became the Italian *Giudeica*, and was then corrupted into "Ghetto." Other scholars derive the word from *gietto*, the cannon foundry at Venice, near which the first Jews' quarter was situated. Both of these opinions are open to the objection that the word is pronounced "ghetto," and not "getto" (djetto); and it seems probable that, even if either of the two words suggested had become corrupted in the vernacular, at least its first letter, the sound of which is the dominating one in the word, would have retained its original pronunciation. A few scholars, therefore, derive the word "ghetto" from the Talmudic *get*, which is similar in sound, and suppose the term to have been used first by the Jews, and then generally. It seems improbable, however, that a word originating with a small despised minority of the people should have been generally adopted and even introduced into literature" (*Jewish Encyclopedia*, V [1903 ed.], 652).

[2] H. Graetz, *Geschichte der Juden*, V, 37; A. Berliner, *Aus den letzten Tagen der römischen Ghetto*, Berlin, 1886.

[3] Berliner, *op. cit.*, p. 2.

back to a medieval European urban institution by means
of which the Jews were segregated from the rest of the population. Other names were originally, and to some extent
still are, in use today to refer to the street or quarter of a
city occupied by Jews. These are *vicus Judaeorum*, later
known as *Judenstrasse, Judengasse* (or just *Gasse*) or *Juden-
viertel* in Germany; *Judiaria* in Portugal; *Juiverie* in France;
and *Carriera* in Provence and Comtat Venaissin.[1]

The varied local names applied to the ghetto from
country to country indicate that by the close of the fourteenth century there already existed in many of the European cities clearly defined areas, predominantly if not exclusively inhabited by Jews. Just as the term ghetto in the
course of time was generally adopted, so the form which the
institution took soon became conventionalized and stand-
ardized throughout Europe.

In Russia, until recently, the ghetto took the form of
the "Pale." This pale of settlement virtually represents a
ghetto within a ghetto. It was established in 1771, to prevent the Jews of White Russia, who came under Russian
dominion at the first partition of Poland, from spreading
throughout the country. While its boundaries have varied,
in 1905 it contained the following fifteen districts: Bess-
arabia, Vilna, Vitebsk, Volhynia, Grodno, Yokaterinoslav,
Kovno, Minsk, Moghilef, Podolia, Poltava, Taurida, Kher-
son, Chernigov, and Kiev. Within these districts, moreover,
the Jewish settlements were restricted to the cities and
towns. The regulations pertaining to the settlement of Jews
prohibited them from living at all in the rest of Russia,
though at some time certain population groups were ex-
cepted, among them graduates from universities, merchants

[1] Philipson, *op. cit.*, pp. 20, 30.

of the first guild, and prostitutes. The Jews were permitted to
live in Poland, but were entirely excluded, for instance, from
Finland, and, except in the case of convicts, from Siberia.[1]

In modern times the word "ghetto" applies not specifically to the place of officially regulated settlement of the
Jews, but rather to those local cultural areas which have
arisen in the course of time or are voluntarily selected or
built up by them. It applies particularly to those areas
where the poorest and most backward group of the Jewish
population of the towns and cities resides. In our American
cities the ghetto refers particularly to the area of first settlement, i.e., those sections of the cities where the immigrant
finds his home shortly after his arrival in America. Sometimes the area in which the Jews once lived but which is
subsequently inhabited by other population groups, particularly immigrants, still retains the designation of ghetto.
Moreover, there seems to be a tendency to refer to immigrant quarters in general as ghettos.

From the standpoint of the sociologist the ghetto as an
institution is of interest first of all because it represents a
prolonged case of social isolation. It is the result of the effort of a people to adjust itself, outwardly at least, to
strangers among whom they have settled. The ghetto, therefore, may be regarded as a form of accommodation between
divergent population groups, through which one group has
effectually subordinated itself to another. It represents at
least one historical form of dealing with a dissenting minority within a larger population. At the same time it is a form
of toleration through which a *modus vivendi* is established
between groups that are in conflict with each other on funda-

[1] Philipson, *op. cit.*, chap. vii. See also *Encyclopedia Americana*, XXI
(1919 ed.), 138.

mental issues. Finally, from the administrative standpoint, the ghetto served as an instrument of control.

Some of these functions, as we shall see, are still being served by the modern ghetto, which, in other respects, has a character quite distinct from the medieval institution out of which it has developed. The ghetto of Western Europe and of America, however, is of primary interest because it shows concretely the actual processes of distribution and grouping of our population in urban communities. It illustrates picturesquely the ways in which a cultural group gives expression to its ancient heritage when transplanted to a foreign setting, the constant sifting and resifting of its members, and the forces through which the community maintains its integrity and continuity. Finally, the ghetto demonstrates the subtle ways in which this cultural community is transformed by degrees until it blends with the larger community about it, meanwhile reappearing in various altered guises of its old and unmistakable atmosphere.

THE NATURAL HISTORY OF THE GHETTO

The ghetto has a written history extending over a period of at least one thousand years. Even before the ghetto became the characteristic form of Jewish community life we find a richly documented history of Jewish settlements that takes us back to the days before the opening of the Christian era. The adventures of the Jewish people since the end of their national sovereignty, which a recent writer has retold under the fitting title, *Stranger than Fiction*,[1] find their setting in every country of Europe, and in almost every corner of the globe. The history of the ghetto offers a rare opportunity, therefore, of converting history into natural history.

[1] Lewis Browne, *Stranger than Fiction*. New York, 1925.

The numerous narratives of ghetto life, the vivid auto-
biographies, the drama, the fiction, and the poetry of the
ghetto; the reports of travelers, the reflections of philosophers, and the argumentation and pronouncements of rabbis
and Talmudists—all these go to make up not merely a history of the ghetto; they also furnish the raw material for a
searching comparative study of an institution—a cultural
community. As we link up an isolated fact and a strikingly
unique detail of ghetto life of one period with that of another,
and of one locality with that of another, we see emerging
similarities in lines of development that furnish the basis for
generalizations, for class concepts, and for sociological laws.
It is with this object in view that we undertake to retell the
story of the ghetto, not confining ourselves merely to a single
community or epoch, but searching for those more universal
truths that hold good irrespective of time and place.

The study of the ghetto, viewed from such an angle, is
likely to throw light on a number of related phenomena, such
as the origin of segregated areas and the development of
cultural communities in general; for, while the ghetto is,
strictly speaking, a Jewish institution, there are forms of
ghettos that concern not merely Jews. There are Little
Sicilies, Little Polands, Chinatowns, and Black belts in our
large cities, and there are segregated areas, such as vice
areas, that bear a close resemblance to the Jewish ghetto.
These forms of community life are likely to become more
intelligible to us if we have before us the natural history of
the Jewish ghetto. The ghetto may therefore be regarded as
typical of a number of other forms of community life that
sociologists are attempting to explore.

In our study of the ghetto we obviously need not allow
ourselves to be swamped by the mass of details that the

material affords, nor need we become involved in the niceties of higher historical criticism. Our task is to reduce the material to a form in which it is stripped of its unique character and becomes typical, or of general significance. At first glance the world of individual experience consists of an endless multiplicity of isolated happenings. Every experience is, in a sense, unique. Only by linking unique phenomena to previous points of reference in the experience of the individual or the culture of the group is some sort of order achieved. By means of an ordered system of reference we are able to reduce the baffling complexity and variety of unique phenomena to a plane where they can be encompassed by the mind. In this process the unique or individual experience is transformed into a representative or typical one.

The enviable rate of progress in the physical and natural sciences is due mainly to the economy of thought and effort resulting from the concentration on crucial experiments and observations. Random observation and experimentation have been recognized as expensive and wasteful. By limiting the locus of observation and choosing the data of experimentation results may be obtained which have significance for a whole class, and not merely for the individual case. On the basis of similarity the results obtained from one experiment may be supposed to hold for a host of related phenomena, provided the nonessential differences between them can be ruled out for the moment.

This, then, will be our procedure in tracing the development of the ghetto from its earliest beginning to the present day in the various localities where Jews gained a sufficient foothold to form typical communities, each having, of course, its own peculiar atmosphere, but all having enough in common to be readily recognizable as forms of the general type of cultural expression characteristic of the group as a whole.

HUMAN NATURE AND THE GHETTO

As the sympathetic historians tell the story of the ghetto it is an amazing record of the tragedies and the adventures of a people. The history of the ghetto is full of human interest, with its peaks of heroism, its miraculous tales of escape, and its frequent and depressing depths of pathos and despair. To tell the full story of the ghetto in all its uniqueness is the legitimate function of the artist and the historian. But the sociologist sees in the ghetto more than the experiences of a given people in a specific historical setting. To him the ghetto is more than a chapter in the cultural history of man. The ghetto represents a study in human nature. It reveals the varied and subtle motives that lead men to act as they do. The sociologist is less interested in the decrees issued by sovereigns and legislatures than he is in the fundamental motives which prompt them and the human relations of which they are a formal expression.

The ghetto is not only a physical fact; it is also a state of mind. The laws that regulated the conduct of Jews and Christians are merely the external forms to which, on the subjective side, there correspond the attitudes of social distance and of self- and group-consciousness. The hostilities and outbreaks of violence with which ghetto history is replete represent the friction and the conflicts to which the living together of diverse cultural groups gives rise. The numerous taboos and restrictions that encumbered the behavior of Jew and Christian toward each other are to be regarded, not merely as the fortuitous and arbitrary decisions of members of either group, but rather as physical expressions of the social distance that was emerging out of a conflict relationship. The conduct of the two groups toward each other did not only involve withdrawal and repulsion, but these were modified by the tendency to become friendly and be attracted. While on the one hand the Jew was coming to be more and more a member of a class—an abstraction —on the other hand there persisted the tendency to react to him as a human being—as a person. The play of these conflicting forces in the interaction of Jew and Gentile constitutes the central thread in the story of the ghetto.

The history of the ghetto from our point of view is the history of an institution. The various stages in the process by which an institution is formed; the fundamental human motives that express themselves in it; the forces that modify it and perpetuate it and finally contribute to its dissolution —these are some of the problems on which we hope to throw light through a study of the ghetto. The history of the ghetto may show the various processes that enter into the origin and the growth of community life in general and the ways in which the community fashions the personality types and the cultural institutions that it harbors. In every community there goes on a process of specialization and integration resulting in the division of labor and co-operation which tie the life within an area into a unit and give it its organized character. The ghetto presents the development of such a community in minute detail, offering an opportunity for observation and generalization.

What we seek to find in the ghetto, finally, is the extent to which isolation has shaped the character of the Jew and the nature of his social life. What are the forces that maintain this isolation, and in what ways has it become modified by contact? How has the isolation of the Jews produced results that hold good, not only for the Jew, but for the Negro, the Chinaman, the immigrant, and a number of other isolated groups in our modern world? While we are concerned mainly with the Jew and the Jewish ghetto in the following pages, and have drawn our material from the history of this one institution, the processes that go on, the motives that are at work, and the consequences that follow are intended to throw light on a much broader subject—on human nature and on culture.

CHAPTER II
THE ORIGIN OF THE GHETTO
SEEKING NEW HOMES

With the year 70 A.D., when the Romans accomplished the conquest of Palestine and the destruction of Jerusalem, begins the period of *diaspora*, or dispersion. With this event there opens up in Jewish history a long chapter of migration and the search for new homes. Not that the Jews were confined to Palestine up to this time, for tradition has it that the Jews were in Italy, Spain, and Germany long before; and it is definitely established that the Jews lived in Alexandria, Antioch, Rome, and the cities of Asia Minor and Egypt before the opening of the Christian era.[1] The Jews were probably not settled anywhere in Europe in any considerable numbers, however, before that time, except in Rome, where they are heard of as early as 76 B.C. The Jewish colony there was considerably increased when the Roman general Pompey entered Jerusalem and carried numbers of Jews back to Rome. Titus deported thousands of Jews to the western Roman provinces. Many of them were put to work in the Sardinian mines, and from Rome they drifted to other Italian cities. "As for Spain," says Philipson, "the earliest authentic notice is by the apostle Paul, who, in his Epistle to the Romans, says: 'Whensoever I take my journey into Spain, I will come to you; for I trust to see you in my journey, and to be brought on my way thitherward by you'; and 'I will come by you into Spain.' Paul, we know,

[1] Frederic Huidekoper: *Judaism at Rome, B.C. 76 to A.D. 140* (New York, 1883), p. 6; David Philipson, *op. cit.*, p. 5.

journeyed only to places in which Jews dwelt, or in which Jewish teachings had been established, for only those acquainted with Jewish doctrines could understand him."[1]

The best evidence for the early presence of the Jews in the western Christian lands is to be found in the numerous decrees passed by church councils affecting them. The presence of Jews in considerable numbers in Spain by the beginning of the fourth century is attested to by the fact that a church council held in the year 305 A.D. passed several decrees forbidding Christians to live on terms of intimacy with Jews. A section of one of these decrees reads: "If heretics are unwilling to join the Catholic Church, Catholic girls must not be given to them in marriage; but neither to Jews nor to heretics should they be given, because there can be no association for the faithful with the unbeliever. If parents act contrary to this prohibition, they shall be cut off from communion for five years."[2] Another says: "If, then, any ecclesiastic or any of the faithful partakes of food with Jews, he shall be deprived of communion so that this may be corrected."[3] And again: "Owners [of land] are warned not to permit their products which they receive from God to be blessed by Jews, lest they make our blessing useless and weak. If any one shall presume to do this after this prohibition, he shall be excluded from the church."[4]

Joseph Jacobs[5] finds evidence of the presence of Jews in England before the Norman conquest in the canon laws of

[1] Philipson, *op. cit.*, pp. 6-7. See also Rom. 15:24, 28.

[2] Labbe et Cosartii, *Concilia Sacrosancta*, I, 1273-76; also *Conciliarum omnium generalium et provincialium collectio regia*, I, 645. Quoted from Philipson, *op. cit.*, p. 7.

[3] *Ibid.*, p. 8.   [4] *Ibid.*

[5] *The Jews of Angevin England* (London, 1893), pp. ix and 2-3.

the archbishops of Canterbury and of York from 669 on:
"A document issued by King Witglaff of Mercia, in 833, con-
firms the right of the monks of the cloister of Croyland to
all the possessions given them by earlier Kings of Mercia,
nobles, and other faithful Christians, and also to those received from Jews as gift, pledge or otherwise."[1]

The settlement of the Jews in France is placed as early
as the second century.[2] In the various trading centers of
Western and Southern Germany, such as Cologne, Magde-
burg, Ratisbon, Mayence, Speyer, Worms, Treves, Nuremberg, the Jews are found some time around the eleventh
century in considerable numbers,[3] although their presence
may here and there be established at a much earlier date.[4]

In all these countries the Jews, during this early period,
led a precarious existence. The uncertainty of life during
the Dark Ages, particularly for strangers, made the Jew a
nomad, and has earned for him the epithet "Wandering
Jew." Mobility and adaptability to strange and constantly
shifting conditions were the chief qualities required for survival. The Jewish traditions of this period are full of tales
of suffering and adventure, of heroic exploits, and of shrewd
dealing with none too friendly neighbors and rulers. The
measures adopted by the Jews in self-defense closely parallel
some of the rationalizations and myths invented to meet
such present-day crises as the Nordic propaganda. Philipson
tells of two of these:

According to tradition, Jews settled in Germany in hoary antiq-
uity. When, in the time of the crusades, the Jews of Western Europe

[1] Philipson, *op. cit.*, pp. 10-11.   [2] Graetz, *op. cit.*, V, 55-56.

[3] Otto Stobbe, *Die Juden in Deutschland während des Mittelalters*. Braun-
schweig, 1866.

[4] G. B. Depping, *Les Juifs dans le Moyen Age* (Paris, 1834), p. 4.

were held responsible for the death of Jesus, and thousands upon thousands of them were slaughtered by the wild mobs on that account, some tale had to be invented to disprove the charge, and the Jews put forth the claim that they had had a congregation in Worms long before the time of Jesus; in fact, as early as the days of Ezra, and that, therefore, they were not concerned with nor responsible for the crucifixion.[1]

According to another tradition, the Jews of Southern Germany were descendants of the soldiers who had sacked Jerusalem. These soldiers, the Vangiones—so ran the story—had selected beautiful Jewish women as their portion of the spoil, carried them to their quarters on the Rhine and the Main, and there consorted with them. Their children were reared as Jews by their mothers, and were the founders of the Jewish communities between Worms and Mayence. This, however, is all legendary.[2]

Leading a life full of uncertainty, the Jews were scarcely more than transients in Western Europe during the darker centuries of the Middle Ages, regarding their settlements, such as they were, as mere stopping-places on a road that led they knew not where. In his rôle of stranger the Jew left, however, more than a passing impression upon his hosts. "That the Jews were the great scientific, commercial, and philosophical intermediaries of the Middle Ages is not denied," says the distinguished English Jewish scholar, Israel Abrahams, "but what is not usually admitted is, how much of progress consists simply in the transmission of ideas and the exchange of articles of commerce..... To assert for the Jews this claim—that they were intermediaries of ideas as well as commercial products—is, I submit, to claim for them a great and not ignoble rôle."[3]

[1] Philipson, *op. cit.*, p. 9.

[2] *Ibid.*, pp. 9–10.

[3] Israel Abrahams, *Jewish Life in the Middle Ages* (New York, 1897), pp. xx–xxi.

THE JEW AS A STRANGER

Compared with what was to follow, the lot of the Jews in Europe during the first one thousand years of the Christian era was bearable if not ideal. With the beginning of the Crusades, however, there set in a sharp reaction of the general population. Not that there were no persecutions before 1096, but they were sporadic and mild compared to the persistent and organized mob violence that began with the First Crusade. Up to that time the Jews were free individuals, on the whole, and lived generally on friendly, and sometimes even on intimate, terms with their neighbors of other faiths. The decrees of many church councils forbidding this intimacy corroborate this. The spectacular mass movements accompanying the Crusades upset the settled life of medieval Europe. Suddenly the population became aware of the strangers in their midst. It needed but little stimulation to transform these strangers into enemies, especially at a time when a scapegoat was needed to give concrete and immediate expression to the remote and idealistic goals of pilgrimages to and conquest of the Holy Land, in which, after all, only a minority could participate. In this predicament the Jews turned to those who were not their neighbors and who were far enough removed in space and station to see them objectively—as a utility; they turned to the emperors and popes for protection. They became the servants of the chamber (*servi camerae*)[1] and acquired formal and impersonal *rights*, which assured them of some sort of status in a society in which every member of the population had a fixed place. The medieval serf was tied to his lord, the tenant to the land which he tilled, the craftsman to his guild. Only the Jew's place in this world was not definitely fixed. He

[1] Philipson, *op. cit.*, pp. 12–13.

was a stranger, but he lived on terms of intimacy with his neighbors. Personal relationships are not based upon rights; it is only when relationships become formal and distant that rights and laws are invoked to regulate the conduct of individuals. As a person the Jew needed no rights to protect him; but as a utility he needed them and acquired them. Empty as this protection often was, and in spite of the instability of the sovereigns who sold it at a high price, the Jews nevertheless regarded it as a privilege. According to Graetz, this protection began in Germany, with Frederick Barbarossa, and was continued under Henry IV, in 1103. During the reign of Conrad III, at the time of the Second Crusade, the Jews applied to him for protection in Nuremberg.[1] The institution of *servi camerae* came into general use, however, in the thirteenth century.[2] There still remains in the Jewish prayer books a special prayer for the sovereign which is based upon this medieval institution.

As Europe emerges from the medieval period, the Jews pass more and more emphatically into a special relation toward the government. Instead of becoming a part of the general population, as the Jews had often been in the earlier centuries of the Christian era, they are thrust out of the general life into a distinct category. One has but to compare the Prayer for the Queen as it still appears in the Anglo-Jewish ritual with its form in the Book of Common Prayer. "May the supreme King of kings," says the Jewish version, "in his mercy put compassion into her heart and into the hearts of her counsellors and nobles, that they may deal kindly with us and with all Israel." The modern Jew resents this language, but it cannot be denied that its medieval tone remains the keynote of millions of Jewish lives.[3]

The Jews, on their part, were seeking status and security while the rulers looked upon them as mere sources of

[1] Graetz, *op. cit.*, VI, 269. [2] Stobbe, *op. cit.*, p. 12.
[3] Abrahams, *op. cit.*, pp. xvii–xviii.

revenue. One of them, Emperor Rupert, in 1407 "commanded that the Jews be not too heavily burdened, lest they be forced to emigrate, and the cities so suffer a diminution of income. In 1480 Frederick III commanded that the Jews of Ratisbon be treated in such a manner that they might restore their fortunes in five years to an extent sufficient to enable them to pay the emperor 10,000 gulden."[1] The Jews, as a result, virtually became the tax collectors for the rulers, since, of course, the necessity of having to pay this tribute affected their charges for goods or services which they were rendering to the population at large. The Jews, through this relationship to the government, proved themselves so desirable that the emperor often found it expedient, when in financial distress, to sell the privilege of protecting the Jews, which meant to tax them, to some prince or churchman. Thus, in 1263, the Jews of Worms were turned over to the Bishop of Speyer, and in 1279 the Jews of Strassburg and Basle were transferred to the Bishop of Basle. This right was sometimes sold to private individuals and to cities, and became one of the important fiscal assets of medieval sovereigns.[2] Generally the Jews also had to buy the right to live in a community in which they had not as yet lived. This was known as the right of *Judaeos tenere* or *Judaeos habere*. This right of keeping or holding Jews that the emperor was free to sell to local authorities or individuals, much as a city nowadays sells a street-car franchise, implied, of course, that the status of the Jews was a precarious one. They were not citizens—not even men—in the eyes of the law, but rather were taxable property. Even this right, as we shall see, was greatly limited and subject to the arbitrary change of will or fortune of the grantor. "The chattel of the ruler, the Jew

[1] Philipson, *op. cit.*, p. 15.   [2] Stobbe, *op. cit.*, p. 19.

had no room for hope but in the ruler's personal clemency
and humanity."[1] This status did not change in fundamental respects until about the era of the French Revolution.

The earliest history of the Jews in Europe shows a
gradual transition from the personal, spontaneous relationship that naturally had grown up between Jew and Christian
to a formal, legalistic, abstract form of intercourse. This
transition began as soon as the ordinary, primary contacts,
through which neighborhood and community life ordinarily
are maintained, broke down, and crises arose which called
for the intervention of the imperial or papal authority. In
the course of this change the Jew acquired a special status,
which not only heightened his own self-consciousness, but
marked him as a *tertium quid* in the eyes of his neighbors.

THE VOLUNTARY GHETTO

The segregation of the Jews into separate local areas in
the medieval cities did not originate with any formal edict
of church or state. The ghetto was not, as sometimes mis-
takenly is believed, the arbitrary creation of the authorities,
designed to deal with an alien people. The ghetto was not
the product of design, but rather the unwitting crystallization of needs and practices rooted in the customs and herit-
ages, religious and secular, of the Jews themselves. Long
before it was made compulsory the Jews lived in separate
parts of the cities in the Western lands, of their own accord.

Though the era of the ghetto proper begins with the sixteenth
century, numerous records are extant of the seclusion of Jews in special
quarters several centuries earlier. The *voluntary* congregation of Jews
in certain parts of the towns, due to the needs of the communal organization, was very common by the thirteenth century. In Cologne
there was a Jews' quarter at that period, though in that city, as well as

[1] Abrahams, *op. cit.*, p. xviii.

in most places where voluntary Jewish quarters existed, Jews also resided outside the Jewish district. But the distinction that one achieves is not as the distinction which is thrust on one. Nowhere is this more strikingly seen than in the case of Prague. There the Jews who lived outside the *Judenstadt* determined in 1473 to voluntarily throw in their lot with their brethren in the Jewish town. . . . . In 1555, when Paul IV established the ill-omened ghetto in Rome, there were very few Jewish families resident anywhere else than in the *serraglio delli hebrei*, or *septus hebraicus*, as the Jewish quarter at the left bank of the Tiber was called. But though few Jews dwelt elsewhere, many of the noblest Christians resided in the very heart of the Jewish quarter. Stately palaces and churches stood in the near neighborhood of the synagogue, and the Roman Christians held free and friendly intercourse with their Jewish fellow-inhabitants. . . . . At first the ghetto was rather a privilege than a disability, and sometimes was claimed as a right when its demolition was threatened.[1]

The Jews drifted into separate cultural areas not by external pressure nor by deliberate design. The factors that operated toward the founding of locally separated communities by the Jews are to be sought in the character of Jewish traditions, in the habits and customs not only of the Jews themselves, but those of the medieval town-dweller in general. To the Jews the geographically separated and socially isolated community seemed to offer the best opportunity for following their religious precepts, of preparing their food according to the established religious ritual, of following their dietary laws, of attending the synagogue for prayer three times a day, and of participating in the numerous functions of communal life which religious duty imposed upon every member of the community. In some instances it was the fear of the remainder of the population, perhaps, which induced them to seek each other's company for the sake of security. Sometimes the prince or ruler under whose pro-

Abrahams, *ob. cit.*, pp. 62–65.

tection they stood found it desirable to grant them a separate quarter for this purpose, as a privilege. The general tenor of medieval social life must also be reckoned with in this connection. It was customary for members of the same occupational group to live in the same street or locality, and the Jews, forming, as a whole, a separate vocational class and having a distinct economic status from the rest of the population, were merely falling in line, therefore, with the framework of medieval society.[1] In addition, there were the numerous ties of kinship and acquaintanceship which formed the basis of that *esprit de corps* which is a significant factor in developing community life. There was the element of a common language, of community of ideas and interests, and the bare congeniality that arises even between strangers who, coming from the same locality, meet in a strange environment.

The voluntary segregation of the Jews in ghettos had much in common with the segregation of Negroes and immigrants in modern cities, and was identical in many respects with the development of Bohemian and Hobohemian quarters in the urban community of today. The tolerance that strange ways of living need and find in immigrant colonies, in Latin quarters, in vice districts, and in other localities is a powerful factor in the sifting of the population and its allocation in separate cultural areas where one obtains freedom from hostile criticism and the backing of a group of kindred spirits.

Finally, the voluntary ghetto was an administrative device, at least in part. It facilitated social control on the

[1] See, for instance, Stobbe, *op. cit.*, p. 176; and Höniger, "Zur Geschichte der Juden im früheren Mittelalter," *Zeitschrift für die Geschichte der Juden in Deutschland*, I, 90.

part of the community over its members; it made tax collection much easier; and it made the supervision that medieval authorities exercised over all strangers and non-citizens possible.

The gradual transition from direct, spontaneous, personal, to indirect, formal, and legalistic relationships between the Jew and his Christian neighbors is indicated in the earliest document available granting to a local group of Jews a separate quarter. This first written charter emphasized the fact that a ghetto was being assigned to the Jews as a right. The security that comes with such written instruments can hardly be overestimated when it is remembered that the powers of the medieval authorities were almost unlimited and the person of the sovereign was likely to change frequently. It must be recalled, furthermore, that during the Middle Ages strangers were generally not allowed to remain in a community for any length of time, and were subjected to heavy taxation. In purchasing this right, however, the Jews both gained and lost something. They obtained the formal protection of a sovereign power, but they lost that personal relationship and self-evident status in the community which every member of a primary group enjoys without being conscious of any formal and legal right. The rights of residence and of trade which the Jews acquired marked a break with their former spontaneous symbiosis with their Christian neighbors and a transition to a secondary relationship in which they constituted a distinct class. The document reads as follows:

In the name of the holy and indivisible Trinity, when I, Rüdiger, also called Huozmann, Bishop of Speyer, changed the town of Speyer into a city, I thought that I would add to the honor of our place by bringing in Jews. Accordingly, I located them outside of the community and habitation of the other citizens, and that they might not readily be disturbed by the insolence of the populace, I surrounded them with a wall. Their place of habitation I had acquired in a just manner; the hill partly with money, partly by exchange; the valley I had received from [some] heirs as a gift. That place, I say, I gave over to them on the condition that they would pay three pounds and a half of the money of Speyer annually for the use of the [monastery] brothers. Within their dwelling place and outside thereof, up to the harbor of the ships, and in the harbor itself, I granted them full permission to change gold and silver; to buy and sell anything they pleased, and that same permission I gave them throughout the state. In addition, I gave them out of the property of the church a burial place with hereditary rights. I also granted the following rights: If any stranger Jew lodge with them [temporarily], he shall be free from tax. Further, just as the city governor adjudicates between citizens, so the head synagogue officer is to decide every case that may arise between Jews or against them. But if, by chance, he cannot decide, the case shall be brought before the bishop and his chamberlains. Night watches, guards, fortifications, they shall provide only for their own district, the guards, indeed, in common with the servants. Nurses and servants they shall be permitted to have from among us. Slaughtered meat which, according to their law, they are not permitted to eat, they can sell to Christians, and Christians may buy it. Finally, as the crowning mark of kindness, I have given them laws better than the Jewish people has in any city of the German empire.

Lest any of my successors diminish this favor and privilege, or force them to pay greater tribute, on the plea that they acquired their favorable status unjustly, and did not receive it from a bishop, I left this document as a testimony of the above-mentioned favors. And that the remembrance of this matter may last through the centuries, I have corroborated it under my hand and seal, as may be seen below.

Given on the fifteenth of September, in the year of the Incarnation 1084, in the twelfth year since the above-mentioned bishop commenced to rule in this state.[1]

The concessions granted to the Jews of Speyer in this document were notable, and, as the bishop states, more favorable than elsewhere. It gave them local autonomy,

[1] *Orient* (1842), p. 391. Quoted from Philipson, *op. cit.*, pp. 36–38.

with juridical powers vested in the hands of the Jewish communal authorities themselves, which the Jews generally did not acquire until considerably later. The document furthermore defines their economic relations to the general population, which, for instance, permitted the Jews to have servants from the Christian population for their necessary services in the synagogue and the homes during the Sabbath, and at other required times, and to sell to the Christians that part of the meat (generally the hind part of the carcass) which the Jews were not permitted to eat. Without the privilege of disposing of this, meat consumption among the Jews would have been a very expensive indulgence. All these circumstances fostered the development of autonomous Jewish institutions, and gave the organized community such control over its members as to assure its continuity and reduce the individual to a state of dependence upon community life which made for effective subordination and strict discipline. The physical barrier which the document calls for, in the form of a wall, was characteristic and was indicative of the insecurity of town life in the Middle Ages. That the Jews did actually look upon this protection as a privilege is indicated by the fact that the Jews, in instances when the demolition of the ghetto was threatened, resisted these attempts, and sometimes repurchased their right to a separate residence at considerable cost to the community.[1]

The document just cited indicates that the Jews, from the standpoint of the ruler, were a mere utility. Just as contract labor may be imported to a community, so the Jews were brought in because, as the Bishop says, they "would add to the honor of our place," and served a number

[1] See Abrahams, *op. cit.*, p. 65.

of functions which the inhabitants of the town were incapable of exercising. The Jews were allowed to trade and engage in exchange—occupations which the church did not permit Christians to engage in. Besides, the Jews were valuable taxable property and could be relied upon to furnish much needed revenue. On the other hand, the Jews, too, regarded the Christian population as a means to an end—as a utility. The Christians could perform functions such as eating the hind quarters of beef, and could purchase the commodities that the Jews had for sale; they could borrow money from Jews, and pay interest. The Christians could perform services for the Jew, such as lighting his fires on the Sabbath and holidays, which the Jew himself was not allowed to undertake by his strict religious ritual. In the religious and the social life of both groups, then, we find those factors which are responsible for the genesis of a relationship of utility between the two groups. This was quite in accord with the whole tenor of medieval life when the place of every individual in a community was rigidly defined, and the functions of each class were definitely circumscribed by custom and by law.

As the life of the Jews changed, it became more and more, what life always is, an adaptation to the physical and social surroundings of a locality. In the locality in which the Jews now found themselves, everyone was tied to something—the soil, the feudal lord, the house in which he and his ancestors lived, or the guild of which he was a member. In this rigid structure the Jews found a strategic place. The attitude of the medieval church had coupled trade and finance with sin. The Jews were at least free from these taboos, which made the occupation of merchant and banker seem undesirable to the Christian population. The Christian churchmen were not troubled about the "perils of the Jewish soul," for, as far as they knew, the Jew had no soul to be saved, since he was damned anyway.

What made the trade relationships possible, however, was not merely the fact that they were mutually advantageous, since they offered a living to the Jew, and prosperity and revenue to the community at large, but the fact that trade relationships are possible when no other form of contact between two peoples can take place. Trade is an abstract relationship, a form of symbiosis, physical rather than social in its nature. It is rational, and the emotions drop into the background. One can trade with one's enemies because trade involves none of the elements of personal prejudice. The less personal, the less emotional, and the more impersonal and the more abstract the attitude of the trader, the more efficiently and successfully can he exercise his function. One cannot very easily trade with relatives and friends, because personal considerations interfere with the abstractions on which trade rests.

The Jew being a stranger, and belonging, as he did, to a separate and distinct class, was admirably fitted to become the merchant and banker. He drifted to the towns and cities where trade was possible and profitable. Here he could utilize all the distant contacts that he had developed in the course of his wanderings. His attachment to the community at large was slight. As a result he was free from sentiment, and when necessity demanded it he could migrate to a locality where opportunities were greater. He had no real property to which he was tied, nor was he the serf of a feudal lord. His mobility in turn developed versatility. He had a sense of perspective, and his ignorance of local traditions and taboos enabled him to discover opportunities in places where no native could see them.

While his contacts with the outside world were categoric and abstract, within his own community he was at home. Here he could relax from the etiquette and the formalism by which his conduct in the gentile world was regulated. The ghetto offered liberation. The world at large was cold and strange, his contact with it being confined to abstract and rational intercourse. But within the ghetto he felt free. His contacts with his fellow-Jews were warm, spontaneous, and intimate. This was especially true of his family life. Within the inner circle of his own tribal group he received that appreciation, sympathy, and understanding which the larger world could not offer. In his own community, which was based upon the solidarity of the families that composed it, he was a person with status, as over against his formal position in the world outside. His fellow-Jews and the members of his family, to whom he was tied by tradition and common beliefs, strengthened him in his respect for and appreciation of the values of his own group, which were strangely different from the alien society in which for the time being he lived.

Whenever he returned from a journey to a distant market, or from his daily work which had to be carried on largely in a gentile world, he came back to the family fold, there to be re-created and reaffirmed as a man and as a Jew. Ever when he was far removed from his kin, he lived his real inne. life in his dreams and hopes with them. With his own kind he could converse in that homely and familiar tongue which the rest of the world could not understand. He was bound by common troubles, by numerous ceremonies and sentiments to his small group that lived its own life oblivious of the world beyond the confines of the ghetto. Without the backing of his group, without the security that he enjoyed in his inner circle of friends and countrymen, life would have been intolerable.

Through the instrumentality of the ghetto—the voluntary ghetto—there gradually developed that social distance which effectually isolated the Jew from the remainder of the population. These barriers did not completely inhibit contact, but they reduced it to the type of relationships which were of a secondary character—trade and other formal intercourse. As these barriers crystallized and his life was lived more and more removed from the rest of the world, the solidarity of his own little community was enhanced until it became strictly divorced from the larger world without. The voluntary ghetto marked, however, merely the beginning of a long process of isolation which did not reach its fullest development until the voluntary ghetto had been superseded by the compulsory ghetto.

Talmudic Student

CHAPTER III
THE GHETTO BECOMES AN INSTITUTION
THE COMPULSORY GHETTO

The forms of community life that had arisen naturally and spontaneously in the course of the attempt of the Jews to adapt themselves to their surroundings gradually became formalized in custom and precedent, and finally crystallized into legal enactments. What the Jews had sought as a privilege, and what was hitherto merely sanctioned by personal courtesies and custom, was soon to become a measure forced upon them. There had been a great deal of intimacy and friendly intercourse between the Jews and their neighbors. Jews played the rôles of merchants, bankers, physicians, and soldiers, among others, and not a few became distinguished advisers of the rulers, and teachers in the seats of learning of the day. Except for their dress and customs, they could scarcely be distinguished from the rest of the population. Their religious ideas and practices, however, or rather the notion that the churchmen and the populace had of their religion, brought them at times into sharp conflict with the established order. When, with the beginning of the Crusades, the church became militant, there set in a period of active oppression of which the ghetto regulations were the culmination, but which, in some instances, notably in Spain and Poland, took the form of wholesale slaughter and expulsion.

By the fifteenth century the ghetto had become the legal dwelling place of the Jews. The motives which actuated the church and the state in taking these repressive measures are sufficiently obvious in the numerous decrees that were pro-

mulgated by rulers or passed by various church councils.
The following is part of the proceedings of the ecclesiastical
synod held at Breslau in 1266:

> Since the land of Poland is a new acquisition in the body of Chris-
> tianity, lest perchance the Christian people be, on this account, the
> more easily infected with the superstition and depraved morals of the
> Jews dwelling among them . . . . we command that the Jews dwelling
> in this province of Gnesen shall not live among the Christians, but
> shall have their houses near or next to one another in some sequestered
> part of the state or town, so that their dwelling place shall be sepa-
> rated from the common dwelling place of the Christians by a hedge,
> a wall, or a ditch.[1]

The fears of the church were not altogether without foundation, as is evidenced by the "Judaizing heresy" of Poland
in the fifteenth century,[2] although they were based generally
upon unconfirmed rumors of hyper-zealous churchmen, or
were deliberate inventions of interested sections of the population. At various periods during the Middle Ages conversions to Judaism occurred, but on the whole the Jews were
not seeking converts, and had a feeling of the superiority of
their own group.[3]

The mere fact of the presence of a foreign, dissenting
population, however, was sufficient to arouse fears as to the
possible effect with reference to heresy on the natives.
Heretical movements within the established church were
not infrequently blamed on the Jews.

The intellectual movement in the majority of the nations of
Europe was everywhere preceded by a revolt against the Church. In
France the revolt occurred in the twelfth and thirteenth centuries, and

---

[1] Philipson, *op. cit.*, pp. 39–40.

[2] S. M. Dubnow, *History of the Jews in Russia and Poland* (Philadelphia,
1916), I, 36.

[3] Abrahams, *op. cit.*, p. 411.

is associated with the Albigensian heresy. In England the fourteenth century saw the rise of Lollardism; in Bohemia the real foundation of the great Prague University was connected, in the fifteenth century, with the reform of the Hussites. Now the second of these movements was, from the theological point of view, undoubtedly a Judaic reaction. As to the first and third, it is sufficient to say that the ruling powers regarded the Jews as the fomenters of the movements, and paid them in bloody coin for their assumed participation.[1]

How the church met the danger of the Jews is illustrated by the following instance:

The third provincial council of Ravenna, held in 1311, desiring to put an end to the free commingling of Christians and Jews, apparently in vogue in that province, decreed, among other restrictive measures, one in regard to the habitation of the Jews: "Jews shall not dwell longer than a month anywhere, except in those places in which they have synagogues."

It appears, however, that the commands of this council were not very much respected, for another held in the same place in 1317 deals more stringently with the same subject. The fourteenth rubric of this council begins, "Although the Jews are tolerated by the church, yet they ought not to be tolerated to the detriment or severe injury of the faithful; because it frequently happens that they return to Christians contumely for favors, contempt for familiarity. Therefore, the provincial council held at Ravenna some time since, thinking that many scandals have arisen from their too free commingling with Christians, decreed that they should wear a wheel of yellow cloth on their outer garments, and their women a like wheel on their heads, so that they may be distinguished from Christians," and then it continues, in reference to our subject: "And Jews shall not dwell longer than a month anywhere except in those places in which they have synagogues. But because some, not being able to abstain from forbidden things, disregard the sound decree of the aforementioned council, and pretend ignorance, a penalty shall teach them to know how grave an offence it is to disregard ecclesiastical decrees; and with the approbation of the sacred council, desiring to prevent this offence hereafter, we warn all

[1] Abrahams, *op. cit.*, p. xxi.

clerics as well as laymen of our province, and we decree no one shall erect houses for Jews, nor rent or sell them any already built, nor under any pretense grant them [any of their houses], or permit them to occupy them. If any one acts contrary to this, he shall by that very deed incur excommunication, from which he cannot be absolved until he shall satisfy the above-mentioned requirements."[1]

Decrees of this general tenor were enacted in every country of Europe, in Turkey, and in Morocco. Some of the decrees read:

. . . . The faithful incur serious danger of body and mind.[2]

That too great converse with them [Jews] may be avoided, they shall be compelled to live in certain places in the cities and towns, separated from the dwelling place of the Christians, and as far from the churches as possible.[3]

We strenuously demand of the rulers that they shall designate in the different cities a certain place in which Jews shall live apart from Christians. And if Jews have houses of their own in [other portions of] the city, they [the rulers] shall command them to be sold to Christians within six months, in actuality and not by any pretended contract.[4]

With the example of the Roman ghetto, instituted by Pope Paul IV, in 1556, before them, ghettos became general throughout Christendom, in every city where there was a Jewish community. These ghettos were generally walled in and had one or more gates, which were locked at night. At sunset the Jews had to be inside the gates, or suffer severe punishment. They were generally not permitted to appear on the streets outside the ghetto walls on Sundays and important Christian holidays. The fact that some authorities refused to grant the Jews more space than had originally been designated for the ghetto generally led to overcrowding when the population grew.

[1] Philipson, *op. cit.*, pp. 40–42.   [3] *Ibid.*, p. 44.
[2] *Ibid.*, p. 42.   [4] *Ibid.*

Besides the isolation which the ghettos more or less effected—I say more or less, for it is quite certain that many Jews contrived to secure the privilege of living outside the ghetto gates—the most serious effect of the new persecution was the terrible overcrowding that necessarily followed from herding thousands of Jews in confined spaces. The Jewish population grew, but the ghettos remained practically unchanged. Enlargements were occasionally permitted, but on the whole the original limits of the ghettos were not expanded. Hence even when the localities in which the ghettos were constructed were not slums, they rapidly became so. Sometimes the Jewish quarter, as in Cologne in the thirteenth century, was the narrowest part of the town, and was even called the "Narrow Street."[1]

Not infrequently the Jews were expelled from their ghettos, the most notable of these occasions being the expulsions of Vienna, in 1670, and Prague, 1744–45. The latter was during the wars of the Austrian succession, when Maria Theresa, on the ground that "they were fallen into disgrace," ordered the Jews to leave Bohemia. The decree was revoked under pressure of the powers, but the Jews, being ignorant of the revocation, petitioned for readmission on payment of a yearly tax, which they paid until 1846.[2]

The motives actuating the authorities to confine the Jews in ghettos have already been in part indicated. The occasions of open conflict with the established church were rare, but there was great fear that the presence of the Jews would weaken the faith of Christians. The argument was often made that the Jews were out to make converts. One decree already cited indicates that there was fear that they might interfere with Christian worship, and for that reason they were to live as far as possible from Christian churches. The greatest factor of all, among overt reasons, was the fear of heresy, which more often was the fear of enlightenment

[1] Abrahams, *op. cit.*, p. 67.
[2] *Encyclopædia Brittanica*, XI (11th ed.), 920.

that might come from the people who had a more cosmopolitan outlook on life and were more widely traveled and read than their neighbors. A somewhat contradictory admixture of reasons is indicated by the following instance:

When a ghetto was about to be established in Vienna in 1570 the citizens objected to having a place outside the city assigned to the Jews for the following three curious reasons: (1) They feared that if the Jews lived alone outside the city they could more easily engage in their "nefarious practices." (2) The Jews would be liable to be surprised by enemies. (3) The Jews might escape!

The citizens therefore proposed that all the Jews should live in one house having only one exit, that windows and doors should be well fastened, so that no one might go out at night; and that the possibility of entrance or exit by secret passages should also be guarded against. As the Jews objected to this scheme, the project was soon dropped.[1]

GHETTO ATMOSPHERE

It will probably be worth while in this connection to reconstruct, as well as possible, the atmosphere of ghetto existence. The effect of this involuntary isolation from the world is dramatically stated by Philipson:

The solution had at last been found; the Jew was effectually excluded. The Christian no longer would be corrupted and contaminated by the close proximity of the followers of the *superstitio et perfidia Judaica*, "the Jewish superstition and perfidy." For four centuries this lasted. As we today remove the victims of a pestilence far away from the inhabited portions of our cities, so the Jews were cut off by the walls of the ghetto as though stricken with some loathsome disease that might carry misery and death unto others if they lived in close contact with them. The ghetto has been well stigmatized as a "pest-like isolation." Speaking of the sixteenth century, one writer says: "Stone walls arose in all places wherein Jews dwelt, shutting off their quarters like pest-houses; the ghetto had become epidemic.[2]

---

[1] *Jewish Encyclopedia*, V, 652.   [2] Philipson, *op. cit.*, pp. 21-22.

What a picture the ghetto recalls! The narrow, gloomy streets, with the houses towering high on either side; the sunlight rarely streaming in; situated in the worst slums of the city; shut off by gates barred and bolted every night with chains and locks, none permitted to enter or depart from sundown to sunrise![1]

In some cities the houses of prostitution were transferred to the ghetto, because the ghetto was a fitting place for an institution of ill repute.[2] Several families often lived in a single building, and the location of the quarter was usually in the least desirable region of the city. One writer speaks of the ghetto of his native town as an "outcast quarter, which stretches along the unhealthy morasses of the river of our town. Pestilential vapors poison the atmosphere, which remains gloomy in spite of the clearest sunshine."[3] The protests which emanated from the Jews with the establishment of the compulsory ghetto were numerous but unavailing. Even when calamities such as fires and epidemics visited the ghetto and often destroyed it or great portions of its inhabitants, the conditions of their settlement were not improved. And yet, in spite of all misery and oppression, the life in the ghetto had a sunny side. It is necessary to view a typical ghetto concretely to appreciate the fact that when active persecution ceased for the time being, the life within the ghetto walls was as rich and as human as in the world outside. In fact, ghetto existence sometimes stood out amidst the darkness of the world surrounding it.

The historians of the ghetto are usually inclined to over-

[1] *Ibid.*, p. 21.

[2] Stobbe, *op. cit.*, p. 276. In the town of Schweidnitz the Jews complained, and the council promised that no women of ill repute should thereafter be transferred to the Jews' street.

[3] Karl Emil Franzos, quoted by Philipson, *op. cit.*, p. 30.

emphasize the confining effect of the barriers that were set up around the Jew, and the provincial and stagnant character of ghetto life. They forget frequently that there was nevertheless life within the walls of the ghetto; "life with ideals and aspirations; with passions, and even human nature."[1] It has taken the artists and poets to rediscover this life of the ghetto. The life in the ghetto was probably always more active and teeming than was life outside. The ghetto made the Jews self-conscious. They lived on the fringe of two worlds: the ghetto world and the strange world beyond the ghetto gates. Life in the ghetto was possible only because there was a larger world outside, of which many Jews often got more than a mere glimpse.

The Jews of the Middle Ages certainly had more contacts and more varied and extensive contacts than their Christian neighbors. They traveled from one town to another, and even when they themselves were unable to see much of the world, their ghetto was visited by Jews from all the corners of the earth. Particularly in the synagogue we find the center of thought, the meeting place where strangers often dropped in to tell of what went on in distant lands. The Jewish communities thus came to share the life of their distant co-religionists, and probably knew more of what was going on in the world than even the most educated Christians. In fact, for a long time the Jews were the intellectual intermediaries between Orient and Occident. They were the physicians and emissaries of the secular princes.

There was always some movement to get out of the ghetto on the part of individuals who were attracted by the wide world that lay beyond the horizon of the ghetto walls.

[1] Abrahams, *op. cit.*, p. xxii.

Sometimes a Jew would leave the ghetto and, enticed by the opportunities that were supposed to await him outside, become a convert to Christianity; and sometimes these converts, broken and humiliated, would return to the ghetto to taste again of the warm, intimate, tribal life that was to be found nowhere but among their own people. On such occasions the romance of the renegade would be told in the ghetto streets, and the whole community would thereby be welded into a solid mass, clinging more tenaciously than ever to its old traditions. The occasional estrangements from family and community ties of rebellious spirits served only to strengthen the bonds of family and community solidarity when the stray members would return to the fold and become reincorporated, amidst solemn ceremonies, into the communal organization.

The real inner solidarity of the ghetto community always lay in the strong family ties. In this inner circle deep bonds of sympathy had been woven between the members through a colorful ritual. Here each individual, who was just a mere Jew to the world outside, had a place of dignity, and was bound to the rest by profound sentiments. The adventures of each were shared by all, and enriched the store of familial lore. Through the organization in the synagogue, in turn, the family unit was given a definite status, based not so much on wealth as on learning, piety, the purity of family life, and services rendered to the community. The community, in turn, acquired a reputation—sometimes of world-significance—through its outstanding personalities, particularly through its philanthropists and scholars.

Ghetto life was hardly ever at a standstill. There were always new problems to be faced, which called for the col-

lective action of its members. There were countless subjects of great importance to its inhabitants to be discussed
and acted upon. Sometimes it was not possible to offer a
united front to the hostile world outside without long de-
bates and serious rifts within the community. Confined as
the province of the ghetto was, there was ample opportunity
for the display of capacity for leadership. There were probably more distinct types of personality and well-marked
characters within the narrow ghetto streets than in the larger
world outside. The ghetto community was minutely spe-
cialized and highly integrated. At the same time it afforded
a rich, intense, and variegated life to its members.

The outward manifestations of separateness, the ghetto
wall, the gates, the Jewish badge, all tended to enhance the
group- and self-consciousness of the Jews. They became the
physical symbols of the social isolation which manifested
itself in the social distance that was preserved between Jews
and Christians. In the course of time the Jews adjusted
themselves to these restrictions and managed to build up a
society of their own, in which life was bearable and at times
even exciting. From this little world of kinsmen they gained
courage to live and venture into the larger cosmos that
loomed enticingly beyond the high walls. The ghetto offered
security and status in a narrow but intimate community,
sheltered from the storms that raged without; but these
storms were frequently too alluring to keep the Jew effectively in his place. It took a larger world to satisfy the crav-
ing for new experience, for excitement and adventure on the
part of the restless spirits among the ghetto inhabitants.
The formal restrictions that bound them served merely as
an additional stimulus which made entrance into the forbidden world all the more enticing.

In order to show in concrete terms something of the structure of the society that grew up in the ghetto, and the life that went on in it, we shall turn to a ghetto which was typical of the institution as it developed in most of the countries of Europe.

Kabbalist

CHAPTER IV

FRANKFORT: A TYPICAL GHETTO

HISTORICAL ASPECTS

The most famous ghetto in history is that of Frankfort
on the Main, in Germany. What transpired there may be
taken as typical of the history of ghettos everywhere in
Western Europe.[1] The Jewish congregation of Frankfort
came into being in the latter part of the twelfth century.
Until 1349, when the city bought the right over them, the
Jews stood under the direct protection of the emperor. In
that year, remembered by the Jews of Europe as one of the
darkest in their history, the Black Death was ravaging the
continent. The Jews, it was said, suffered fewer casualties
than did the rest of the population. They were accused of
having poisoned the wells, and reports spread by the Flag-
gelants, who were sweeping from town to town, led the mobs
to unspeakable excesses against the Jews. Fire was set to the
Jewish ghetto, and apparently the whole community per-
ished. For a consideration the Jews were again granted the
right, in 1360, to settle in Frankfort, by the city council. At
this time they could own real estate and fix their residence
at will, but as a matter of fact most of the Jews did live in
the Jewish quarter, where, however, many Christians, including the mayor, resided.

Every three months, from the fifteenth century on, the
Jews had to renew their lease permitting them to live in the

[1] The literature on the ghetto of Frankfort is extensive. See Isidor
Krakauer, *Geschichte der Juden in Frankfurt*. The details of this account
are taken mainly from Philipson, *op. cit.*, chap. iv.

city. The city council, on these occasions, had to pass an act known as *Judenordnung*, which the Jews, by means of money, were always successful in having passed. In one of these acts, that of 1460, the Jews were compelled to leave their homes and move to a segregated area, thus establishing the *Judengasse*, or ghetto. This decree gives as the reason for instituting the ghetto the fact that many Jews lived in the immediate neighborhood of the chief church and were thereby exercising a profaning and contaminating influence. Besides, the decree states, it was nothing short of an affront to the Christian religion for Jews to worship so near the church, since their noises while chanting their prayers disturbed the Christian worshipers. Furthermore, the Jews could see the holy host and hear the church songs, which was nothing less than shameful. These reasons, or rationalizations, rather, are probably not worth serious consideration in themselves, but they indicate that in the course of social contact between Jews and Gentiles there had developed certain areas of friction which found formal expression in the segregation of the Jews.

The *Judengasse* established by this decree, which had been urged by the Emperor himself, was situated in a sparsely inhabited portion of the city, far removed from the rest of the inhabitants, on the border between the old and the new city, on a part of the dried-up moat which ran along the wall of the old city. This area, from all accounts, might be described as an interstitial area. This, together with the circumstance that the ghetto was located near the market place, was characteristic of all the ghettos of Europe.

Besides the wall, a typical medieval symbol of town life, the ghetto had three gates, one each at the beginning, at the end, and in the middle of the wall. They were locked at night, and superintended by watchmen.

The Jews did not submit passively to this stringent order. They pleaded and protested, urging upon the council that the decree be revoked. In their petition they set forth the strongest reasons they could find. The street, they said, would be so far removed from the rest of the city that if they ever needed the help of the townsmen they would not be able to assist. The Jews complained that of late they had been stoned and mocked in the streets which led to the ghetto, and that this practice would be all the more troublesome if they had to continue to walk through those very same streets. They pointed out that during the fairs they might be attacked by visitors. They offered to sell their houses near the church, and to build a higher wall around their dwellings and content themselves with one gate, to be locked at night. The order went into effect, however, and the Jews were locked up in what was at once termed "New Egypt," recalling the slavery of the Jews in biblical times. To the Jews the most oppressive features of the order were, not the discomfort and the loss of freedom of movement which was involved in the ghetto edict, but rather something which they did not mention in their petition, namely, the surrender of status and self-respect which the ghetto implied.

The density of settlement is pictured by Philipson in the following terms:

It was a most gloomy street, twelve feet broad, in its widest portion fifteen or sixteen feet. A wagon could not turn in it, and that the great confusion incident to the many stoppages thus caused might be avoided, the city council had the middle entrance widened. The *Gasse* contained 190 houses, built very close together, some of them very high and containing many souls, the 190 houses harboring 445 families. In each house there were two or three families, and as the community consisted of between twenty-five hundred and four thousand persons, each house contained, on an average, between thirteen and twenty persons. On account of the extreme narrowness of the street and the height of the buildings on either side, the tops of the buildings seemed almost to touch each other.[1]

To this must be added the fact that the Jews could not leave their street at will, not even for recreation. They were excluded from the rest of the city, and were locked in behind the ghetto walls nightly. If Jews dared make their appearance at places in the city, such as on the promenades, or the public squares, their hats were snatched from their heads by passers-by. The story is told that in certain German cities, in Hanover until a few years ago, a sign was displayed prominently at the entrance to the public park, bearing the legend: *Ein Jude und ein Schwein dürfen hier nicht herein.* (A Jew and a pig are not permitted to enter here.) There was one occasion, however, when the Jews were permitted to enter the city hall through the front entrance, and that was on New Year's Day, when they were expected to bring their annual gifts of spices to the city fathers and to express their allegiance and gratitude for the privileges which they enjoyed. At all other times they had to use the rear entrance. When Jews made their appearance even at specified places where their presence was not prohibited, they were usually subjected to insults and abuse. The cry "Hep! hep!" which has been revived lately in antisemitic parts of Germany, usually followed them as they were chased through the streets. A law passed by the city council prohibiting anyone from striking or insulting a Jew on the streets proved of little avail.

[1] Philipson, *op. cit.*, p. 56.

There are three dramatic events in the history of the Frankfort ghetto which, while they give to the ghetto of Frankfort a great deal of its historical fame, might stand as typical of what crises ghetto life brought almost anywhere in Europe. The first of these concerns a converted Jew, John Pfefferkorn, who, in order to give overt evidence of his loyalty to his newly adopted faith, wrote several diatribes against the Jews, accusing them of anti-Christian expressions in the Talmud and their prayer books. He gained favor with the Dominican order, and got the backing of the Emperor. On a feast day he appeared in the synagogue of Frankfort, accompanied by priests and councilmen, and confiscated what books he could find. The Jews were able to obtain the intervention of the Archbishop, whom Pfefferkorn had affronted, in their behalf. Pfefferkorn was able to get the Emperor to appoint a committee of inquiry.

Among its members were Hoogstraten, the grand inquisitor of the Dominican order; John Reuchlin,[1] and Viçtor von Carben, "formerly a rabbi and now a priest." To the great surprise of the conspirators, Reuchlin declined to serve, and wrote a defense of all Jewish books except such as contained direct aspersions on Christianity. In it he told, in rather plain words, his opinion of Pfefferkorn. The Jews were saved, as the fight was now on between Reuchlin and the Pfefferkorn party, that is, the Dominicans.[2]

The second and more tragic incident arose out of the hostility of the guilds toward the Jews. Having failed in their attempt to have the Jews expelled from the city, they organized an attack on the Jewish quarter under the leadership of a baker, Vincent Fettmilch. The Jews were prepared for the attack. They removed their families to the cemetery, and met the mob with arms, after having prayed and

[1] The famous humanist and scholar.
[2] Philipson, *op. cit.*, pp. 65–66.

fasted. The mob broke through the gates, and in spite of determined resistance the Jews were overcome. With the aid of armed citizens and on the advice of the council, they left the city for over a year, and took up their abodes in the neighboring towns.

In the meantime, order had been restored, and steps were taken looking to the return of the Jews. The leaders of the mob, Fettmilch and six others, were beheaded. On the very day that this took place, February 28, 1616, the Jews returned. Their return was celebrated with music. When they arrived in front of the *Gasse*, they were formed into a circle, and the new *Judenordnung*, drawn up by the imperial commissioners, was read to them. The town council having shown itself so powerless to guard them, the protection of the Jews reverted to the emperor; they once again became his private property. After their return into their "street," a large shield was placed upon each of the three gates, upon which was painted the imperial eagle, with the inscription, "Under the protection of the Roman Imperial Majesty and of the Holy Empire." Strange to say, the Christian population was compelled by imperial mandate to pay the Jews 175,919 florins indemnity for the loss they had sustained. In memory of these events, the Jewish congregation of Frankfort annually celebrated two events, the nineteenth of Adar, as a fast day commemorative of their departure from the city, and the twentieth as a holiday, called Purim Fettmilch, in memory of their return.[1]

It was events such as these that stood out in the traditions of the ghetto and that still linger in the memory and lore of the people, although the ghetto walls have long ago ceased to exist.

There was a third great crisis that the Jews of the Frankfort ghetto still recall, which is even more typical of ghetto

[1] Philipson, *op. cit.*, pp. 68–69. Purim refers to the Jewish holiday in commemoration of the deliverance from Haman through Mordecai and Esther. There is also a Purim Prague, commemorative of a similar event in another celebrated European ghetto. See A. Kisch, "Die Prager Judenstadt während der Schlacht am Weissen Berge," *Allgemeine Zeitung des Judenthums*, LVI, 400.

experiences generally than the other two events cited, namely, the great fire of 1711, which completely destroyed the *Gasse*.

The population had greatly increased, but the space for habitation was not enlarged. The number of houses did not increase, and the 190 houses that, in a former day, had sheltered but two thousand persons, were now the homes of some eight thousand, according to the smallest calculation the Jewish population at this time. Each house, therefore, on an average, harbored forty-one persons. The *Gasse* is an example of the worst evils of the tenement system. On January 14, 1711, the fire broke out in the house of the chief rabbi, which stood in the middle of the "street." The cause of the fire was never discovered. It wiped out the Jewish quarter completely, and was called the great Jewish conflagration, in contradistinction to the great Christian conflagration eight years later. The Christian population, as soon as the fact of the raging of the fire became known, hurried to the *Gasse* to give assistance. But the Jews, in an agony of terror, and remembering former days, had locked the gates for fear of plunder, and kept them closed for an hour. When at last they opened them, the flames had gained great headway. The fire spread throughout the quarter, and with the exception of three houses standing at the extreme end of the street, everything was destroyed. The Jews, now homeless, had to look about for shelter. Some were harbored in Christian houses. After the "street" was rebuilt, they lingered in these houses with the hope that they might be permitted to remain outside the *Gasse*, and have freedom of residence, but they were all ordered back in 1716.[1]

Other fires, less disastrous, followed, but the ghetto was rebuilt on the same site each time. Gradually the streets were widened and modernized, so that today, when most of the houses have disappeared, the Börne Strasse bears little resemblance to the old *Gasse*. In other ways as well the Jews began to fare better. In 1811 they gained political emancipation, being accorded the right of citizenship, which they lost

[1] Philipson, *op. cit.*, pp. 69–71. The street is named in honor of Löb Baruch, known in German literary history as Ludwig Börne.

again after the fall of Napoleon, to regain it in 1848, to lose it again in 1850, and finally to receive it a third time in 1864.

While still known among the population as the *Juden-gasse*, few Jews have lived there since the beginning of the nineteenth century. Two great reminders still stand: the ancestral home of the Rothschild family, which has been turned into a museum, and the Jewish cemetery. Even the cemetery shows some signs of the tenement conditions of the old ghetto, for the graves are close together, and two or three on top of one another.[1] The Frankfort Jewish community of today is scattered all over the city. The ghetto seems to have vanished more completely than in most large American cities, where the compulsory ghetto has never been known.

GENERAL CHARACTERISTICS

The ghetto of Frankfort occupies a conspicuous place in the history of the Jews in Europe, for several reasons. In the first place, Frankfort was one of the largest Jewish communities during the Middle Ages. But it was not size alone that placed the Frankfort ghetto in the front rank. Other and smaller communities, such as Rothenburg ob Tauber, one of the most interesting medieval towns of Germany, had an inconspicuously small Jewish population, but was known throughout the world wherever Jews lived. It gained its fame because of the great renown of its learned Rabbi Meyer of Rothenburg, whose Responsa[2] were accepted as authoritative by medieval Jewry. An outstanding personality was able to give his community world-wide prestige.

Frankfort had other claims to fame. It was the home of

[1] H. Bäerwald: *Der alte Friedhof der israelitischen Gemeinde zu Frankfurt am Main*, Frankfort, 1883.

[2] Responsa is the technical name applied to the discourses of rabbis in response to questions propounded to them (see chap. vi, p. 85).

the noted Rothschild family, whose wealth and social position gave to the ghetto of their native town a glamor which has not yet vanished. Frankfort became one of the most significant commercial and banking centers of Europe. The Jews, with their partial monopoly of trade and finance, were the very core of the commercial and industrial life of that city. The Rothschilds became the counselors and bankers of kings, who sent their emissaries to the Jewish financial magnates to negotiate loans and advise them about their fiscal policies. The Jews have left their impress on the life of Frankfort as they have on no other city in Europe. In time of need, it was Frankfort that came to the rescue of Jews everywhere.

There was a third reason for the pre-eminence of the ghetto of Frankfort. As has already been indicated, Frankfort gave birth to Ludwig Börne, whose personality profoundly influenced the romantic movement in European literature. He was representative of the intellectual life that animated the Jews of Frankfort. In spite of their narrow ghetto street, they led a cosmopolitan existence. Frankfort, during the eighteenth century, became the literary center of Germany, and the *liaison* station between the thinkers and poets of France and the rest of Europe. In this intellectual current the Jews had a conspicuous rôle. The Jews of Frankfort had a *Weltanschauung* which far transcended the confines of their ghetto. It was Heine who, in his essay on Ludwig Börne, said: "'Juden' und 'Christen' sind für mich ganz sinnverwandte Worte im Gegensatz zu 'Hellenen'! mit welchem Namen ich ebenfalls kein bestimmtes Volk, sondern eine sowohl angeborene als angebildete Geistesrichtung und Anschauungsweise bezeichne." The Jews of Frankfort had tasted sufficiently of the life of the country in which they lived to feel themselves a part of its fabric. The ideas that were current in the world were their own. It is no accident, therefore, that the Jews of Frankfort should form the cultural nucleus of the Jews of Central Europe. In spite of all conversions and intermarriages that have taken place in that city, the Jewish community there still remains one of the most influential in the whole of Europe. Its older families are probably more decidedly orthodox than those of any other German city. They have a noticeable pride of ancestry and a strong feeling of group solidarity.

Besides the ghetto of Frankfort there were a great many other ghettos in Europe whose history would be worth retelling. There were the ghettos of Worms and Speyer, of Regensburg and Nuremberg, and smaller ghettos all along the important trade routes of Western and Southern Germany. Perhaps the most famous ghettos outside of Germany were the ghettos of Prague, of Vienna, of Rome, and of Venice. Some of them achieved fame through the important schools of rabbinical thought which were centered there, others through the spectacular rôle they played in the political, military, and economic history of Europe. Still others are remembered in Jewish folklore for the massacres and the heroisms of their inhabitants. But as the ghetto of Frankfort, so, in general, were the ghettos everywhere throughout Europe.

The ghetto arose, in the first instance, out of a body of practices and needs of the Jewish population. Gradually it became an established institution without the Jews themselves being aware of the invisible walls that they were building around their community. Only when it became formally recognized and sanctioned by law, or, rather, decreed by law, however, did it become an object of resentment because is was a symbol of subjugation.

The typical ghetto of the sixteenth century is a densely populated, walled-in area usually found near the arteries of commerce or in the vicinity of a market. But before the segregation became expressed in physical barriers the Jews already had in all cities where they lived in considerable numbers what was in every respect a cultural community definitely set apart from the Christian or Moslem culture about them. The forcible confinement within ghetto walls merely served to give the community a more definite geographical expression on the one hand, and to intensify the self-consciousness of the members of the community on the other.

The ghetto was the product of a sifting process that went on for several centuries, in the course of which the Jews, a mobile, transient, homeless people, became set apart from the natives, whose cultural life was of a different character from their own. Even when conditions were fairly settled and the community had made a fairly stable and satisfactory adjustment to the circumstances imposed by the times, the ghetto was hardly ever more than a mere stopping-place. Centuries of shifting fortune and ceaseless wandering ever since the beginning of the *diaspora* had left on the Jew something of the character that we associate with the gypsy. The Jew was a person of many contacts, and often of many "homes." In the course of his migrations he established himself in the remotest parts of the globe. He was not a lone "hobo," however, for, as a rule, Jews settled in groups.

The reason for this must be sought in the religious traditions of that people.

The simplest and commonest form of Jewish solidarity is the organized community, which will be found in any town containing even a handful of Jews. The motor force in its organization is the desire for public worship, which cannot be properly conducted according to religious law without a minimum of ten adult males. The primary force is thus religious, and its external expression gradually materializes into a synagogue. This institution forms the pivot and centre of communal life throughout Jewry, and its establishment is followed by the growth of a cluster of other institutions, each answering some definite social need or aspiration. . . . .[1]

This institution was of such significance as an organizing factor in Jewish communal life as to merit more detailed description.

THE SYNAGOGUE

The Jewish quarter, even before the days of the compulsory ghetto, "seems to have grown up round the synagogue, which was thus the center of Jewish life, locally as well as religiously."[2]

This concentration round the synagogue may be noted in the social as well as in the material life of the Middle Ages. The synagogue tended, with ever increasing rapidity, to absorb and to develop the social life of the community, both when Jews enjoyed free intercourse with their neighbors of other faiths, and when this intercourse was restricted to the narrowest possible bounds. It was the political emancipation, which the close of the eighteenth century witnessed, that first loosened the hold of the synagogue on Jewish life. . . . . But throughout the Middle Ages proper the synagogue held undisputed sway in all the concerns of Jews.[3]

The dominant position held by the synagogue in Jewish life is to be accounted for on the basis of the function of religion in that life and the synagogue as an expression of that func-

[1] Israel Cohen, *Jewish Life in Modern Times* (London and New York, 1914), p. 23.

[2] Abrahams, *op. cit.*, p. 1.   [3] *Ibid.*, pp. 1–2.

tion. Whatever else they may have been, the Jews were certainly and primarily a group of people held together by common religious traditions and practices. This bond, which found expression through the synagogue, as the center of religious life, colored the whole of their existence.

It is not enough to say that the Jew's religion absorbed his life, for in quite as real a sense his life absorbed his religion. Hence the synagogue was not a mere place in which he prayed; it was a place in which he lived; and just as life has its earnest and its frivolous moments, so the Jew in the synagogue was at times rigorously reverent, and at others quite at his ease.[1]

In the synagogue the members of the community assembled for prayer three times a day, and in the synagogue they remained almost throughout the day on special occasions, such as the Day of Atonement. Prayer was not merely a ritual performed by the rabbi, but it was a communal activity, in which all the adult males participated actively, at least ten being required for this purpose.

In other ways than this was the synagogue the center of Jewish life in the Middle Ages. Their "religion was truly their life,"[2] and every act of daily conduct was in need of religious sanction. The synagogue had three traditional functions. It was, of course, first of all, a *Beth Hattefilah*, a "house of prayer," in the widest sense of that term. Here not only was the scene of the routine services and ritual, but here too gathered the Jews for those more spontaneous prayers in time of crises, when death threatened a member of the community, or when enemies assailed the gates of the ghetto, or when disease or pestilence swept the country, or when their political fate was in the balance.

The synagogue was also a *Beth Hammidrash*, a "house of

[1] *Ibid.*, p. 15.   [2] Philipson, *op. cit.*, p. 31.

study." The association between school and synagogue in the Jewish community has always been close. Before and after the services the Jews studied in the synagogue, read, and argued about the "Law" and the commentaries of the rabbis. The rabbis were generally not only the religious but also the intellectual leaders of the community, and learning has always been a primary duty and a mark of distinction for every Jew. Here, at the synagogue, moreover, was the meeting place for strangers, who brought news from the world without, and here one gathered such knowledge of conditions of affairs in foreign lands from wandering students, scholars, and merchants as the medieval world afforded. In the synagogue centered those currents of thought that gave the Jewish medieval life some of its distinctiveness, in strange contrast to the intellectual stagnation in the world outside.

The synagogue was, finally, a *Beth Hakkeneseth,* a "house of assembly." In the synagogue centered all those activities that were vital in the life of the community and held it together. The synagogue was the administrative center of the ghetto and at the same time the community center. Most of the public announcements that concerned the entire community were made there, and through the synagogue the secular authorities were able to reach the Jews. Here taxes were assessed and such functions as were left to the Jewish community itself by their civil or ecclesiastical overlords, such as local regulations, passed and proclaimed. The synagogue officers had important judicial functions which they sometimes exercised with the assistance of the secular government. In the synagogue centered the educational, the philanthropic, and much of the recreational life of the community. The synagogue organization remained for several centuries a highly integrated and undifferentiated unit, and thus strengthened its hold on the community.

As the ghetto became more and more an autonomous community, there arose, as differentiations from the synagogue, several well-defined functionaries.

The democratic constitution of Jewish society in the Middle Ages shows itself in the method of electing the governing body .... the voting being always secret. The officials elected were essentially the same in all Jewish congregations; they differed little from those enumerated in the Talmud, or from those familiar to students of the New Testament records. There was the President or par excellence Parnass, the Treasurer or Gabay; there were sometimes special officers to whom the care of the poor and the care of the sick were entrusted, and—except that differentiation of functions is now more complete— the modern organization of the synagogue existed in the Middle Ages with very slight variation. The other unpaid officials were the Council, mostly of seven, and, until the thirteenth century, the Rabbi and two Dayanim (or members of the court). These became later salaried officers, and the class of paid officials included the *Schochet* (or officer to superintend the slaughtering of cattle for Jewish use), the *Chazan* or precentor, and the teacher. But the most powerful officer of all was the *Shamash* or beadle. This functionary rapidly became ruler of the synagogue. His functions were so varied, his duties placed him in possession of such detailed information of members' private affairs, his presence so permeated the synagogue and the home on public and private occasions, that the *Shamash*, instead of serving the congregation, became its master. Unlike the parish beadle, the characteristic of the *Shamash* was not pompousness so much as overfamiliarity. He did not exaggerate his own importance, but minimized the importance of everyone else. He was at once the overseer of the synagogue and the executor of the sentences of the Jewish tribunal or *Beth Din*.[1]

The Jewish tribunal, before mentioned, was far from being the external, powerless institution that it might appear to be, judging from the extent that Jewish communal

[1] Abrahams, *op. cit.*, pp. 54–56.

life was regulated from without. The communal life of the Jews was strictly regulated by ordinances or *Tekanoth* which covered every phase of life. If a distinction between the religious and secular applies to most modern ghettos and other communities, no such distinction existed in the medieval ghetto. The punishment for violations ranged all the way from fine, imprisonment, corporal punishment, to excommunication and even the death penalty. These ordinances were usually passed by the community council, with the consent of the rabbi. In some instances the individual ghettos were bound into a sort of federation, such as the "Union of the Four Districts," which practically ruled Polish Jewry for a long time. Generally, however, the local communities were jealous of their autonomy. The rabbi exercised power over his congregation fairly unmolested by civil authorities, although in some instances his election had to be confirmed by them.

The rabbis of the Middle Ages exercised an influence over the whole of Jewry, however, through their reputation rather than their official position. The legal decisions and opinions rendered by these rabbis were of world-wide significance to the Jews, and were regarded as a sort of supreme court.

EXTRATERRITORIALITY

There was one fact which contributed probably as much as any other toward the communal solidarity of the ghetto, and that was the fact that the civil authorities treated the ghetto as a community. The Jewish community as a whole was held responsible in very essential matters for the conduct of its members. This was true first of all in matters of taxation.

Though .... the Jews were jealous of the right to manage their own communal affairs, their internal organization was largely affected by their relations to the external civil powers. Their organization, indeed, revolved on the pivot of the taxes. Wherever and whenever one casts his eye on the Jewish communities of the Middle Ages, the observer always finds the Jew in the clutches of extortionate tax-collectors. .... In most cases, if not in all, the various medieval governments exacted the taxes *en masse* from the Jewish community, and left the collection of this lump sum to the officials of the synagogue.[1]

Through the circumstance that the wealthy members of the community paid more than their share of the taxes, and virtually paid the taxes of the poorer Jews, there arose gradually in the ghetto an aristocracy of wealth which displaced in prestige that of learning of a former day. This is very marked by the close of the seventeenth century.[2] This arrangement gave the community organization tremendous strength, for it tightened the hold of the community on the individual members. Furthermore, it gave to the officials of the community an intimate knowledge of the private affairs of each member, vastly increasing the force of communal control. These taxes ranged all the way from the "protection" tax, permitting the Jews to live in the ghetto, to a tax to pay for the king's dinner, or to contribute to the popular sports, such as the Roman circuses.[3] Some special forms of this communal responsibility will bear mention.[4]

One of these has to do with the *jus gazzaga*, or tenant rights, which were governed by equity rather than statute.

[1] Abrahams, *op. cit.*, pp. 40–41.

[2] H. Graetz, *History of the Jews*, Vol. V, chap. vi.

[3] A. Berliner, *Geschichte der Juden in Rom*, II, 61; see also Abrahams, *op. cit.*, p. 47.

[4] A scholarly account of the nature and development of the self-government in the ghetto is to be found in Louis Finkelstein, *Jewish Self-Government in the Middle Ages*, New York, 1924.

The Jewish community discouraged and even punished members who would avail themselves of the power of the civil courts or civil law against fellow-members of the ghetto. Informers, those who betrayed the Jewish community to outsiders, were severely punished. In this respect the attitude of the Jewish community was much the same as that of the Sicilians toward their North Italian conquerors.

The *jus gazzaga* made it unlawful for a Jew to oust another Jew from property which he rented or had leased, even though that property was owned by a Christian. This arrangement arose to prevent the charging of exorbitant rents by owners of houses in the ghetto. The Roman ghetto shows an interesting result of the exercise of this right.

In reference to this *jus gazzaga*, or possession of leaseholds of the houses in the ghetto, Alexander VII (1655–67) issued a decree favorable to converted Jews. The popes made continual efforts to convert the Jews by every method in their power. . . . . At times they succeeded, and naturally these converted Jews were not regarded with the most affectionate feelings by their former brethren in faith. Now, it happened at times that a converted Jew was in possession of a *jus gazzaga*. He, of course, could move out of the ghetto, and live wherever he desired; that was one of the inducements held out for conversion. Thereby his house in the ghetto, of which he held the perpetual lease, became vacant, and he was anxious to rent it, since he had to pay rent to the Roman owner. The Jews, however, banded themselves together, and agreed not to rent such houses, in order to injure the faithless and keep others from accepting Christianity. Alexander, therefore, issued a brief in 1657 to the effect that the Jews of the ghetto, as a community, had to make good the rent of such houses as long as they stood empty.[1]

Pope Paul II, in 1468, compelled a certain number of Jews to participate in the races for the amusement of the Roman populace. This custom was discontinued two centuries later,

[1] Philipson, *op. cit.*, p. 134.

when the Jews promised to pay 300 scudi yearly to the papal treasury.[1]

One final, striking arrangement of the Roman ghetto will be introduced here to illustrate the measures by which the authorities were unwittingly welding the bonds of community life of the Jews:

> One of the great objects of the popes was to convert the Jews to Christianity by any means whatsoever, since they firmly believed that by this they were accomplishing an important and holy work. From their standpoint they looked upon the Jews as lost. They attributed the refusal to accept Christianity to obstinacy and blindness. Various methods were employed by them, but the strangest of all was that introduced by Pope Gregory XIII, at the instigation of a converted Jew, Joseph Tzarfati. In his bull, *Sancta mater ecclesia*, of September 1, 1584, he commanded that in all places where there was a sufficient number of Jews, a sermon be preached to them on the truths of Christianity every Saturday. . . . . All Jews above the age of twelve, unless prevented by sickness or some other adequate excuse, to be given to the bishop, were to attend, so that always at least one-third of the Jewish population was to be present. This was carried out in Rome, especially in the eighteenth century. On Saturday afternoon the strange sight of the police driving men, women, and children over twelve to church with whips could be witnessed in the Roman ghetto. Saturday afternoon was chosen because it was thought that the words preached to them in the church, setting forth the doctrines and truths of Christianity, compared with the teachings of Judaism listened to in the morning in the synagogue, would appear so far superior and so much more worthy of acceptance that they would be converted easily. At first one hundred fifty had to appear, but the number was later made three hundred. At the entrance to the church stood a watchman, who counted those that entered, to make sure that the number was full. In the church, the police made the people pay attention; if anyone appeared inattentive, or under the soporific influence of the sermon fell asleep, he was roused by blows of the whip. . . . . Needless to say, the effort proved entirely fruitless; from a weekly it dropped

[1] *Ibid.*, pp. 141–42.

into an occasional service held five times a year. It was gradually
dying out when Leo XII revived it in 1824, and it was finally abolished in 1847, the first year of Pius IX.[1]

By these forces from within and without the synagogue was
perpetuated as the center of ghetto life, and the ghetto maintained as a cultural community.

COMMUNITY INSTITUTIONS

Besides the synagogue there were a number of other
institutions that made up the framework of the ghetto community. A common feature of all ghettos was the cemetery.
Around the cemetery centered the most sacred traditions of
the group. Here, as in the instance already cited from
Frankfort, the Jews often made their last stand against invading enemies. The cemetery was variously referred to as
the "house of life" and the "good place." The care of the
cemetery was one of the chief collective responsibilities of
the community. The dead were treated with kindly reverence, and the cemetery was left undisturbed even though
the growing population within the ghetto walls made every
foot of land precious.

Most large communities had a house for the poor and
the sick, a public bath, and a ritual bath-house (*mikvah*),
since in most instances the Jews were prohibited from bath-
ing in rivers, and they were unable to find refuge in those
institutions for the care of the sick which were located outside the ghetto, in the few places where they existed, even if
it had not been for their religious scruples about following
the dietary laws. A communal bake-house and slaughtering
place could generally be found in the ghetto. The larger
communities had a guest-house, where strangers could find

[1] Philipson, *op. cit.*, pp. 143–45.

shelter and refuge. The larger Jewish ghettos also had a dance-house, where the Jewish girls could appear without the identifying two blue stripes on their veils, and the men without the distinguishing mark on their clothes, or the peaked hats on their heads.[1] Here, too, the celebrations and often the weddings, pageants, and dramas were staged. It was the bright spot of the humdrum ghetto existence.

In connection with the synagogue, as has been indicated already, there were the house of justice and the school. The fact that the term *Shul* (German *Schule*) is still often used among orthodox Jews to refer to the synagogue attests to the traditional close relationship between house of worship and house of study. The school was a fairly distinct institution, however, though often housed in the synagogue building. There were two kinds of schools: the elementary school, or *Cheder*, and the advanced institution of higher learning, the *Yeshiba*. This distinction still survives in the modern community.

There were also a number of less concretely crystallized institutions in the ghetto, such as a board of guardians to care for the poor and to carry on the philanthropic enterprises of the community, and usually a committee to deal with the civil authorities, "holy leagues" or burial societies, and various other cultural and economic organizations. In the close life within ghetto walls, almost nothing was left to the devices of the individuals. Life was well organized, and custom and ritual played an organizing and institutionalizing rôle, which still accounts for the high degree of organization of Jewish communities, often verging on over-

[1] A. Berliner, *Aus dem inneren Leben der deutschen Juden im Mittelalter*, p. 52; and Philipson, *op. cit.*, pp. 33–34.

organization, and the persistence of old, outworn institutions long after their *raison d'être* has ceased to operate.

These institutions did not arise ready made. Every one of them, and particularly those that had to deal with the conflict and disorder within the group, was the characteristic form of accommodation to the situation created by the ghetto and the isolation which it symbolized and enforced. This is true, not only of the typical institutions of the ghetto, but it may even be said that the race itself, as we know it, is a product of the ghetto.

CHAPTER V
THE JEWISH TYPE
THE JEWS AS A RACE

Who are the Jews? The traditional view is that they are a Semitic people, and that throughout many centuries of dispersion their purity of blood has been preserved. Recent accumulations of material, however, indicate that the Jews are by no means uniform in their physical characteristics, and that the majority of them are of a type different from that found among other Semitic-speaking peoples, for the Semites are primarily a linguistic group.[1]

Anthropologists and sociologists are becoming more cautious in generalizing about biological and temperamental differences between races, nationalities, and cultural groups. There is probably no people that has furnished the basis for more contradictory conclusions than the Jews. The traits with which they have been credited by their friends, their enemies, and themselves fairly exhaust the vocabulary. Still, the elementary question as to whether the Jews are a race, a nationality, or a religious or cultural group remains unsettled. There are those who, with Chamberlain, believe that the Jew constitutes a clear racial type whose characteristics are unmistakable. His amazing words are worth quoting:

Very small children, especially girls, frequently have quite a marked instinct for race. It frequently happens that children who have no conception of what "Jew" means, or that there is any such thing in

[1] Roland B. Dixon, *The Racial History of Man* (New York, 1923), chap. vi.

63

the world, begin to cry as soon as a genuine Jew or Jewess comes near them. The learned can frequently not tell a Jew from a non-Jew; the child that scarcely knows how to speak notices the difference. Is not that something? To me it seems worth as much as a whole anthropological congress. . . . . Where the learned fails with his artificial constructions, one single unbiased glance can illumine the truth like a sunbeam.[1]

Hilaire Belloc prefers to think of the Jews, not as a race, but primarily as a nationality. In fact, he points out that the Jews themselves **have** adjusted their notions of themselves to suit the varying circumstances with which they were confronted. They were a race when it suited them, a nationality when necessity demanded it, a religious group, and, finally, a cultural unit when their situation made such a status desirable.[2]

The distinctive physical character of the Jew is important in this study because the presence or absence of such characteristics would be a significant consideration in determining the basis of group-consciousness, race-prejudice, and the rôle played by social and non-biological factors in the historical isolation and cultural development of that people. A physical mark may facilitate the singling out of a member of a group and therefore serve as a sort of racial uniform, as is the case with the Negro because of his color, for instance, in a white community. In the absence of any distinctive physical traits, however, artificial and external marks may come into use which will serve as efficient substitutes for the branding of a people. This is, in fact, what happened in the case of the Jews.

[1] Houston Stewart Chamberlain, *Foundations of the Nineteenth Century*, II, 537.

[2] Hilaire Belloc, *The Jews*, Boston and New York, 1923.

That the Jewish face is characteristic, and that a Jew can be singled out from among a thousand Christians, is a recent opinion. In medieval ages the tormenters of the Jews did not place much confidence in the so-called "Jewish" type as a safe, distinguishing mark. It seems they knew that appearances are often deceptive, that one who has a hook nose, black eyes and hair, thick lips, etc., may be a Christian, a Mohammedan, or a heathen, as well as a Jew, and that one devoid of these traits is not necessarily a Gentile. They were, however, determined to know a Jew when they met one, and to avoid mistakes, many enactments were promulgated compelling Jews to wear badges in order that they might be easily distinguished from non-Jews.[1]

In the isolating effect that it produced, and in the degradation which it heaped upon the Jews, the device of the badge is second only to the institution of the ghetto itself. In fact, the ghetto and the badge became twin institutions. Pope Innocent III, who proposed the Jewish badge, advanced the argument that "the measure was imperative if intermarriage or concubinage was to be prevented between Christians and non-believers."[2] It was decreed by the Fourth Lateran Council, in 1215, and thereafter by most church councils of that century—from that of Oxford in England in 1222 to that of Buda in Hungary in 1279—that every Jew was to wear on his clothes a mark, usually a piece of yellow cloth, by which he might at once be known as a Jew. "From that time on the Jew was a marked creature. The command was received by the unfortunates with a wail of despair resounding throughout Europe. Effort upon effort was made to have it revoked or to evade it, but all in vain."[3]

Among modern anthropologists the notion of "pure"

[1] Maurice Fishberg, *The Jews: A Study in Race and Environment* (New York, 1911), p. 92.

[2] Abrahams, *op. cit.*, p. 296.

[3] Philipson, *op. cit.*, p. 10.

races is no longer seriously entertained. The Jews are apparently a hybrid people, like all the rest. It has been held, however, that their peculiar historical experiences have contributed to maintaining a fairly close adherence to the characteristics which they displayed when they first appeared on the European scene, nearly two thousand years ago. In speaking of their dark skin, Ripley says:

Perhaps the most conspicuous example of the racial fixity of this trait of pigmentation is offered by the Jews. They have preserved their Semitic brunetness through all adversities. Socially ostracized and isolated, they have kept this coloration despite all migrations and changes of climate. In Germany today 42 per cent of them are pure brunets in a population containing only 14 per cent of the dark type on the average. They are thus darker by 30 per cent than their gentile neighbors. As one goes south this difference tends to disappear. In Austria they are less than 10 per cent darker than the general population; and finally, in the extreme south, they are even lighter than the populations about them. This is especially true of the red-haired type common in the East.[1]

Ripley attributes this darker complexion to the sedentary, indoor iife which the Jews have led for centuries. Ever since the days of Darwin, isolatioɩ. has been recognized as one of the basic factors in the development of biological variants. The Jews therefore furnish a crucial experiment.

Behind the walls of the ghetto the Jewish type was carefully protected from the influence of its alien environment, and there it also received a special impress, the product of exile and oppression. The chronic outbreaks of massacre and banishment, the unceasing reign of petty despotism, economic misery, and nervous alarm, have wrought traces upon the organism of the Jew; they have bent and stunted his body, whilst they have sharpened his mind and brightened his eye; they have given him a narrow chest, feeble muscles, and a pale complexion; they have stamped his visage with a look of pensive sadness,

[1] W. Z. Ripley, *The Races of Europe* (New York, 1899), p. 73.

as though ever brooding upon the wrongs of ages. But the frame that has endured and survived so much suffering is also endowed with a high degree of resistance.[1]

Not only this rather strict isolation, but the consequent inbreeding which had its foundation in the religious scruples of the Jews, has tended to develop a physical type. There is a great deal of evidence to support the contention that the Jews, even in the dark ghetto days, frequently intermarried with non-Jews; but the consequence of such intermarriage was that usually the member of the group who did this was thereafter no longer considered a part of the Jewish community, but rather was merged with the Christian population. The Negro in the United States gets credit for all mulattos, while the offspring of mixed marriages between Jews and Christians are usually accredited to the latter.

Since the time of Ezra and Nehemiah, that is, from about 400 B.C., marriage between Jew and non-Jew has been strictly prohibited. The *Kohanim* (priests) were not allowed even to marry with those who had been converted to Judaism. The common people, however, were permitted to do this, and during the Hellenic period, and in the *diaspora*, it was very common; of this the Judaised Chazars are a good example. On the other hand, during the *diaspora* such marriages were denounced by the Christians as well as by Jews, and were forbidden, under pain of heavy penalties. . . . . But intermarriage, toward the end of the Middle Ages, as the social position of the Jews deteriorated, became very rare, and has been since the sixteenth and seventeenth centuries till recently a negligible quantity. The social and religious gulf between Christian and Jew had become so wide that alone precluded the possibility of intermarriage and rendered the legal prohibition quite unnecessary. Nevertheless this prohibition stands to this day, and still holds good in Spain, Portugal, Russia, and all countries belonging to the Greek Church.[2]

[1] Cohen, *op. cit.*, p. 116.

[2] Arthur Ruppin, *The Jews of Today* (New York, 1913), pp. 157–58.

While the Jews on their part had thus only limited opportunities for intermarriage with Gentiles, the latter were scarcely ever attracted to Judaism, which, in view of the disabilities that the group was under, together with its own strict ritual, especially dietary laws, was not inviting to proselytes. The ghetto from the standpoint of population was a relatively closely inbreeding, self-perpetuating group, to such an extent that it may properly be called a closed community.

The combination of various features of ghetto existence tended toward the development and perpetuation of a definite type, which to a marked extent persists to the present day, especially in countries where the circumstances of Jewish communal life have remained relatively unchanged, as, for example, in Eastern Europe and the Orient. One of these features was the strenuous effort that was made to embark every member of the group on a matrimonial career. No strict restrictions against intermarriage between close relatives existed; in fact, such marriages were frequently encouraged.

This fact, it has been pointed out by many students of the subject, tended to increase the proportion of defectives in the population.[1] The insanity rate, it has also been observed, is inordinately large among the Jews. The same is said to hold true for similar inbreeding groups, such as the population of the Orkneys and the Society of Friends.

The explanation of the frequency of insanity among Jews is to be found in social considerations. . . . . The outstanding fact in regard to social environment of the Jews is that they are today mainly an urban population, and in the past have been a ghetto population. . . . . An ordinary population is spared the degenerating effects of many generations of town life, because any incipient decadence is neutralized and

[1] J. Snowman, "Jewish Eugenics," *Jewish Review*, IV, 173.

compensated for by the infusion of fresh country blood, as the stream of life is constantly flowing toward the large cities. A Jewish population, on the other hand, has not this reserve of vitality, and thus the evils generated by city life are so liable to remain impressed upon future generations.[1]

Not only is the circumstance of urban life to be noted as a powerful influence in shaping the physical characteristics of the Jews, but the special conditions under which they, as a persecuted and segregated population, lived must be added.

The ghetto life was not only unwholesome physically, but unwholesome mentally, emotionally, and spiritually. Living in constant dread of massacre, exposed to ridicule, degradation, and more sinister disaster, the race developed an apprehensiveness and acquired a lower threshold for fear stimuli. This kept up by the drawing in toward an overintimate family life.[2]

If, as is generally conceded, psychic conflict is the most important cause of neuroses, the Jews have had ample opportunity to cultivate the most fruitful soil for their development. For centuries they lived in an acutely hostile environment which always threatened their destruction and regularly put the threat into partial execution. Segregation became the usual mode of existence.[3]

The Jews have frequently been pointed out as the classic illustration of the great force of religious and racial prejudices in giving rise to a distinct physical type. Little did the medieval enemies of the Jews dream that by their very measures against them they were unconsciously helping to develop and preserve a distinct population in their midst. Ripley says of them, "Social ostracism, based upon differences of belief in great measure, has sufficed to keep them

[1] *Ibid.*, p. 168.

[2] Abraham Myerson, "The 'Nervousness' of the Jew," *Mental Hygiene,* Iv, 69.

[3] I. S. Wechsler, "Nervousness and the Jew," *Menorah Journal,* X, 121.

truer to a single racial standard, perhaps, than any other
people of Europe."[1] It would be difficult to cover briefly all
the material that has accumulated in recent years on the
description, not to speak of explanation, of the physical
type, or types, of the Jews in the world today.[2] Instead, it
will suffice to introduce the conclusions of Fishberg, whose
views seem to conform most nearly to the facts, which, in
this case, have been perverted and confused on many an
occasion by partisan bias.

What is that "Jewish type," that Jewish physiognomy, which
characterizes the Jew?

It is the opinion of the present author that it is less than skin deep.
Primarily it depended upon the dress and the deportment of the Jews
in countries where they live in strict isolation from their Christian or
Moslem neighbors. A striking example is furnished by the side-locks of
hair which most oriental or semi-oriental Jews allow to grow on their
temples. In Austrian Galicia one of the Jewish faith may be of any
ethnic type; he may be a Slavonian pure and simple, as many of them
are; still, as long as he wears side-locks anyone can distinguish him as
a follower of Judaism, because nobody of any other creed wears side-
locks. . . . . A man in Galicia dressed in a long caftan or frock-coat,
an under-cap (skull cap), a hat pushed to the back of the head, and
two spiral locks hanging down in front of his ears, can only be a Jew,
no matter what his face looks like. If the same individual should one
day shave off his beard, cut his ear-locks, and don the dress of his
Christian neighbors, the change might be magical. All the so-called
"Jewishness" might disappear, and a Slavonian pure and simple
might be evident to anyone who knows the physical type of the Eastern European races. This can best be seen among the Jewish immigrants to the United States.

[1] Ripley, *op. cit.*, pp. 32–33.

[2] Professor Roland B. Dixon in his *Racial History of Man*, pp. 162–75,
furnishes an excellent brief summary of the physical anthropology of the
Jews, emphasizing not merely the fact that they are a hybrid people, but
indicating that the physical differences between the Jews of the different
countries today are very marked.

Next to dress and deportment, the Jew in Eastern Europe has often a peculiar attitude of the body which is distinctly characteristic. The inferior hygienic, economic, and social conditions under which he was compelled to live in the ghettos have left their mark on his body; he is old prematurely, stunted, decrepit; he withers at an early age. He is emaciated, his muscles are flabby, and he is unable to hold his spinal column erect [the "ghetto bend"]. . . . . As an acquired character it is not transmitted by heredity.

. . . . It is not the body which marks the Jew; it is his soul. In other words, the type is social or psychic. . . . . Centuries of confinement in the ghetto, social ostracism, ceaseless suffering under the ban of abuse and persecution have been instrumental in producing a characteristic psychic type which manifests itself in his cast of countenance which is considered as peculiarly "Jewish." The ghetto face is purely psychic, just like the actor's, the soldier's, the minister's face.[1]

THE SOCIAL TYPE

Whatever may be said concerning the effect of ghetto life on the physical characteristics of the Jews applies with even greater force to the social characteristics.

If their sojourn in the ghetto for many generations was potent in producing the ethnic type of the Jew, it has been more effective in producing and maintaining the social conditions which may be called characteristic of the children of Israel. Isolation, which has been called by Darwin the cornerstone of breeders, is more effective in engendering social types than ethnic types; in man isolation is seen to be mostly of two kinds, geographical and social, and it was mostly social isolation which was operative in moulding the Jew as we meet him today. In fact, geography played only a minor rôle, in his case. Notwithstanding that the seed of Israel were scattered in various parts of the habitable globe, in spite of the fact that the different Jewish communities have been separated geographically from each other in a manner unknown among any other social group, they still lived everywhere in the same milieu. It was only after their emancipation in Western Europe during the first half of the nineteenth century that

[1] Fishberg, *op. cit.*, pp. 162–66.

there were to be noted differences in the environments of the Jews in different countries.[1]

The limitations which the world imposed upon the Jews did not merely affect the range and the kind of their contacts with other people, but also determined to a great extent the life they had to live in their own provincial ghettos. Furthermore, they were excluded from the many important spheres of public life, such as politics and civic and social functions, that were open to the members of the community about them. They were, in most instances, prohibited from owning land, or living outside the cities (except in the East); they were excluded from the guilds, and the number of occupations open to them was narrowly prescribed. In addition, their own religious ritual and community life closely defined the conduct of the individuals and restricted their contact with the outside world. "Who can say what would have been the effect of such a treatment prolonged throughout several hundreds of years?" asks Leroy-Beaulieu. "If the Mohammedans could have tried the experiment on the Christians, they probably would have obtained as clearly marked a type in ten generations."[2]

The Jew is a much more clearly defined social type than physical type. What is typical of the Jews as a group is their characteristic "run of attention," or the direction of their habits and interests which have become fixed through centuries of communal life in segregated areas: "Judaism has been preserved throughout the long years of Israel's dispersion by two factors: its separative ritualism, which prevented close and intimate contact with non-Jews, and

[1] *Ibid.*, p. 533.

[2] Anatole Leroy-Beaulieu, *L'antisemitisme*, Paris, 1897; quoted from Fishberg, *op. cit.*, p. 534.

the iron laws of the Christian theocracies of Europe, which encouraged and enforced isolation."[1]

There is probably no people that has been subjected to the persistent influence of so rigid a social pattern as have the Jews. This pattern was furnished by their religious ritual, and this ritual pervaded every sphere of their existence. Though widely scattered, they were subject to a fairly uniform set of customs throughout the world. The folkways and the mores of the Jews stood in strange contrast to those of their neighbors. Besides, the Jews were segregated from the rest of the population by rigid customs and explicit laws. Living, as they were, in segregated areas, they were enabled to develop and perpetuate a cultural life barely touched by the happenings in the outside world. When suddenly the Jews awoke in the midst of the modern world they found themselves outstripped in every important sphere of activity with the exception of commerce. Their culture seemed archaic in comparison.

All the devices that operated to keep the Jew apart, at the same time made him crave the contacts that were taboo. He lived on the periphery of two worlds, and not fully in either. As a result, he developed that keen sense of self-consciousness which is often expressed in his awkwardness and lack of poise when in the company of strangers. He is either shy and self-effacing, or he overcompensates in the direction of aggressiveness. In either case he is seldom himself. He finds himself haunted by loneliness in the outer world, and when he returns to his familial hearth he is restless and anxious to escape.

The Jew was tied to this ritual not merely through the relative isolation of his social life, but through the ties of

[1] Fishberg, *op. cit.*, p. 555.

sentiment on which this ritual rested. His life was full and real only where the values to which he was accustomed were dominant. The Jew is not merely a product of his past social life, but his character is constantly being re-created along the old pattern because his past experience has so indelibly impressed upon him the value of this heritage that he inevitably sets to work to shape his environment to conform to his accustomed pattern. But ultimately, as is indicated in a subsequent chapter (chapter vii), the so-called Jewish racial type disappears with the disappearance of the ghetto.

CHAPTER VI
THE JEWISH MIND
MENTALITY AND THE DIVISION OF LABOR

To the modern psychologist mind is not so much the cause as it is the result of activity. If we would know the mentality of a people, we must get acquainted with their activities and experiences. Isolation has exercised the most significant influence upon the Jew as a physical and social type. In the following pages we shall undertake to show the effect which the social life of the ghetto produced upon the mind of the Jew. The most striking index of the mentality of a community is perhaps to be found in the degree to which the division of labor has been carried, and the number of distinct occupational groupings that the community supports.

If there is a "Jewish mentality" it ought, therefore, to become apparent through an examination of the occupational aspects of Jewish life, and the place of the Jews in the division of labor of medieval society.

All that we know of Jewish life in the *diaspora* points to the conclusion that only an insignificant number of Jews devoted themselves to agriculture even in those lands where no difficulties were placed in their path. Perhaps Poland in the sixteenth century is the best instance. There they appear to have taken up farming. But even in Poland they showed a preference for city life. For every 500 Christian merchants in the Polish towns of the period, there were to be found 3,200 Jewish merchants.

Yes, they became town-dwellers—whether voluntarily or by stress of circumstance is of no consequence—and town-dwellers they have remained. . . . .

Now the modern city is nothing else but a great desert, as far removed from the warm earth as the desert is, and like it forcing its
inhabitants to become nomads. The old nomadic instincts have thus
through the centuries been called forth in the Jew by the process of
adapting himself to his environment, while the principle of selection
has only tended to strengthen those instincts. It is clear that in the
constant changes to which the Jews have been subjected, not those
among them that had an inclination to the comfortable, settled life of
the farmer were the ones likely to survive, but rather those in whom
the nomadic instincts were strong.[1]

Whether one agrees with Sombart's explanation or not is
unimportant; the fact to which he refers, that the Jews became a dominantly city people, is indisputable. Sombart
goes on to show how the Jew, by nature and by experience,
was eminently fitted to find a place in, and to give great
impetus to, the whole capitalistic movement that has transformed the world in the past few centuries into a highly
complex interdependent unit. He says:

Unlike most other writers on the subject, I will begin by noting
a Jewish quality which, though mentioned often enough, never received the recognition which its importance merited. I refer to the
extreme intellectuality of the Jew. Intellectual interests and intellectual skill are more strongly developed in him than physical [manual]
powers. . . . . No other people has valued the learned man, the scholar,
so highly as the Jews. "The wise man takes precedence of the king,
and a bastard who is a scholar, of a high-priest who is an ignoramus."
So the Talmud has it. Anyone who is acquainted with Jewish students
knows well enough that this overrating of mere knowledge is not yet
a thing of the past. And if you could not become "wise," at least it was
your duty to be educated. At all times instruction was compulsory in
Israel. In truth, to learn was a religious duty; and in Eastern Europe
the synagogue is still called the *Shool*. Study and worship went hand
in hand; nay, study was worship, and ignorance was a deadly sin. A

[1] Werner Sombart, *The Jews and Modern Capitalism* (New York, 1913),
p. 334.

man who could not read was a boor in this world and damned in the next. In the popular saying of the ghetto, nothing had so much scorn poured upon it as foolishness. "Better injustice than folly," and "Ein Narr ist ein Gezar" (a fool is a misfortune) are both well known. The most valuable individual is the intellectual individual; humanity at its best is intellectuality at its highest..... One consequence of this high evaluation of intellectuality was the esteem in which callings were held according as they demanded more "headwork" or more "handwork." The former were almost in all ages placed higher than the latter..... As Rabbi said, "The world needs both the seller of spices and the tanner, but happy he who is a seller of spices." ...

The Jews were quite alive to their predominant quality and always recognized that there was a great gulf between their intellectuality and the brute force of their neighbors. One or two sayings popular among Polish Jews express the contrast with no little humour. "God help a man against Gentile hands and Jewish heads." "Heaven protect us against Jewish moach (brains) and Gentile koach (physical force)." Moach vs. Koach—that is the Jewish problem in a nutshell. ....

.... He will look at the world from the point of view of end, or goal, or purpose. His outlook will be teleological, or that of practical rationalism. No peculiarity is so fully developed in the Jew as this, and there is complete unanimity of opinion on the subject.[1] Most other observers start out with the teleology of the Jew; I, for my part, regard it as the result of his extreme intellectuality, in which I believe all the other Jewish peculiarities are rooted..... No term is more familiar to the ear of the Jew than *Tachlis*, which means purpose, aim, end or goal. If you are to do anything it must have tachlis; life itself, whether as a whole or in its single activities, must have some tachlis, and so must the universe.[2]

[1] The writings of Sombart have aroused considerable controversy. The criticisms directed against him have been, mainly, that his facts do not justify his conclusions, and that they have been gathered from a biased point of view. For a more recent account, see H. Waetjen, *Das Judentum und die Anfänge der modernen Kolonisation*, Berlin, 1914. See also Joseph Jacobs, *Jewish Contributions to Civilization* (Philadelphia, 1919), pp. 265 ff.

[2] Sombart, *op. cit.*, pp. 258–66.

Sombart points out a number of other characteristics besides these which tended to fit the Jew for his rôle as capitalist. Among these was his mobility, his adaptability, his flexibility, which fitted him to be a successful undertaker, organizer, trader, and negotiator. As to the Jews' experience, he adds that the Jew, by the nature of his contacts—largely of a categoric and secondary sort—was especially fitted to become the commercial individual and less fitted to become the artisan, who requires close and intimate personal contacts with his clientèle. The Jew had wide and scattered contacts; he knew languages; he had connections; and he had some wealth—these were the foundations that served him for a commercial career. Moreover, the Jew was not prevented by his religion, as were others, from dealing in money. He therefore became the money lender and the banker. By the time that the medieval church relaxed its stand on the question of usury the Jews had already a fair start.

In other ways than these the Jews found for themselves an important place in medieval society. They were frequently the physicians and emissaries of rulers and princes. What there was of Oriental medicine they had brought to the West, and their wide contact and correspondence placed them in a favorable position for extending their knowledge. They were, as Simmel has pointed out, the typical stranger, and in that rôle they acquired the objectivity and built up the relationship of the confidant, which served them well as counselors and diagnosticians.

The Jews did not, however, avoid the crafts and arts, as one might be led to believe by the generalizations of Sombart. They plied numerous trades, they peddled many articles, but in many cases they were also the manufacturers of their wares. There were numerous Jewish dyers, silk weavers, gold- and silversmiths, tailors, and printers,[1] besides a great variety of other occupations. The restrictions placed upon them by the government, the church, and the guilds, besides their own religious ritual, account for their predominance in some, and their scarcity in other, occupations. In Poland, where they were less of an urban people and lived in self-sufficing areas of settlement, their occupations tended to approximate those of the Christians.

It must not be supposed that the Jew was always or even typically successful and rich. He was often nothing more than the indirect tax-collector for the ruler, and periodically his fortune was taken from him by force. The number of poor Jews in the medieval ghettos was large, and the provision made for them by their more prosperous fellow-Jews was generous. "Although the Jew has acquired the reputation of being the personification of the commercial spirit, he is sometimes quite shiftless and helpless, failing miserably in everything he undertakes, as though pursued by some mocking sprite, and good-humouredly nicknamed by his brethren a *Schlemiel*."[2]

Not only do we find in the ghetto distinct vocational types, but the religious and community life tended to develop other numerous specializations of activity and status which gave rise to distinct personality types. Some of these, such as the *Rabbi*, the *Shamus* or sexton, the *Parnass*, or councilman, have already been mentioned. There are others, such as the *Shochet*, or slaughterer, the *Mohel*, or circumciser,

---

[1] See Abrahams, *op. cit.*, chaps. xi and xii, and Appendixes A to H. Also Joseph Jacobs, *Jewish Statistics* (London, 1891), chaps. iv–vi, and Ruppin, *op. cit.*, chap. iii.

[2] Cohen, *op. cit.*, p. 186.

and the *Shadchan*, or marriage broker. The last of these is a picturesque character that finds frequent expression in fiction, and that still serves an important function in the Eastern European communities:

> In Eastern countries, such as Morocco, Persia, and India, the marriage is arranged by the parents of the young couple, who submissively acquiesce in their fate. In Eastern Europe the parental negotiations are preceded by the activity of a matrimonial agent, who is rendered necessary by the segregation of the sexes still observed in most of the communities of Eastern Europe. The Shadchan, as he is called, is a prized visitor in the home of every marriageable girl, whose chances depend, apart from natural charms, upon the size of her dowry and the family reputation for piety, learning, and philanthropy.[1]

His services were in constant demand, and his area of operations was not even confined to any particular country, but extended throughout the Russian Pale and into Galicia, Roumania, and more distant regions. Frequently the markets and the fairs were places at which marriages could be arranged, for here Jews of various localities had opportunity to meet and to discuss such problems.

Something has already been said of the emphasis on learning and scholarship. This scholarship was usually of a religious nature. The talmudical student, known as *Yeshiba Bachur*, enjoyed a favored position in the community.

> The highest virtue of the bridegroom is excellence in talmudic study, which surpasses in value a splendid pedigree or a dazzling income bedimmed with ignorance. In most of the teeming communities of Russian and Galician Jewry the father still regards sacred learning as the noblest possession in a son-in-law, and if he can ally his daughter to a budding rabbi he believes the union will find especial grace in Heaven. The lack of worldly means on the part of the bridegroom forms no deterrent, for it is customary for the father of the bride to

[1] *Ibid.*, p. 41.

keep his son-in-law in his own house for the first two years after marriage, and then to set him up in a home and business of his own.[1]

Here is an instance in which the values that the group attaches to a certain type of behavior become an important selective agency in the perpetuation of a social type. In modern times secular knowledge has in great measure been able to take the place of religious learning.

A number of other types center around the religious life of the ghetto. Among them are the *Zaddik*, or righteous individual, the leader of the community; the *Batlanim*, or the men of leisure or hangers-on in the synagogue, who, like a modern coroner's jury, are always at hand when a *minyan*, or assembly of ten men, is required for prayer. The old ghetto also had its professional jester, known as *Marshallik*, and *Badchan*, who entertained at weddings, on holidays, and particularly at the feast of Purim. Finally, there was the *Meshumed*, or apostate, whose lot was an unhappy one in the ghetto. He was shunned by the community, and was often ostracized. These are some of the types that life in the ghetto brought forth, and that have acquired a distinctive place in the memories and attitudes of the group. There were others, some of them specializations of types already mentioned; there were even some types that the Jews recognized among the *Goyim*, or Gentiles, with whom they had occasional contact. One more type is worthy of special mention, namely, the beggar, or *Schnorrer*. The relation between the giver and the receiver of charity was a peculiar one in ghetto society. Charity was more or less synonymous with justice, and to give to the poor, the orphans, and the helpless, was a religious duty.

[1] *Ibid.*

It cannot be too strongly emphasized that this relation between giver and taker was in itself a strong preventive to pauperism in the modern sense. But it is undeniable that it led to that insolence in the Jewish beggar which, growing out of the theory that the recipient of the gift was enabling the donor to perform a religious duty, and was, in a sense, the benefactor of the donor, made the *schnorrer*, or beggar, come to be a most persistent and troublesome figure in modern Jewish society.[1]

INTELLECTUAL LIFE

The enforced confinement of the Jews in ghettos throughout the major part of the Middle Ages, especially during that brighter period of the Renaissance almost up to the beginning of the nineteenth century, left profound effects upon not only their bodies, but upon their minds. When the rest of the world about them had already outgrown feudalism, the Jews were still living in a social milieu whose patterns had been cut by the feudal order. While the Jews were on the one hand spared the effect of the ecclesiastical morass of the Christian church in the Middle Ages, they built up an intolerant medieval theology of their own which governed conduct and restricted thought:

Shut off from all contact with the world at large, the Jew within the walls of the ghetto naturally did not respond to the culture of the world. Learning, certainly, there always was, and learning was held in the highest respect; but it was the learning of the ancients, the Talmud and rabbinical dialectics. These studies sharpened the mind, it is true, and later, when emancipation came, the Jewish intellect, exercised for centuries in this dialectical training school, readily mastered the difficulties of the various branches of learning in the universities. But in the ghetto, notably in Germany and the countries of Eastern Europe, this terrible, systematic exclusion of the Jews from all contact with the outer world contracted the mind and prevented all cultivation of learning outside of Jewish studies.[2]

[1] Abrahams, *op. cit.*, pp. 310–11.   [2] Philipson, *op. cit.*, pp. 195–96.

There were some mitigating circumstances in this domination of the synagogue over Jewish life, however:

The synagogue was the centre of life, but it was not the custodian of thought. If Judaism ever came to exercise a tyranny over the Jewish mind, it did so, not in the Middle Ages at all, but in the middle of the sixteenth century. A revolt against medievalism such as occurred in Europe during and at the close of the Renaissance may be said to have marked Jewish life towards the close of the eighteenth century.[1]

From the sixteenth to the eighteenth century the Jews were about as closely bound by rabbinical authority and ritualistic customs as the Roman church ever had bound the Christian peoples of medieval Europe. During the Middle Ages proper, however, the Jews played an important rôle in the intellectual life of Europe. The medieval universities were not altogether closed to the Jews, and where their personal influence was lacking, there was the indirect influence which they exerted in mediating between the culture of the Orient and the barbarism, or rather the incipient civilization of the West.[2] It was not so much external pressure as internal control in response to that pressure that left a marked effect upon the mental life of the ghetto.

The Jews suffered more from the dispiriting calms of life within the ghetto than from the passionate storms of death that raged without it. The anti-social crusade of the medieval church against the Jews did more than slay its thousands; it deprived the Jews of the very conditions necessary for the full development of their genius. The Jewish nature does not produce its rarest fruits in a Jewish environment. I am far from asserting that Judaism is a force so

[1] Abrahams, *op. cit.*, p. xvii.

[2] See Andrew White, *Warfare of Science with Theology*, II, 33; also Rashdall, *Universities of Europe in the Middle Ages;* also H. O. Taylor, *The Medieval Mind;* and especially Joseph Jacobs, *Jewish Contributions to Civilization* (Philadelphia, 1919), chaps. iv and v.

feeble that its children sink into decay so soon as they are robbed of the influence of forces foreign to itself. But it was ancient Alexandria that produced Philo; medieval Spain, Maimonides; modern Amsterdam, Spinoza. The ghetto had its freaks, but the men just named were not born in ghettos. And how should it be otherwise? The Jew who should influence the world could not arise in the absence of a world to influence.[1]

Quite early in the medieval history of the Jews there grew up partisan camps in the larger Jewish community. On the one hand were the Spanish, or Sephardic Jews, who prided themselves on the purity of their stock and the superiority of their status; on the other were the German Jews, or Ashkenazim, whose ghetto history considerably lowered their status.

But it is a striking fact that the "German" Jews, more characteristically Jewish than their Spanish brethren, ended by gaining control of the whole of European Judaism. The Jewish schools in the Rhineland flourished, not, as in Moorish Spain, in imitation of neighbouring illumination, but in contrast to surrounding obscurantism. There was no Christian university till the middle of the fourteenth century, but the Rhinelands had what were practically Jewish universities in the era of the first Crusade.[2]

Jewish life in the Middle Ages was by no means identical in the various countries, nor unified, much as the ghetto exercised a uniformizing influence. In each country and locality the Jews worked out their problems created by local circumstances as the situation permitted. There were gradually arising certain integrating currents which began to weld the scattered communities of Jews into something resembling a unit, which, however, did not take the form of a nationalistic movement. Perhaps the most potent influence in this direc-

[1] Abrahams, *op. cit.*, pp. xxi–xxii.
[2] *Ibid.*, pp. xxii–xxiii.

tion was the prestige attaching to the opinions of certain rabbis whose reputation for piety and learning gave them a unique position in the intellectual life of the Jews.

The Geonim of Persia, who swayed Judaism during the seventh to the eleventh century, and their spiritual successors, the rabbis of North Africa and Spain, carried on a world-wide correspondence. The answers which they made to questions addressed to them constitute one of the most fertile sources of information for Jewish life in the Middle Ages. . . . . Meir of Rothenburg was probably a greater man with a greater mind than some of his Spanish contemporaries, but the latter corresponded with a far wider circle of Jews. True, the codification of Jewish law was inaugurated by Spanish Jews in the "golden age," but the code which finally became the accepted guide of Judaism was the work of the sixteenth century. Codification implies the suppression of local variation, but in the Responsa[1] of the later French and German rabbis there is already far less heterogeneity of habits than in the Responsa of the Spanish Jews, and certainly of the Geonim. And this is quite natural. If your horizon is narrow, you regard your own conduct as the only normal or praiseworthy scheme of life. Hence, without any conscious resolve to suppress varying customs, these were as a matter of fact much contracted by the local tendencies of the great French rabbis who became the authority for all Judaism from the fourteenth century onwards. After the end of the twelfth century even the Spanish Jews relied on their German brethren for guidance in the Talmud.[2]

It is important to point out that the isolation of the ghetto was, after all, only relative. Before confinement in the ghetto became effective the Jews had set in motion a number of currents of thought and activity which brought them into contact with the outside world, and which the ghetto wall was not able to shut out completely.

[1] The answers to the questions propounded to the rabbis are known as Responsa. The Responsa literature is quite extensive.

[2] Abrahams, *op. cit.*, pp. xxv–xxvi.

The seventeenth was the gloomiest century in the pre-emancipation history of the Jews, but until the beginning of the sixteenth century they were never for long cut off from the common life around them. Nay, their interests were wider than those of their environment, for they had the exceptional interest of a common religion destitute of a political centre. It is hard to exaggerate the importance of this factor in molding Jewish life. Thus was begotten that cosmopolitanism which broke through the walls of the ghettos and prevented the life passed within them from ever becoming quite narrow and sordid.[1]

Through the synagogue, which, as has already been indicated, became the center not only of religious but of intellectual life, the isolated communities were kept in intermittent contact with each other, and a social movement that had its origin in one was likely to be propagated by travelers, students, and rabbis, who, first of all, of course, sought the synagogue whenever they arrived in a new community. "Thus Jewish life was not narrow, though its locale was limited."[2]

The Jews continued to share to some extent the larger life about them, often in a measure exceeding that of their Christian neighbors, so that "in the Middle Ages proper, Jewish life, with all the innate 'provincialism' from which it has never, in all its long and chequered history, contrived to free itself, was freshened and affected by every influence of the time."[3] Abrahams has an eloquent passage in which the contrast between medieval life at large and the Jewish aspect of that life is contrasted:

When one thinks what human life was for the majority of men in the Middle Ages, "how little of a feast for their senses it could possibly

[1] *Ibid.*, p. 4.   [2] *Ibid.*, p. 5.

[3] *Ibid.*, p. 6. See also I. Husik, *Medieval Jewish Philosophy*, New York, 1916.

be, one understands the charm for them of a refuge offered in the heart and the imagination." More than to any others, this remark applies to the Jews. As the Middle Ages closed for the rest of Europe the material horizon of the Jew narrowed. Prejudice and proscription robbed them of the attractions of public life and threw them within themselves, to find their happiness in their own idealized hopes. But the fancies on which they fed were not of the kind that expand the imagination.

Jews were not inaccessible to ideas, for they never confused the land of Philistia with the land of the children of light. But the ideas which came to them in the really dark ages of Jewish life were not the ideas which freshened Europe and roused it from its mystic medieval dreams. Indeed, Judaism became more mystical as Europe became more rational; it clasped its cloak tighter as the sun burned warmer. The Renaissance, which drew half its inspiration from Hebraism, left the Jews untouched on the artistic side. The Protestant Reformation, which took its life-blood from a rational Hebraism, left the Jews unaffected on the moral side. It was, in a sense, a misfortune for the Synagogue that it had not sunk into the decadence from which the Reformation roused the church. As it was not corrupt it needed no rousing moral regeneration, and so it escaped, through its own inherent virtues, that general stirring-up of life which results from great efforts for the redress of great vices.[1]

During the period of the Renaissance the Jewish communities, still suffering from the effects of the persecutions begun during the Crusades and continuing during the fourteenth and fifteenth centuries, and culminating in the Spanish Inquisition, were split up into numberless local and factional cliques. Under this continuous oppression "the Jew found relief in an unreal world conjured forth by an unbridled imagination. The great wave of mysticism in the thirteenth century, and the great wave of Chassidism of the eighteenth century, are the historic evidences of the psychological reaction."[2]

[1] Abrahams, *op. cit.*, p. 160.
[2] E. M. Friedman, *Survival or Extinction* (New York, 1924), p. 131.

By the middle of the sixteenth century we find evidences of consolidation of the scattered local settlements and the isolated and provincial thought of the ghettos. The codified Jewish law, known as Shulchan Aruch (table prepared), compiled by Joseph Caro, stimulated the accommodation of practices and beliefs of the various Jewish communities to each other. The uniformity produced in religious and social life of the Jews everywhere as a result of the wide circulation and acceptance of this code was due in large measure to the fact that "it had the good fortune of being compiled in an age of printing," and the fact that during the age of the ghettos it was primarily through the religious channel that life could be influenced at all.[1]

Until the dawn of the social and political emancipation of the Jews at the end of the eighteenth century their intellectual life, on the whole, was of a uniform and specifically Jewish character, for they were sundered by ghetto walls from external influences. They were trained in traditional Hebrew lore in the schools of the Synagogue, and nurtured on Jewish ideals; with the exception of a Spinoza or a Süsskind of Trimberg, they devoted themselves mainly to the study and enrichment of their own national literature; and even when they occupied themselves with alien subjects they still laboured in a Jewish milieu and retained a Jewish outlook. But with the advent of emancipation a radical change sets in.[2]

LIFE IN THE PALE

The general outline of the description of the Western ghetto, given in the preceding pages, applies also to the Eastern pale. There remain a few facts of special significance, however, with reference to Jewish settlements in Eastern Europe, on which it is proposed to dwell briefly here.

[1] Abrahams, *op. cit.*, p. xxvi.
[2] Cohen, *Jewish Life in Modern Times*, p. 224.

Contemporaneous with the migrations of the Jews along the Mediterranean to Italy, Spain, and Western Europe, there went forth another wave of immigrants through Asia Minor, the Caucasus, up to the shores of the Caspian and the Black seas. It is even possible that this movement antedated that toward the West.[1] From the East had also come a pagan people, the Khazars, who around the year 740 A.D. became converted to Judaism. By the year 1100 the Jews had a considerable community at Kiev. With the conversion of Russia to the Greek Orthodox faith their fate gradually changed. By the beginning of the twelfth century they had already experienced their first massacre or pogrom. Occasional merchants and scholars visited these Eastern settlements from the West; and from the East, by the time of the Crusades, studious young men came to study with the German rabbis. During the Crusades, beginning with the first in 1096, a steady stream of Jews who found themselves persecuted in the provinces of the Danube and the Rhine began to find their way to Poland, which by this time had already come under the influence of the Roman church, but took a less active part in the persecution of the Jews incident to the Crusades.

From their German brethren the Jews of Poland received their communal organization, their religious culture, and their language, which was a German dialect interspersed with Hebrew and Polish expressions and forms which gradually developed into what is known at the present time as Yiddish. The special relationship to the ruler, the hostility of the church, and the partial local autonomy of the Jewish

[1] Most of the details of this section are taken from S. M. Dubnow, *History of the Jews in Russia and Poland from the Earliest Times until the Present Day* (3 vol., Philadelphia, 1916, 1918, 1920).

communities were transferred from the West to the East almost in their entirety. In Lithuania, however, the Jews enjoyed a great deal more autonomy and tolerance than in Poland. This accounts for the superior status which the Lithuanian Jews have maintained to the present day as over against the rest of Eastern European Jewry. On the whole, the Jews were not so closely confined to the cities in the East as they were in the West, and they had more lenient regulations as to land tenancy than they enjoyed in the West. But in general they drifted into the same economic functions that they had practiced in Germany: "By the beginning of the fourteenth century Polish Jewry had become a big economic and social factor with which the state was bound to reckon. It was now destined to become also an independent spiritual entity, having stood for four hundred years under the tutelage of the Jewish center in Germany."[1] In Poland, unlike Germany, the Jews frequently settled in villages and engaged in farming, while in the towns they were not chiefly absorbed in petty trades and money-lending, but had open to them a varied field of economic activities. They engaged in the trades, handicrafts, and many other economic functions, including the leasing of crown and *Shlakhta* estates,[2] with the right of propination (distilling and selling spirituous liquors), which they continued to exercise on behalf of nobles even after the partition of Poland. The Jews were also the leading tax-farmers of the country. They found themselves favored by royalty and partly by the big *Shlakhta*, or estate owners, and opposed by the clergy and the burghers. The changes of the position of the Jews in Poland depended upon the shifting dominance of these classes in the Polish state.

[1] Dubnow, *op. cit.*, I, 65.

[2] *Shlakhta* refers to landed nobility.

The Jews found themselves the intermediaries between the nobles and the peasantry on the one hand, and the keen competitors of the burghers on the other.

In their *Kahals*, or communities, the Jews of Poland enjoyed even greater autonomy than the German Jews did in their ghettos. These *Kahals* were, moreover, more closely knit together into larger units than they were in the West. These conferences, or councils, as they were called, the most noted of which was the "Council of the Four Lands," were not only the guardians of the Jewish civil interests in relation to the government, but they appointed rabbis, passed laws for the Jews, decided upon religious ritual, education, taxes, and sat as a sort of supreme court in matters Jewish. The *Kahals* had compulsory education, which centered around the Bible and the Talmud, for all children between the sixth and thirteenth year. The elementary schools, or *cheders*, were either public or private, while the higher education, carried on in the *yeshibas*, was entirely under community control. Poland, during the sixteenth and seventeenth centuries, rapidly became the center of Jewish religious study, and was less influenced by secular interests than had been the case in France and Germany.

By the middle of the seventeenth century the Jews of Eastern Europe began to suffer from periodical massacres at the hands of military peasant bands or Cossacks, and later the invading Muscovites. The clergy fomented many ritual murder accusations[1] against the Jews, and the pans, or rural estate owners, together with the guilds in the cities, contrived to make the next century and a half a period of almost uninterrupted massacres of Jews.

[1] The charge that the Jews slaughtered Christian children and used human blood in their religious ritual has often been made the basis of massacres and lately of judicial persecution. The Beilis case is a recent example.

The social and economic decline of the Polish Jews, which set in after 1648, was not conducive to widening the Jewish mental horizon, which had been sharply defined during the preceding epoch. Even at the time when Polish-Jewish culture was passing through its zenith, Rabbinism reigned supreme in school and literature. Needless to say, there was no chance for any broader intellectual currents to contest this supremacy during the ensuing period of decline. The only rival of Rabbinism, whose attitude was now peaceful and now warlike, was Mysticism, which was nurtured by the mournful disposition of a life-worn people, and grew into maturity in the unwholesome atmosphere of Polish decadence.[1]

During this period of decadence the masses became increasingly ignorant and superstitious, while the talmudic culture, narrow and circumscribed as it was, became the exclusive possession of a small circle of scholars. The magic and superstition of Cabalism gained not only a strong hold upon the masses but on the spiritual leaders of the various communities as well.

During this period the Sabbatian movement, started by the self-appointed messianic liberator, Sabbatai Zevi, swept like wildfire through the superstitious masses of Jews. This was followed later by another messianic movement known as Chassidism, which, however, was outlawed by the orthodox rabbis. They were followed by another sect, known as the Frankists. These movements were in part a revolt against the dry-as-dust Rabbinism of the day, but could not have flourished had it not been for the degraded social and intellectual position of the Jews, and the restlessness incident to the political disturbances of the period of persecution.

Up to the partitions of Poland the Jews had been fairly consistently excluded from Russia proper. With Poland

[1] Dubnow, *op. cit.*, I, 198–99.

partly incorporated in the Russian Empire, the rulers of that empire had also inherited the problem of the Jews in their new domain. Their fate from now on was decided on a larger scale and from a more distant center than ever before. Furthermore, with the ascendancy of the Greek Orthodox church the history of the Eastern Jews takes on a more local and special aspect. The Jews of the East share less and less the fate of their Western brethren. A new device develops, commensurate with the new problems presented by the vast territory of Russia, namely, the pale of settlement. By these measures, which were enacted, revoked, and re-enacted several times in the course of the latter part of the eighteenth, the whole of the nineteenth, and part of the twentieth, century, the Jews are restricted to certain provinces of the empire. Furthermore, within these provinces the Jews are restricted to certain localities, particularly the towns and cities. Occasional expulsions from the rural districts, in which they had at various times been permitted to settle, resulted in the overcrowding of the Jewish quarters of the cities and in the duplication in aggravated form of the slum conditions of the Western ghettos. Meanwhile the Jewish population was often decimated by pogroms. With all this came the exclusion from public life, from many occupations, and from popular education and the universities. Not only was the ghetto life of the East, during this specific period at least, in many instances more confining and isolating than that of the West, but it persisted long after the walls of the Western ghetto had vanished, and the Jews of the West had come to share the cultural life of the Western European peoples.

The Jews of the pale, the Russian, Polish, and in part the Roumanian Jews, came, as a result, to be differentiated from those of Western Europe, the German, French, Dutch, and English Jews, in several fundamental respects. For a long period the Jews of the East were merely a cultural dependency, an outpost of Western Jewry. When an independent cultural life did develop in Russia, Poland, and Lithuania, it was self-sufficient and self-contained, apart from the larger world beyond the pale. Not so with the Jews of Western Europe. They were never quite impervious to the currents of thought and the social changes that characterized the life of Europe since the Renaissance. While the Jews of the East lived in large part in rural communities—in a village world—those of the West were predominantly a city people, in touch with the centers of trade and finance near and far, and in touch also with the pulsating intellectual life of the world. While the Jews of the Rhine cities were associating with kings and princes, with men of thought and of practical affairs, their brethren in Russia were dealing with peasants and an uncultured class of decadent, feudal landlords. When the Jewries of the West were already seething with modernist religious, political, and social movements, those of the East were still steeped in mysticism and medieval ritual. While the German Jews were moving along with the tide of progress in science and modern industry, those of Russia and Galicia were still sharing the backwardness and isolation of the gentile world of villagers and peasants. Although, until the middle of the last century, the Jews of the East were, as a rule, never quite so confined in their physical movements as were the ghetto Jews of the West, they lived in a smaller world—a world characterized by rigidity and stability—and when they were herded into cities in which they constituted the preponderant bulk of the total population they merely turned these cities into large villages that had little in common with the urban centers of the West. When we characterize the Jews as an urban people, therefore, we do so with the important qualification that the Jews of Eastern Europe occupied until recently the status of a village people. This distinction between the two large camps of modern Jewry goes far to explain the features of Jewish communal life in the New World to be dealt with in subsequent chapters.

Holy Emissary

CHAPTER VII
THE GHETTO IN DISSOLUTION
SOCIAL MOVEMENTS

Scarcely had the medieval Jewish communities attained the position of fairly autonomous settlements with a culture more or less distinct from that of their neighbors when profound currents from without and within the ghetto began to stir the imagination and the activity of their inhabitants. Some of these, such as Cabalism and Chassidism, have already been alluded to in the previous chapter. These, however, were just the beginning of a whole series of social movements which agitated the life of the people. While some were intended to preserve what there was of separatism and sectarianism, others tended to break down the ghetto walls both in the literal and the figurative sense.

Toward the end of the sixteenth century the Cabalistic movement was making headway, especially in Eastern Europe, rapidly enveloping Jewish life in a deep veil of mysticism and superstition. Intellectual activities were at their low ebb. The air of the ghetto and the pale was stagnant with ignorance, religious bigotry, and fanaticism which fed on the exclusion from the world without and the violent persecution.

The intellectual life of the Jews was then limited to the study of the Bible and Talmud. These studies, principally encouraged in the Talmudic schools in Poland, were not primarily directed to finding out the spirit of these books. They made of the text of the Bible a palaestre for interpretations which, though clever, were hair-splitting and fantastic; nor did the Talmud, upon which they piled commentary upon commentary, and supercommentary upon supercommentary, fare much better. By the side of these flourished the Kabbala, which in its most important book, the Zohar, professed to have revealed the key to all wisdom, and to be able thereby to dispense with all other knowledge. The innumerable ritual ceremonies were slavishly followed and made the pivot of daily life. Nothing gives us clearer insight into the mental attitude of the Jews of that period than that event which moved the whole of the seventeenth century Jewry to its very depths— the appearance of the Messiah, Sabbatai Zevi, and the subsequent cult of Sabbataism in the eighteenth century, led by Nehemiah Chija Chajon and other less scrupulous adventurers. On the same level was the quarrel between Emden and Eybenschütz in Hamburg (1750–56), a quarrel which raised the passions of Jews all over Europe to the boiling point, raising the question whether or not the life-saving amulets sold to midwives by Rabbi Eybenschütz contained the name of Sabbatai Zevi in their formula. Such was the intellectual standard of Jewry in the eighteenth century.[1]

The Chassidic movement was an outgrowth of the Cabalistic lore. It was essentially rustic in origin, and at first was taken up only by the most provincial and ignorant masses of Jews residing in isolated towns and villages. Israel Baal Shem Tob (known by the abbreviated form of his name, "Besht," the "master of the good name"), born around 1700 on the border line of Podolia and Wallachia, became the founder and leader of the sect. He had great advantages for his calling: he was poor, he was ignorant, he was enthusiastic, and he was obscure. More important, however, was the fact that he began his practice as wonder-worker at a time when the whole mass of Jewry was looking for a messiah, and when the orthodox rabbis had become detached from the people.

Besht became the favorite of the masses. Warm-hearted and simple in disposition, he managed to get close to the people and to find out

[1] Ruppin, *op. cit.*, pp. 4–5.

their spiritual wants. Originally a healer of the body, he imperceptibly grew to be a teacher of religion. He taught that true salvation lies, not in Talmudic learning, but in whole-hearted devotion to God, in unsophisticated faith and fervent prayer. . . . . Besht preached that the plain man, imbued with naïve faith, and able to pray fervently and whole-heartedly, was dearer and nearer to God than the learned formalist spending his whole life in the study of the Talmud. Not to speculate in religious matters, but to believe blindly and devotedly, such was the motto of Besht. This simplified formula of Judaism appealed to the Jewish masses and to those democratically inclined scholars who were satisfied neither with rabbinic scholasticism nor with the ascetic Cabala of the school of Ari.[1]

The opponents of Chassidism called themselves *Mithnagdim*, "Protestants," and persecuted and excommunicated the Chassidists wherever they could lay their hands on the members of the sect which had grown powerful and had become harder to manage because it had transformed itself into a secret society. Meanwhile, in Lithuania Jewish scholarship had taken an intellectualistic turn, but remained definitely within the restricted horizon of talmudical learning.

During the second half of the eighteenth century a new light began to shine for the Jews of Western Europe which sent some of its rays to the East and left profound impressions upon the whole complexion of Jewry. This was the wave of the so-called "Enlightenment," the inception of which is usually associated with the name of Moses Mendelssohn. Partly influenced by the enlightenment of the whole of Western Europe during the latter half of the eighteenth century, and particularly by the French philosophers of that period, and partly by the development of commerce and industry, which took off some of the stigma of the usurer from the Jew and facilitated numerous contacts, a new social

[1] Dubnow, *op. cit.*, I, 224-25.

and economic outlook began to characterize the Jews of the West. The old separatism began to break down, and left its marks upon Jewish religious and communal life.

While in the West the increased personal intercourse between Jews and Christians also stimulated the Jews to participate in the wider world of thought, to read French and German books, to abandon their ghetto jargon (*Jüdisch-Deutsch*) in favor of the language of the country in which they lived, in the East matters stood differently.

The breezes of Western culture had hardly a chance to penetrate to this realm, protected as it was by the double wall of Rabbinism and Hasidism. And yet here and there one may discern on the surface of social life the foam of the wave from the far-off West. From Germany the free-minded "Berliner," the nickname applied to these "new men," was moving toward the borders of Russia. He arrayed himself in a short German coat, cut off his earlocks, shaved his beard, neglected the religious observances, spoke German or "the language of the land," and swore by the name of Moses Mendelssohn. The culture of which he was the banner-bearer was a rather shallow enlightenment, which affected exterior and form rather than mind and heart. It was "Berlinerdom," the harbinger of the more complicated Haskala of the following period, which was imported into Warsaw during the decade of Prussian dominion (1796–1806).

The contact between the capitals of Poland and Prussia yielded its fruits. The Jewish "dandy" of Berlin appeared on the streets of Warsaw, and not infrequently the long robe of the Polish Hasid made way timidly for the German coat, the symbol of "enlightenment."[1]

The Eastern interpretation of "enlightenment" was considerably influenced by the Russian government's zeal to have the Jews "enlightened" by compulsory methods, among which was forcible recruiting of Jewish boys into the army, there to be made into good Christians and Russians. Another feature of the government's program was the partial

[1] *Ibid.*, pp. 284–85.

abolition of the communal autonomy of the Jews and compulsory instruction in secular subjects, without, however, permitting the Jews to participate in civil functions or to attend the secular educational institutions. Finally, the Russian government sought by decree to force the Jews to abandon their characteristic Jewish dress and appearance. All these efforts, while they made for great numbers of conversions—feigned as well as genuine—to Christianity, on the whole merely tightened the hold of ritualism and provincialism upon the Jews of Russia.

Two other social movements of profound significance swept Judaism before the era of emancipation opened: nationalism and socialism. Since Zionism has grown into a formidable movement, attempts have been made at various times to show that the Jews had never lost the desire of at some time returning to Palestine and there re-establishing their national sovereignty. The Zionists point to the frequent references by medieval thinkers and poets to the Holy Land as indicative of the fact that Jewish nationalism had never ceased to play a rôle even at a time when the morale of the Jews in the *diaspora* was at its lowest ebb. This is to be attributed to the necessity of such a movement as Zionism to find a *raison d'être*, to justify itself and seek support for its aims in the historic experiences of the people. But a more objective study reveals the contrary:

Judaism became nationalized by the fall of feudalism and the rise of the ghettos. The superficial appearance of a national entity has, I fear, originated the movement now popular with some modern Jews in favor of creating a Jewish state, politically independent and perhaps religiously homogeneous. I speak regretfully, because one does not like to see enthusiasm wasted over a conception which has no roots in the past and no fruits to offer for the future. The idealized love of Zion which grew up in the Middle Ages had no connexion whatever with this process of nationalization through which Judaism passed. Still less was it connected with an aspiration for religious homogeneity which did not exist in the Middle Ages, and is not likely to survive in Judaism now that it has once more become denationalized. National aspirations are nursed by persecution, but the medieval longing for the Holy Land grew up, not in persecution, but in the sunshine of literature. The Spanish-Jewish poet, to use Heine's famous figure, came to love Jerusalem as the medieval troubadour loved his lady, and the love grew with the lays. Jehuda Halevi used the very language of medieval love in this passionate address to his "woe-begone darling":

> O! who will lead me on
> To seek the spots where, in far distant years,
> The angels in their glory dawned upon
> Thy messengers and seers?
>
> O! who will give me wings
> That I may fly away,
> And there, at rest from all my wanderings,
> The ruins of my heart among thy ruins lay?

The same Jehuda Halevi who sings thus declared that Israel was to the nations as the heart to the body—not a nation of the nations, but a vitalizing element of them all.[1]

Whatever parallels may be found by the historian between Zionism and the European nationalism of the nineteenth century, the former had the added stimulus of the messianic hopes which repeatedly stirred the Jewish world during the Middle Ages, and which had found vivid expression in Jewish literature.

In the ghettos the Jews spoke a jargon of Judeo-German, Judeo-Spanish, Judeo-Polish, or whatever the admixture might be in accordance with local circumstances. These Yiddish dialects had already developed something of a literature. The movement of enlightenment, however, which

[1] Abrahams, *op. cit.*, pp. xxiv–xxv.

was given great impetus by Moses Mendelssohn's translation of the Pentateuch into pure German, put a stigma upon the use of Yiddish, which thereafter was not considered a polite language. The talmudic scholars, even, who used the jargon in their study and conversation began to look with horror upon the occasional translation of the Scriptures into Yiddish. By the opening of the nineteenth century the enlightenment movement, especially in the East, had taken the form of a neo-Hebraic Renaissance, known as the Haskalah movement. Plays, poems, scientific, political, and religious treatises began to appear in Hebrew, and many translations of literary works from other languages into neo-Hebrew were perfected. This literary revival lent itself readily to the propagation of nationalism.

From quite another source the Jewish nationalistic movement gained strong support. During several attempts to "solve the Jewish problem" in Russia on the part of the government, efforts had been made to settle the Jews on the land in some uncolonized areas. These Jewish settlements received only half-hearted encouragement from the government, but in spite of that some had a fair measure of success. Large parts of the Jewish population began to feel that a territorial basis for the Jewish communities on a sufficiently large scale to assure economic self-sufficiency, accompanied by religious and political autonomy, was the only way to save the Jews from persecution on the one hand, and from conversion and disintegration on the other.

The social and political disabilities that hampered even those Jews who had achieved something in the secular world, especially the Jewish students, added strength to the Zionist movement. These "intellectuals" found themselves rebuffed as undesirables and inferiors in European society, and many of them returned to their people enthusiastic about the movement to establish a Jewish nation.

Zionism did much to reunite Eastern and Western Jews whom the different historical experiences and the unequal rate of social and economic progress of the East and the West had widely separated. Toward the middle of the nineteenth century numbers of Jews, particularly aged Jews, journeyed to Palestine, there to pass their last days. Some of them, and more often their children, became apostles of Zionism.

The advocacy of the colonization of Palestine as the only solution of the Jewish question was made as early as 1818 by Mordecai Manuel Noah, in America, and was repeated in different countries at intervals throughout the century. In France it was urged in 1830 by the historian Joseph Salvador; in Germany, in 1862, independently by Moses Hess, in his *Rome and Jerusalem;* and by Hirsch Kalischer, in his *Quest of Zion,* the one a socialist, the other an orthodox rabbi; in England, in 1876, by George Eliot in her famous novel, *Daniel Deronda;* and in Russia, in 1880, by the Hebrew writers Moses Lilienblum and Perez Smolenskin, and soon after by Leon Pinsker, too, who, in his historic pamphlet, *Auto-Emancipation,* eloquently argued that the settlement of the Jews in a land of their own was the only salvation from their sufferings, though he did not specifically propose Palestine for the purpose.[1]

In 1870 the *Alliance Israelite,* which had been established in Paris in 1860 to assist the Jews of Eastern Europe, established an agricultural school in Palestine. In 1884 the "Society of Lovers of Zion" was founded in Kattowitz, at a representative Jewish conference to promote extensive settlements in Palestine.

The work of colonization, however, lagged at the beginning, partly owing to the early settlers being endowed only with zeal, but with

[1] Cohen, *op. cit.,* p. 328.

little practical knowledge, and partly owing to the obstacles inevitably associated with pioneer settlement; and it was not until Baron Edmond de Rothschild came to its aid with his munificent generosity that it made any appreciable progress. The Lovers of Zion were animated, it is true, by the national sentiment, but the general character of their activity was a blend of philanthropy and religious piety, whilst the aid contributed by Western Jews was also prompted mainly by charitable motives tinged with the racial consciousness. Not until the advent of the feuilletonist and playwright, Theodor Herzl, in 1896, was the Jewish national sentiment propounded as an idea whose expression should not limit itself to the creation of scattered colonies in the Holy Land, but which should expand into an organized endeavour of the Jewish people to work for its national regeneration.[1]

With this, Zionism became a political movement. Herzl's pamphlet, *The Jewish State*, in spite of strong opposition from rabbis and laymen, had the effect of bringing together the first International Congress at Basle, in 1897, to consider the program outlined by him. Since then Zionist congresses have been meeting regularly.

Zionism, it must be remembered, was not a ghetto movement. It began with those who had already partially emerged from the ghetto. It did not start with the Jews of the pale, for they had too little contact with the world of practical politics to inaugurate a nationalistic movement of this sort. The Jew, as long as he finds himself inclosed by ghetto walls, is not only helpless, but is extremely naïve about the world outside. The Zionist movement was, at least in part, the culmination of the attempt on the part of the Western Jews, who had already acquired some experience with politics and civic life, to assist their Eastern brethren, who were still held strictly under the thumb of Tsaristic autocracy. As the Zionist movement gained momentum, however, it was the

[1] *Ibid.*, pp. 328–29.

Jews of Eastern Europe who became its most ardent champions. Pogroms and exclusion from the common life of the country were the levers that compelled their adherence, while the Western Jews, who began to feel fairly comfortable under the changed conditions of the last half of the nineteenth century, maintained a philanthropic interest in the movement and often were compelled by idealistic motives of cultural solidarity or personal motives of leadership to maintain their affiliation and contribute their "shekel," as the annual dues were called; but on the whole the political life of their own locality was much more immediate and absorbing. Not until the recrudescence of anti-Semitism in recent times has their attitude toward Zionism changed. But already it is becoming evident to many who otherwise are favorably inclined to Zionism that the establishment of an independent Jewish state, far from solving the "Jewish problem," would merely result in making the ghetto international.[1]

Side by side with Zionism a great number of Jews thought that they had found another road leading to freedom, the road of political and social revolution, which found expression in the Socialist movement. In France, Germany, and Russia numbers of Jewish workers and intellectuals looked to the general revolt of the masses as the surest means that would bring political and social equality to them. Even while they were still excluded from the sphere of political activities of the various countries, they could participate in the agitation and discussion that first centered around the question of constitutional monarchies and later took the form of utopian socialism, finally culminating in the movements generally identified by the names of two Jews, Karl

[1] See Karl Kautsky, *Are the Jews a Race?* London, 1926.

Marx and Ferdinand Lasalle. The Jews, being predominantly members of the middle class, and particularly the *petit
bourgeoisie*, stood as a whole on a liberal democratic plat-
form. They were represented in the Socialist movement less
by numbers than by enthusiasm and outstanding personalities.

In Russia, socialism among the Jews took partly the
form of Zionism, and became incorporated in the Poale Zion
party. The federation of Jewish socialist organizations,
known as "Bund," exercised an important rôle in the formation of the Russian Social Democratic party. It was composed largely of Jewish workingmen, but received its leadership and enthusiasm from numerous students and intellectuals who joined its ranks. It was a secret movement, of course,
and had about it much of the romantic atmosphere.

Finally there came a movement within Judaism which
confined itself largely to reforming the ritual, known as the
Reform movement. This movement not only brought Jewish religious services in accord with the procedure in Christian churches, such as introducing organs, mixed choirs, and
the substitution of the vernacular for Hebrew, but it also
permitted greater latitude in the personal conduct of the
individual. In the Reform temples praying shawls and philacteries are not worn, and the congregation does not wear
hats, as is required in the orthodox synagogue. In most
instances services are held on Sundays instead of Saturdays,
and the prayers thrice daily, which characterize the synagogue, are omitted. The Reform movement widened the gulf
between the religious and the secular. The emphasis on
Kosher food disappears, and even intermarriage of Jews
with Gentiles is not frowned upon so severely as was the
case in the Middle Ages.

This movement, which started in Germany, looked upon Judaism more as a religious and less as a cultural and national body. In fact, it emphasized the civic and local interests of the Jewish population as over against the "national" and "cultural" aims and the separatist attitude of orthodoxy. It favored cultural assimilation with the general population. But Reform Judaism, too, differs from country to country. It never gained much of a foothold in Russia, is hard to distinguish from orthodoxy in England, and has taken its most radical turn in Germany and the United States. It did away with the *Cheder* and the *Yeshiba*, and relegated the rabbinical literature to the scrap heap. The leaders of Reformism have insisted that only through some such modernizing influence as this can Judaism be saved from complete disintegration; while the defenders of orthodoxy have replied that Reformism is only a step to complete assimilation and apostasy, and is to be regarded therefore as the surest and most direct route toward conversion and desertion.

These movements within the Jewish communities of Europe and America marked the beginning of a new epoch in the *diaspora*. They are indicative of the inner forces that were gradually breaking down the ghetto walls, and were one phase of the process of dissolution of the ghetto, which was paralleled by the political emancipation and the acquisition of social status from the outside.

In view of the religious movements that stirred the European ghettos internally, and the social and political currents that swept upon them from without, historians have been busy attempting to discover the forces that held the Jews together and prevented them from disintegrating into a number of isolated sects. It has been pointed out by some that the conservatism of the group was due to its wide dispersion, while others have held that pressure from without was strong enough to solidify the group and immunize it against disintegrating influences. As one views the experiences of the Jews in retrospect, one cannot help noting that the influences of these sectarian movements are still operative, and that at least one factor in the persistent integration of the life of the group is the constant struggle that is being carried on against them, in the course of which the members have become mobilized in a common combative effort.

It has been suggested, however, that the larger, integrated Jewish community of the Middle Ages no longer exists, and that what we see today is virtually a series of disparate sects. It should be noted, though, that the religious motives, which underlie a great deal of Jewish communal life even to the present day, are essentially rooted in the desire for security, and this need for security has not been effectually satisfied by any of the sectarian movements within Judaism itself. Only to the extent that the solidarity of the family has been affected by modern life has the community been weakened and the allegiance to the old heritage been periled. To the great masses of Jews neither the exotic, orgiastic sects of Cabalism and Chassidism nor the rationalism of enlightenment and reformism, nor, finally, the radical transition to some Christian denomination, could offer an adequate substitute for the warmth, the comfort, and the security that was to be found in the orthodox religious beliefs and practices.

To the Jew, each new movement, whether from without or from within his own group, presented a new avenue of escape from his troubles, and to a fuller and freer life. Like a drowning man, he reached for every object that was thrown out to him, hoping to save himself. Zionism, Socialism, and every other movement that came along has found numbers of Jewish adherents. The Jew lived on the fringe of two worlds. From behind the ghetto wall he was able to steal a glimpse of life in the larger world outside. He never lived fully in either world, and was torn between the impulse to remain in the intimate circle of his own kind, where he found security, and where he had some sort of status, and the conflicting impulse to escape into the life outside, which from a distance looked so free, so varied, and so colorful—where he could find a larger audience to appreciate his talents; where he could meet, not only with ghetto Jews, but with men of the world. As a result he took seriously every movement that went on, looking upon its slogans as the call to freedom.

One other phase of this behavior of the Jew is worth noting. The Jew was more or less at the mercy of his own intellectual qualities. He had become accustomed to look upon every plan with the view of its rational meaning and teleological significance. The Jew had no difficulty in rationalizing, not only Reformism and Socialism, but Zionism and Chassidism as well. He looked upon the programs of these movements as rational solutions of his problems. He failed to see that life was not a series of hurdles which must be overcome by dialectics, but an ongoing process, in the course of which every day brings new situations which cannot be met by nostrums and magic formulas, but which must be lived, and which reappear again and again and never are finally solved.

EMANCIPATION

The change from medievalism to modernism, which we are accustomed to associate with the Renaissance, the rise of cities, the growth of nationalism, and the decay of absolute monarchism, left the Jews of Europe largely unaffected. They were a special class of the population, to be dealt with separately, and to whom the ordinary rights of citizens did not apply. Toward the middle of the eighteenth century, however, there appeared occasional symptoms of a changing attitude toward the Jews on the part of the governments and the general population of central and western Europe. The increasing contact which came with the growth of modern capitalism and the breakdown of the feudal and guild system, and the growing tolerance which was an aftermath of popular enlightenment, had already stirred the Jews more or less profoundly, as evidenced by the social movements within Judaism itself that have just been described.

The Jews were still aliens, however, in the countries in which they had lived for centuries. They were barred from landownership, from many occupations, from the universities and schools, from participation in civil and political affairs, and from the ordinary rights of citizenship. Furthermore, they were restricted in choosing their domicile, and were subjected to special taxation. In some countries their private lives were circumscribed even as regards dress, speech, and worship. They were subject to arbitrary expulsion, and exposed to insult and violence on the part of the populace, without rights of redress. "In short, they had no right except the right to exist, and this was exposed to so many wrongs that it was felt as a burden itself."[1] They did not submit to these measures passively, but so long as they remained in the ghettos they were impotent. Their hands were tied, and they were often censured for not improving their lot.

[1] Cohen, *op. cit.*, p. 135.

Even in England, where the Jews had enjoyed freedom
of domicile, and from the poll tax since they had resettled in
that country in 1655, after an expulsion, an act for the
naturalization of the Jews passed in 1753 was repealed in
the same year as a result of popular indignation. In France
the spirit of toleration preached by the "philosphers of reason" began to have its effects in the gradual removal of the
disabilities of the Jews. But the full "rights of man" were
not extended to the Jews of France until 1791. Napoleon
later confirmed these rights granted by the revolutionary
National Assembly. Meanwhile an interesting episode occurred which was of more significance to the Jews of the rest
of the continent than to those of France:

The Jewish question in France was reopened by the guild merchants and religious reactionaries of Alsace, who exploited the inability of the peasants of this province to repay their debts to the Jews
by petitioning Napoleon to abrogate the civil rights of the Jews. The
conqueror resolved to submit the question to the consideration of the
Jews themselves. He convened an Assembly of Jewish Notables of
France, Germany, and Italy, in order to ascertain whether the principles of Judaism were compatible with the requirements of citizenship, as he wished to fuse the Jewish element with the dominant population. The Assembly, consisting of 111 deputies, met in the Town
Hall of Paris on July 25, 1806, and was required to frame replies to
twelve questions relating mainly to the possibility of Jewish patriotism,
the permissibility of intermarriage between Jew and non-Jew, and the
legality of usury. So pleased was Napoleon with the pronouncements
of the Assembly that he summoned a Sanhedrin after the model of the
ancient council of Jerusalem, to convert them into the decrees of a
legislative body. The Sanhedrin, comprising 71 deputies from France,
Germany, Holland, and Italy, met under the presidency of Rabbi
Sinzheim, of Strassburg, on February 9, 1807, and adopted a sort of
charter which exhorted the Jews to look upon France as their fatherland, to regard its citizens as their brethren, and to speak its language;
and which also expressed toleration of marriages between Jews and

Christians, while declaring that they could not be sanctioned by the synagogue.[1]

The Jews, as this decision shows, were willing to compromise with some of their age-old traditions, such as their attitude toward intermarriage, to purchase their rights of citizenship.

For a time the Jews of Italy, of Westphalia, and of the Hansa towns profited by Napoleon's action and gained civil emancipation, but with the fall of Napoleon there came a reaction. In Rome, during the revolution of 1848, the ghetto was once again abolished, only to be re-established when the revolution was past. In 1870 the Jews of Rome sent a notable petition to the Pope setting forth their grievances and pleading for the abolition of the ghetto. The opening sentences of this petition are indicative of the tenor of the document; it read:

Most Holy Father! The elders and the delegates of the Jewish community of Rome, faithful subjects of your Holiness, prostrate themselves before your exalted throne, and offer the assurance of the continued loyalty of their co-religionists. This feeling of loyalty is the result of the many conspicuous deeds of kindness which we, O Holy Father, have experienced at your hands, and we are now animated by the pleasant sensation of hope, since your exalted will has consented to receive new petitions in its name. In fulfilment of the duty imposed on them, the petitioners presume humbly and reverently to lay before your holy wisdom and mildness the present exceedingly wretched condition of their co-religionists. May you deign to cast a gracious glance from your exalted throne upon those who, though Israelites, are a portion of your people.

And this medieval document, written in 1870, ended as follows:

Accustomed as the undersigned are to bless your name, they hop not to have spoken in vain to your fatherly heart of the sad lot sti theirs; the insalubrity of the old Jewish dwellings; the direct and in

Cohen, *op. cit.*, pp. 137–38.

direct obstacles to the free pursuit of the trades, the fine arts and the larger number of industries; the limited right to possess real estate; the denial on the part of some notaries of their right to act as witnesses; the alarming increase of poverty; the impotence of the Israelitish benevolent institutions to prevent or lessen misery; the impropriety of the yearly appropriations paid by order of the finance commission to two Catholic institutions; the alarm of the rich, who, in consequence of the mentioned burdens, are subjected to many pecuniary sacrifices required by their own religious foundations, and others which the indebtedness of their benevolent institutions demands of them; the inability to take energetic measures for the better education of the greatly increasing poorer class—all this [misery], O Holy Father, must appeal to you, in such a degree, that your own heart will find it advisable not to delay the carrying out of the good deed, for *pauperes facti sumus nimis*, we have become too impoverished, and the prayer which the undersigned whisper in the hearing of your Holiness is the prayer of forty-eight hundred of your subjects.

Hear us, O Holy Father, so that the children of Israel may once again benefit by that noble generosity inseparably connected with your immortal name!¹

Before the Pope had had an opportunity to act upon this servile diplomatic gesture, the Italian king made his entry into the Holy City, and the Jews of Rome were admitted to full citizenship, which the rest of the Italian states had already granted them in 1859, when the papal states came under the rule of Victor Emanuel. The Roman ghetto stood, however, until 1885, when it was the last of the Western European ghettos to be destroyed.

In Germany and Austria the Jews had won minor rights here and there during the eighteenth century, but with Napoleon's fall they were withdrawn. In 1819 the feeling against the Jews ran so high that wholesale massacres and expulsions took place throughout Central and Northern

¹ Philipson, *op. cit.*, pp. 164–74.

Europe. The revolutions of 1848, in which the Jews were actively interested, brought relief. In Prussia the fight for emancipation was led by a Jewish lawyer from Hamburg, Gabriel Riesser. The national parliament at Frankfort passed the decree emancipating the Jews. This was followed by emancipation in Hanover and Nassau in the same year, in Württemberg in 1861, Baden in 1862, and Saxony in 1868. The North German Confederation, formed in 1869, abolished religious disabilities, and with the formation of the German Empire in 1870, full civil equality became an accomplished fact. In Austria-Hungary emancipation came in 1869. In England the first Jew to sit in Parliament was Baron Lionel de Rothschild, in 1858, and the English universities admitted them to full privileges only in 1870. Not until 1890, however, did all positions in the British Empire, except that of monarch, become open to Jews. In Canada the Jews have enjoyed full civil rights since 1832, in South Africa since 1820, and in Australia ever since their settlement.

In Belgium the Jews were emancipated in 1815, in Denmark in 1849, in Norway in 1851, in Sweden they gained most of the rights of citizenship in 1865, and in the same year in Switzerland. Spain gave overt expression of its friendly interest in the Jews, whom it had expelled 350 years earlier, in 1858; Portugal, in 1825. In Bulgaria and Serbia the Jews gained civil rights in 1878, and in Turkey not until 1908. In Russia the Jews did not gain their rights of citizenship until the revolution of 1917, and in Roumania they were subject to all sorts of disabilities until after the World War. Their status even at present is uncertain. In Russia and Roumania active persecution coexisted with political subjection, and in the latter country there is reason to believe on the basis of recent happenings that pogroms are not yet a thing of the past. A similar situation has arisen in post-war Hungary.

An interesting sidelight on the attitude of the orthodox communities toward emancipation is furnished by what happened in Amsterdam:

> Upon the establishment of the Batavian Republic in 1795, the more energetic members of the Jewish community pressed for a removal of the many disabilities under which they laboured. . . . . Some of these disabilities were removed in response to vigorous agitation, but the demand for the full rights of citizenship made by the progressive Jews was at first, strangely enough, opposed by the leaders of the Amsterdam community, who feared that civil equality would militate against the conservation of Judaism, and declared that their co-religionists renounced their rights of citizenship in obedience to the dictates of their faith.[1]

The "progressive" Jews won out, and the Jews of Holland gained civil equality in 1796.

The political freedom which the Jews thus gained throughout Western Europe toward the middle of the last century came to them bit by bit, and not without persistent struggle. The changed social life of Western Europe since the French Revolution, and the mass movements that accompanied it, had loosened the hold of the traditional ties of the provincial Jewish communities and had given some of its members an opportunity here and there to taste the life that lay outside the ghetto. The Jews were not slow to avail themselves of the opportunities that emancipation offered. They entered whole-heartedly into the political life of the countries in which they lived, and as the barriers to residence and occupation were removed, they expanded the horizon of their social life. They flocked to the universities in large

[1] Cohen, *op. cit.*, p. 139.

numbers, and many of them distinguished themselves in the new fields of activity which now were open to them.

This political and social emancipation led to more intimate contacts between Jews and non-Jews, and still more dissolved the hold that tradition and religious ritual had exercised in the past. Those members of the Jewish communities, like the orthodox group in Amsterdam, who saw in the new freedom the decline of the influence of the Jewish religion as a unifying and conservative force and the ultimate dissolution of Jewish communal life had some things left to console them: First, the formal equality decreed by the law did not at the same time bring about social equality. Second, although the official barriers were removed, there remained numerous barriers created by custom which hindered the Jews from entrance into the society of their Christian fellow-citizens; and third, as Ruppin points out, although Western Jewry seemed to be crumbling, there were approximately six million Jews left on the other side of the Vistula who were still clinging to the old bonds that exclusion and oppression had fashioned. But since that time even Russia has been revolutionized, and the "last bulwark" of Judaism threatens to disappear.

MODERN GHETTOS

Just as the ghetto arose before formal decrees forced the Jews into segregated areas, so the ghetto persists even after these decrees have been annulled. But just as the voluntary ghetto differed in important respects from the compulsory institution, so the ghetto that lingers after its formal basis has been undermined is a different sort of structure from its predecessor. Mr. Zangwill has said: "People who have been living in a ghetto for a couple of centuries are not able to step outside merely because the gates are thrown down, nor to efface the brands on their souls by putting off the yellow badges. The isolation from without will have come to seem the law of their being."[1] The formal abolition of the ghetto and the granting of the rights of citizenship did for the Jews about what the emancipation proclamation did for the American Negro. The abolition of Negro slavery did not make the Negro free and equal. In fact, race prejudice against the Negro seemed to arise only as the Negro became emancipated. Slavery was more than a mere legal relationship between master and slave. The ghetto was more than just a legal measure. It had become an institution, and, as such, had come to exist not only in statutes and decrees but in the habits and attitudes of individuals and in the culture of groups. Though the physical walls of the ghetto have been torn down, an invisible wall of isolation still maintains the distance between the Jew and his neighbors.

When, in the Middle Ages, proselytes entered the Jewish community they left their world behind them, outside the ghetto gates. Jews who left their community for the world outside were absorbed into the general population and disappeared within a few generations, without leaving a trace. This exodus of individuals from the ghetto was at times quite large, and the path was made smooth by the church, which meant the state as well. With the formal ghetto abolished, however, even this avenue of escape is made more difficult. An English Jew, Joseph Jacobs, has expressed the typical reaction in the following terms:

. . . . I was just at that stage which comes in the intellectual development of every Jew, I suppose, when he emerges from the ghetto,

[1] Israel Zangwill, *Children of the Ghetto* (Philadelphia, 1907), I, 6.

both social and intellectual, in which he was brought up. He finds the world outside pursuing a course quite oblivious of the claims of his race and his religion. This oblivion is in itself a tacit condemnation of the claims which justified his former isolation. He is forced to reconsider them, and the result is that he either re-enters the ghetto never to emerge, or comes outside never to re-enter.[1]

Zangwill has given this invisible wall literary expression in his poem, "The Goyim" (The Gentiles):

> Beware of the *Goyim*, his elders told Jacob,
> In the holy peace of the Sabbath candles.
> They drink Jewish blood:
> They are fiercer than flame,
> Or than cobras acoil for the spring.
> They make mock of our God and our Torah,
> They rob us and spit on us,
> They slaughter us more cruelly than the *Shochet* our cattle.
> Go not outside the Ghetto.
> Should your footsteps be forced to their haunts,
> Walk warily, never forgetting
> They are *Goyim*,
> Foes of the faith,
> Beings of darkness,
> Drunkards and bullies,
> Swift with the fist or the bludgeon,
> Many in species, but all
> Engendered of God for our sins,
> And many and strange their idolatries,
> But the worst of the *Goyim* are the creatures called Christians.
>
> In the comforting gleam
> Of the two Sabbath candles
> The little boy thrilled with an exquisite shudder
> At the words of his elders.
> For the slums that enswathed with their vileness his nest,
> Pullulated with Christians;

[1] Joseph Jacobs, *Jewish Ideals and Other Essays*, p. xiii.

Easy to recognize
By the stones and the scoffs of their young at his passing,
And the oaths of their reeling adults,
And the black eyes they gave to their females
On Saturday nights,
Preparing for Sunday.
Foul-tongued and ferocious these creatures, the worst of the *Goyim.*

But Jacob grew bigger,
Outgrowing the Ghetto.
He laughed at his elders
With their cowering fears and exclusive old customs
And mechanical rites.
He worshipped the Gentiles,
No savage inferiors to Israel,
But Plato and Virgil, but Shakespeare and Shelley,
But Bach and Beethoven,
But Michael Angelo,
Dreamers and seers and diviners,
Shapers of Man, not a tribe;
Builders of beauty.

O the soul-shaking roll of the organ
In their dim cathedrals
And the sacred trance of the spirit
In their grass-grown colleges.

Poor Ghetto's fusty lore
And the drone it imagined music
And the blind-alley it called the cosmos.
Hats off to the *Goyim,* he cried, hats off e'en in Synagogue.
Great are our brethren the *Goyim,* and the greatest of all are the
    Christians.

But behold him today,
Little Jacob once more,
Bowed small by the years and calamities,
With his tragical eyes,
The Jew's haunted eyes,

That have seen for themselves,
Seen history made
On the old Gentile formula,
Seen the slums written large
In the red fields of Europe,
And the *Goyim* blood-drunken,
Reeling and cursing
As on Saturday night.

Back, back, he cries, brethren.
Back to the Ghetto,
To our God of compassion,
To our dream of Messiah,
And our old Sabbath candles!

For the others are *Goyim*,
Who despite all their Platos,
Their Shakespeares and Shelleys,
Their Bachs and Beethovens,
Drink human blood.
Not only ours but their kinsmen's.

Pitiless fratricides,
Beings of darkness,
Foes of the faith,
Fiercer than cobras acoil for the spring:
Many in species, but all
Engendered of God for our sins,
And many and strange their idolatries,
But the worst of the *Goyim* are the creatures called Christians.[1]

The ghetto still remains a fairly universal institution where-
ever Jews live in considerable numbers. Even in the United
States, where medieval legislation is not a part of the tradition of the general population, and in the countries of
Europe where the legal status of the Jew is that of citizen,
a nucleus of the ghetto persists.

[1] Israel Zangwill, *The Voice of Jerusalem* (New York, 1921), pp. 324–26.

Even in this free country of ours, where a ghetto has never been established by religious canon or civil law, the effects of ghetto life in Europe crop out very perceptibly. In our large cities Jewish quarters are being formed which, though not defined by law, nor enclosed by walls, nor barred by gates, to all intents and purposes are no less ghettos than those of mediaeval days. The poorer Jews who come to this country naturally flock together and inhabit whole districts, which come to assume the appearance of ghettos. So it is also in London, Amsterdam, Paris, Vienna, and other large cities of Europe. The ghetto in law has ceased to be; the ghetto in fact still exists.

Now, this *esprit de corps*, this exclusiveness, this seeking of brethren, is a direct result of the treatment to which Jews have been subjected during the Christian centuries. And not alone the masses of poor, wretched creatures that live in the lowly quarters of the great cities of the world, but even those Jews who have reaped all the benefits of emancipation, and move in the higher circles of life and thought, are often met with the reproach that they are clannish and exclusive, that they shut themselves up within their own social precincts, and are attracted to one another by a magnetism of fellowship. Very true, and very natural; so long were the Jews excluded by legal measure and enactment and religious prejudice and teaching from all intimate contact with non-Jews, so long were they thrown upon one another, that, as a logical result, they became exclusive. People maltreated and oppressed for the same reason cling to one another. Suffering in a like cause attaches them very close to each other, for there is no bond that unites so firmly as suffering. The Jew was excluded, therefore he became exclusive; he was avoided, therefore he became clannish; the hand of the world was against him, therefore he sought protection amongst his own. Even though official exclusion be a thing of the past, the prejudices of men and churches cannot be abolished by law and decree, and largely these still exist against the Jew.[1]

The ghetto gains its recruits, not only from the orthodox countries of the East, but its own children who have at one time or another left the fold frequently return from the cold, artificial life without to the warmth and familiarity of the

[1] Philipson, *op. cit.*, pp. 199–201.

ghetto. They were lost in the outside world, and return to the inner circle where life has meaning and where personality is anchored in a set of values and sentiments on which the group is unanimous. Getting out into the world has made the Jew self-conscious. As long as he remained in the ghetto he had his problems, but they were small in comparison with the friction and the prejudice and the rebuffs with which he, now that he is no longer a utility, but a human being, meets.

The name *Judenschmerz* has been applied to that attitude on the part of the Jew whose talents would entitle him to participate in the work of the world, but who feels himself hampered, excluded, or merely tolerated by the world at large. The more sensitive individuals in the group who find no adequate expression for their impulses, finding themselves avoided by the outside world and not being inclined to revert to their own group and share in the activities that it provides on a smaller scale, settle down to a life of brooding, of apathy, and melancholia.[1]

There is scarcely a city of any considerable size in Europe or America that does not have its ghetto. Even in towns containing only a score of Jews, there is to be found in all parts of the world some more or less definitely organized Jewish community. The center of this community is usually the synagogue, which for orthodox Jews is a prerequisite for public worship. Around the synagogue, as has already been indicated, there cluster a number of other institutions answering to the manifold needs of the traditional habits of life of the Jews.

Some communities contain such an abundance and elaboration of institutions, answering not only to a variety of tendencies and rites

[1] This subject has recently been treated by Ludwig Lewisohn in his *The Island Within*, New York, 1928.

in the religious domain, and to every conceivable social, philanthropic, and intellectual purpose, but also to separate industrial and professional interests, and to rival political aspirations, that they form complete social organisms in themselves.

Cognate in origin, allied by the same traditions and customs, these communities give to modern Jewry the semblance of a vast network of autonomous settlements. The enlightened Jew, in whatever part of the globe he may live, is conscious of this world-wide dispersion. He has acquired this consciousness from his earliest youth, with his initiation into the history of his people; nay, from his early childhood, when he first heard stories of their persecution in barbarous lands told in hushed breath at the family hearth. The knowledge is fostered by his press, which takes as its sphere of interest the conditions of Jewry throughout the world; it is stimulated by contact with fellow-Jews arriving from other lands; it is sustained by the frequent dispersion of the members of a single family, particularly from Russia, to all corners of the globe.[1]

There are several factors that may account for the persistence of the modern ghetto besides the continuity of traditions from within and prejudice from without. Frequently colonization efforts are undertaken by a number of national and international organizations within Jewry, such as the Alliance Israelite, the Hilfsverein der Deutschen Juden, or, in the United States, the Jewish Colonization Society, the Industrial Removal Office, the Hebrew Sheltering and Immigrant Aid Society, the Baron de Hirsch Fund, and kindred organizations, which sometimes transplant entire communities from one country to another and facilitate the re-creation of the old communal organization in the new environment. This is particularly true of many immigrants from Eastern Europe who have been established in new homes in North and South America.

But even where no such organized effort exists it is re-

[1] Cohen, *op. cit.*, pp. 24–25.

markable to what an extent the Jewish community, particularly if it is an orthodox community, tends to perpetuate its old surroundings. From one point of view, what we see here is merely one aspect of the transplantation of all Old World immigrant groups to the New World; but in the Jewish community the forces that make for cohesion are implicit in the organization of the group itself.

To a large extent the modern ghetto is necessitated by the precepts and practices of orthodox Judaism, by the need of dwelling within easy reach of the synagogue, the schoolroom, and the ritual bath, the kosher butcher-shop, and the kosher dairy. But even for those who are indifferent to religious observances and ritual practices, residence in the ghetto is necessitated by social and economic circumstances. Ignorance of the language of the new country, of its labour conditions, and of its general habits and ways of thought, as well as the natural timidity of a fugitive from a land of persecution, compels the immigrant Jew to settle in the colony of his co-religionists. Among them he is perfectly at home; he finds the path of employment comparatively smooth, and if his efforts to attain it be delayed, he is helped in the interval by charity from a dozen hands.[1]

Conversely, in countries where the contact between Jew and non-Jew has been continued for a few generations, and where no new immigration from other countries in which the Jews retained their old status has taken place, the ghetto has, to a large extent, disintegrated.

Under these circumstances not only does the ghetto tend to disappear, but the race tends to disappear with it. Contact with the world through education, through commerce and industry, through literature and the arts tends to bring about a substitution of the cultural values of the world at large for those of the ghetto. This contact, moreover, frequently brings about intermarriage. The figures that are

[1] *Ibid.*, pp. 37–38.

available on the extent of intermarriage indicate that it is most frequent in those countries and localities where intercourse between Jew and Gentile is least restricted, and tends to become more general as marriage becomes a civil instead of a religious matter. Ruppin, who has collected the most adequate statistics on this question, says:

. . . . We find that we can divide countries into four distinct classes, according to the amount of intermarriage which goes on within them.

In the first class we include those countries where mixed marriages are less than 2 per cent: Galicia, Bukovina, Roumania, and the Jewish immigrant areas of England, France, and the United States.

In the second class (intermarriages from 2 to 10 per cent) we place Catholic Germany, Hungary (excluding Budapest), and Bohemia.

To the third class belong Protestant Germany, Holland, Austria (Vienna and Budapest). Here intermarriage goes on to the extent of from 10 to 30 per cent of Jewish marriages, and shows signs of rapid increase. It does not as yet threaten to disrupt the Jewish population, though it seriously reduces its numbers.

Finally, in the fourth class, come Denmark, Australia, and Italy. Here one-third of the Jewish marriages are mixed marriages, and constitute a serious menace to the continued existence of the already scanty Jewish population in those countries, as the children of the mixed marriages are practically all brought up in the Christian faith. The same thing applies to the Jewish communities which have been long established in England, France, and the United States of America. A few large German towns (Berlin, Hamburg) should be included also in this fourth class.[1]

The falling away of the children of mixed marriages and the increased rate of intermarriage among the children and grandchildren of Jewish immigrants are factors of especial significance in the changing character of the Jewish group.

[1] Arthur Ruppin, *op. cit.*, pp. 169–70. For a detailed discussion, particularly in reference to intermarriage in the United States, see Julius Drachsler, *Intermarriage in New York City*, New York, 1921.

It is safe to say that the present fifteen million Jews in the world constitute only a small proportion of the total living descendants of the original settlers in the Western World at the beginning of the Christian era. They constitute merely the residue of a much larger group whose Jewish identity has been lost in the general stream of the population.

What has happened in the case of the Jews is essentially what has taken place in all minority groups in recent times. As the barriers of isolation have receded, assimilation and interbreeding have decimated the size of the group and leveled its distinguishing characteristics in accordance with the milieu. Joseph Jacobs has given voice to the feeling of a great section of Jewry with reference to this tendency:

The great danger of modern times is the tendency toward what may be termed Chinesism, a fatal and monotonous similarity and mediocrity invading all sections of national life. One of the outward signs of this is the deadly monotony of dress and furniture, which is becoming more and more international. The growth of intercommunication is giving a common set of ideas and ideals to the whole world, and making it more and more difficult for any special culture like the Irish, or the Japanese, or the Jewish, to hold its own. Every such specific culture that disappears would make the final form of humanity, which seems so rapidly approaching, less rich and manifold. There would be nothing gained for the world, and much would be lost for it if all Jews were tomorrow to become indistinguishable from their neighbours.[1]

But he, like many others who are conscious of this trend, consoles himself with the thought that, after all, modern culture has much in common with Jewish culture, and the Jews who have taken an active part in the world in which they lived have been, for the most part, able to do so without

[1] Joseph Jacobs, in his introduction to the English edition of Ruppin's *The Jews of Today*, pp. xvii–xviii.

sacrificing their identity completely. They have, in consequence, acquired a "duplex culture," and their nature "has become richer and more irridescent."[1]

A Jewish community may in some respects be said to exist after the obstacles to ready intercourse with the larger community have been removed, but at best it is a nondescript community. Where, however, as is the case in most large cities of Western Europe and the United States, a steady influx of new immigrants has replenished the disintegrating Jewish community, there a ghetto, with all the characteristic local color, has grown up and maintains itself.

The most important feature that distinguishes the communities of the West from those of the East is their voluntary character. . . . . Western communities differ markedly from Eastern in another respect, as they generally comprise two main sections—the native and the foreign, the latter consisting mostly of immigrants from Russia, Rumania, and Galicia, whilst including representatives from many other countries in the East. The native section lived in some sort of concentration in the early history of their community, within a convenient distance of the synagogue and the kosher butcher-shop; but a rise in material prosperity would be followed by removal to a better district, where a new Jewish area might be created, though one less distinguished from its environment by external tokens. The foreign section, however, live in a state of dense concentration. Their poverty makes them settle in a poor quarter of the town, where they reproduce the social conditions in which they have been born and bred, so far as the new environment will allow. They have been accustomed to live as one large family, speaking the same tongue and breathing the same air, and all revolving around the synagogue, which is for them not merely a house of worship and religious instruction, but a center of charity and of social intercourse; and although they are now free to

[1] Horace Kallen has recently presented his notion of cultural pluralism in answer to this argument. See his *Zionism and World Politics*, New York, 1921, and *Culture and Democracy in the United States*, New York, 1924.

settle wherever they please, they cannot easily break away from the engrained habits of generations. The ghetto in the East may be a symbol of political bondage; but in the West the only bondage that it typifies is that exercised by sentiment and tradition.[1]

In the modern ghetto as we see it in the United States, where in some cases the Jews were even among the pioneers that had a hand in founding the town or city, the contrast between the two sections of the Jewish community is even greater. The ghetto is scarcely ever more than a transitional stage between the Old and the New worlds.

The influences from without penetrate slowly and subtly, luring the Jew into the outer world. By dint of industry, sobriety, and thrift he improves his worldly position and moves to a more spacious quarter. By that time he will have mastered the vernacular and become pretty familiar with the principal conditions of the adopted fatherland. He possesses a hereditary gift for adaptability, which is stimulated by his native co-religionists, who make "Anglicization" or "Americanization," or whatever else the local term may be, a cardinal principle in their communal policy. The actual immigrant from the East who settles in a Western ghetto may, by reason of age, poverty, or prejudice, remain there and die there. But his children seldom, perhaps never, do so; their modern education weakens the sentimental attachment to the ghetto, and they prefer to live farther afield and enjoy a sense of actual equality with their non-Jewish neighbours. This steady migration of the children of the ghetto into the outer circle of the communal area exercises a conservative influence upon religious conformity and Jewish life in general, which are everywhere exposed to the corroding effects of a Western environment. But simultaneously with the outflow from the ghetto there is a regular influx from Eastern Europe, which is impelled by the forces of oppression and will continue as long as those forces prevail.[2]

[1] Cohen, *op. cit.*, pp. 36–37.

[2] *Ibid.*, p. 39. As has already been pointed out, however, the changed situations in Poland, Russia, and the Baltic countries have already affected the ghetto, and in America a new departure in the national immigration legislation is bringing about noticeable changes.

It is these ghettos that exercise a profound influence upon the whole Jewish community in the larger cities. It is this ghetto that keeps the Jew, who does not himself live in it and perhaps never has lived in it, from completely merging and being accepted in the non-Jewish community. As one writer has put it: "These voluntary ghettos are a constant menace, for they arouse the worst passions of non-Jewish demagogues, and the Jews are referred to as a class, and discriminated against as a separate body.....These last visible vestiges of ghetto existence must be wiped out. They are fraught with menace."[1]

It is with the study of one of these voluntary modern ghettos, that has emerged within a larger Jewish community in the midst of a great American city, that we shall deal in the pages that follow.

[1] Philipson, *op. cit.*, p. 218.

CHAPTER VIII

THE JEWS IN AMERICA

FIRST SETTLERS: THE SEPHARDIM

The year of the discovery of America marks also an important date in Jewish history: the expulsion of the Jews from Spain. Up to the period of the Inquisition the status of the Jews in Spain and Portugal had been a favored one, compared with that of the Jews in the rest of Europe. They were landowners; they were not confined to ghettos, and numbers of them had won positions of influence in the nobility and in the commercial and political life of Spain and Portugal. A good portion of them had assimilated with the rest of the population.

With the beginning of persecution, however, an abrupt change took place. Thousands of Jews under pressure accepted the dominant religion. These *Marranos*, as the converted Jews who secretly kept up their old Jewish ritual and communal life were called, occasionally relapsed into open confession of Judaism and became one of the most fertile sources of inquisitorial persecutions of the Jews as a whole. With their exile from Spain the Sephardic Jews (so called because of their separate religious forms which distinguished them from the German and Eastern Jews, or Ashkenazim) were scattered throughout Italy, France, Holland, England, and the Near East. The Jews of Amsterdam, from the beginning of the sixteenth century, and great portions of the English Jews, were of this stock. They maintained their distinct religious life in their new homes, and adhered to some of their proud traditions, the products of relatively free surroundings, which made them regard the Ashkenazim as a much inferior group.

Although it has been ascertained that there were several converted Jews in Columbus' first expedition to land in the West Indies, and although the Jews were closely connected with the early American exploration projects, it was unlikely that any of them, having just been expelled from the mother-country, would settle in its colonies in the New World. During the sixteenth century, after the violence of the Inquisition had somewhat abated, Jews and *Marranos* gained a foothold in the West Indies, in Brazil, Peru, and in Mexico. The Jews who settled there had generally been in Holland and countries other than Spain and Portugal before they finally drifted to the New World. While Brazil was under the domination of the Dutch a considerable wave of Jewish immigration swept that country. They established numerous congregations on the Old World model. As political fortunes changed, however, and the Dutch were replaced by the Portuguese, the same experiences that the Jews of Europe underwent at that time were duplicated in America. They were expelled, and great numbers of them were massacred. It was under circumstances such as these that the first settlers came to the American colonies.

The exact date of the first arrivals in North America is unknown, but there is reason to believe that some soldiers and sailors came to New Amsterdam, as New York was then called, as early as 1652, having been given certain grants and privileges by the Dutch West India Company, in which the Jews of Holland were interested.[1] The first evidence of

[1] Madison C. Peters, *The Jews in America* (Philadelphia and Chicago, 1905), p. 27.

Jewish immigration to New York, however, does not antedate 1654. In that year two Jewish immigrants from Europe are known to have arrived on a boat named "Pear Tree," and later a party of emigrees from Brazil, consisting of twenty-three members, arrived in the "St. Catarina," which has come down in tradition as the Jewish "Mayflower."

These early settlers were received in none too cordial a fashion on the new continent. Most of them being refugees, and having been expropriated in their old homes, were poor. Not being able to pay for their passage, their goods were sold at auction. They were dealt with, not as individuals, but *en masse*, and two members of the group were placed under arrest until the bill was paid. Peter Stuyvesant, the governor of the colony, wrote to the directors of the Dutch West India Company in Amsterdam, requesting them to confirm him in his opinion that "none of the Jewish nation be permitted to infest New Netherland." He apparently did not reckon with the fact that the Jews of Amsterdam were financially interested in the company that employed him and were represented in the board of directors. He was ordered by the directors to admit the Jews, "provided that the poor among them shall not become a burden to the company or to the community, but be supported by their own nation." The conditions of the admission of the Jews were such as to indicate that their status in the New World would be patterned after the Old. Fortunately, it was Holland, and particularly Amsterdam, that was chosen as the model for the American ghetto, for in that city the Jews enjoyed great privileges, compared with the rest of Europe. When the Jews complained to the company that Stuyvesant was disobeying instructions, he was reprimanded, in the following letter, dated Amsterdam, June 15, 1655:

We have seen and heard, with displeasure, that against our orders of the 15th of February, 1655, issued at the request of the Jewish or Portuguese nation, you have forbidden them to trade at Fort Orange [Albany] and the South River [Delaware], also the purchase of real estate, which is granted to them without difficulty here in this country, and we wish it had not been done, and you have obeyed your orders which you must always execute punctually and with more respect. Jews or Portuguese people, however, shall not be employed in any public service [to which they are neither admitted in this city] nor allowed to have open retail shops; but they may quietly and peacefully carry on their business as beforesaid and exercise in all quietness their religion within their houses, for which end they must without doubt endeavor to build their houses close together in a convenient place on one or the other side of New Amsterdam—at their choice—as they do here.[1]

The status of the Jews in New York changed little when that city was taken over by the British in 1664. Under King James II they were permitted to establish a synagogue. This synagogue, established in 1695, and probably preceded by a temporary semipublic place of worship by three or four years, was the first on the North American continent. It was called Shearith Israel (Remnant of Israel). The first structure was located on Beaver Street, between Broadway and Broad Street, and when it became too small for the community, a new edifice was erected on Mill Street (corresponding to South William Street), which existed from 1728 (the year of its erection) on for about a century. A cemetery had been established as early as 1656, on Oliver Street and New Bowery, then outside the city. The Jews engaged primarily in trade, and made use of their European connections for exchange of articles of commerce. They exported some wheat to Europe, and had commercial connections with the West Indies.

[1] Peter Wiernik, *History of the Jews in America* (New York, 1912), p. 65.

Most of the Jews of this period were of Sephardic stock, having come primarily from Spain and Portugal, but there are indications that a small number from other countries had already arrived during the first decade of the eighteenth century. The older immigrants maintained an attitude of exclusiveness and hauteur toward their co-religionists from other countries of the Ashkenazim branch. They were prosperous, and they had a European tradition of superiority which the newcomers from Germany, England, and especially from the east of Europe, lacked.

There was a time when a Spanish Jew or Jewess who married a German or Russian co-religionist would be promptly disowned; the hostility to such alliances was much stronger than it has ever been between Protestant and Catholic. The Sephardim have always had their own graveyards in which German and Russian Jews have not found rest.

Part of this feeling has been due to ancestral pride; part had a more rational basis, for it is incontestable that, from most points of view, the Spanish Jews are superior to other representatives of Israel. There are only a few of them; they are nearly all rich, or at least prosperous; they are merchants, bankers, and landowners; they are not pawnbrokers or peddlers or rag-pickers; and they have a distinct talent for public life.[1]

The writer of the foregoing is somewhat misinformed as to the early history of these Sephardic Jews, for there were peddlers and pawnbrokers among them, and they did not form a homogeneous and aristocratic body. They frequently led a transient, unstable existence in other countries before they came to America. They became group conscious only upon the arrival of the next tide of immigration, occupying, because of its poverty and its lack of experience in the new country, an inferior status. It is true, however, that the

[1] Burton J. Hendrick, *The Jews in America*, p. 17.

conception which the Sephardim built up of their own worth has made them a distinct aristocracy in the communities in which they were the original Jewish settlers.[1]

The earliest mention of a Jew in New England is in connection with an order directing him to leave the colony of Massachusetts, in 1649. During the seventeenth century there is repeated mention of the presence of Jews in Connecticut. The most important center of Jewish settlement was in Newport, where fifteen Jewish families arrived from Holland in 1658. Newport had by this time come to be the most important commercial center of the colonies, excelling even Boston and New York. In Rhode Island the Jews seem to have found a greater measure of tolerance than anywhere else on the new continent. Occasionally during this period Jews are mentioned in legal documents as violating some of the Sunday closing laws and incurring the displeasure of the Puritans. In Maryland the Jews found no favorable habitat, although an occasional individual was able to settle there. The religious liberty for which the colony was known did not apply to Jews. Toward the middle of the eighteenth century Jews began to drift to the colony of Georgia, where they were favorably received by Governor Oglethorpe. A prominent Jewish congregation was organized in Charleston, South Carolina, in 1750, and a benevolent association shortly thereafter. In the last quarter of the eighteenth century a German-Jewish congregation also established itself there.

Altogether there were only about two thousand Jews in the Colonies when the Revolutionary War broke out. By that time some Jews had already become converted under the pressure of the Puritan churchmen and the restrictions

[1] See Werner Sombart, *The Jews and Modern Capitalism*, pp. 347-49.

to which Jews were subjected in most of the colonies. In the revolution itself numbers of Jews took part, predominantly on the side of the Colonists. They were active particularly in the provisioning of the armies and in financing the revolution. When the Constitution was adopted, the clauses referring to religious liberty, of course, gave the Jews the equal status before the law which they had not formerly enjoyed, but in several of the states religious test clauses still disfranchised them. In North Carolina the Jews were not fully enfranchised until the Constitutional Convention of 1868.

THE GERMAN WAVE

During the latter part of the eighteenth century the Jewish communities in America began to assume a somewhat different complexion. German Jews had begun to trickle in, and at first had been received into the established Sephardic congregations. They intermarried and adopted a good deal of the Sephardic ritual. But as, toward the beginning of the nineteenth century, and especially after the fall of Napoleon and the beginning of the European reaction, these German Jews came in larger number and were reinforced by slowly increasing numbers from other non-Sephardic countries, a new complication set in.

The small Sephardic communities, in defence of their own individuality, could not, and, by reason of their hidalgo pride would not, continue to absorb the new element. On the other hand, the prominent, useful individuals of the German section felt the propriety of devoting themselves to the needs of their countrymen.[1]

One of the earliest symptoms of this rift is to be found in the secession of the Ashkenazic element from the Jewish

[1] Henrietta Szold, "Elements of the Jewish Population in the United States," in Charles S. Bernheimer, *The Russian Jew in the United States* (Philadelphia, 1915), p. 11.

community in Philadelphia in 1802, when the Hebrew-German Society Rodef Shalom, one of the earliest German-Jewish congregations in America, was formed. The organization of a separate congregation was soon followed by the establishment of benevolent and educational activities around the synagogue, which served as somewhat of a model for subsequent efforts of other cities.

The population composing this second wave of Jewish immigration to the United States differed from the original settlers in several important respects. The German Jews were poor, but meanwhile conditions in the country had changed. Through the Louisiana Purchase an immense new territory had been opened up, and while the early Spanish and Portuguese Jews brought much-needed wealth with them, and, what was equally important, had business connections with the Old World, the newcomers came when men were needed even more than wealth. Some of them settled in the old centers of population where Jewish communities already existed, but an ever increasing number went West and South and founded new Jewish congregations. They were dependent, however, upon the older established communities in the East. This is shown by the following letter which the Cincinnati Jews sent to those of Charleston, asking for aid in the building of a synagogue, which they received. The letter indicates also the close bond between the members of the various Jewish communities throughout the country. They were beginning to feel a common consciousness, which expressed itself not only in the organization of mutual aid societies, but in frequent interchange of visits and in the participation of certain common social and intellectual interests of American Jewry and of Jewish communities throughout the world.

To the Elders of the Jewish Congregation at Charleston

GENTLEMEN: Being deputed by our Congregation in this place, as their committee to address you in behalf of our holy Religion, separated as we are and scattered through the wilds of America as children of the same family and faith, we consider it as our duty to apply to you for assistance in the erection of a House to worship the God of our forefathers, agreeably to the Jewish faith; we have always performed all in our power to promote Judaism and for the last four or five years we have congregated where a few years before nothing was heard but the howling of wild beasts and the more hideous cry of savage man. We are well assured that *many Jews are lost in this country* from not being in the neighborhood of a congregation, they often marry with Christians, and their posterity lose the true worship of God forever; we have at this time a room fitted up for a synagogue, two manuscripts of the law, and a burying ground, in which we have already interred four persons, who, *but for us, would have lain among the Christians;* one of our members also acts as Shochet. It will therefore be seen that nothing has been left undone, which could be performed by eighteen assessed and six unassessed members. Two of the deceased persons were poor strangers, one of whom was brought to be interred from Louisville, a distance of near 200 miles.

To you, Gentlemen, we are mostly strangers and have no further claim on you than that of children of the same faith and family, requesting your pious and laudable assistance to promote the decrees of our holy Religion. Several of our members are, however, well known both in Philadelphia and New York—namely Mr. Samuel Joseph, formerly of Philadelphia; Messrs. Moses Jonas and Mr. Joseph Jonas; the two Mr. Jonas's have both married daughters of the late Rev. Gerson Mendes Seixas of New York. Therefore with confidence, we solicit your aid to this truly pious undertaking; we are unable to defray the whole expense, and have made application to you as well as the other principal congregations in America and England, and have no doubt of ultimate success.

It is also worthy of remark that there is not a congregation within 500 miles of this city, and we presume it is well known how easy of access we are to New Orleans, and we are well informed that had we a synagogue here, hundreds from that city who now know and see nothing of their religion would frequently attend here during holidays.

We are, Gentlemen, your obedient servants,

S. Joseph Chan
Joseph Jonas
D. I. Johnson
Phineas Moses

I certify that the above is agreeable to a Resolution of the Hebrew Congregation of Cincinnati.

July 3, 1825   Joseph Jonas, *Parnas*[1]

The credentials which the Jews of Cincinnati presented in this letter are characteristic and noteworthy. They were relying first of all upon their "connections" in other cities. Even in a new country under pioneer conditions, family and community ties were not forgotten. Wanderers that they were, the Jews were never quite in the same class with the gypsies, adventurers, or hobos, for the Jew, when he traveled and settled abroad, took not only his family with him, but he remained a member of that family wherever he went. Moreover, the Jew always had a destination; he was not without aim.

It seems that the cause for which the Cincinnati Jews were pleading needed no lengthy argument to justify itself in the eyes of their fellow-Jews. Its merit was self-evident. Without a synagogue there would be no community. To be sure, a synagogue was needed to keep members of the community from straying, to prevent intermarriage, and to make possible communal worship. But the main strength of the appeal is to be found in the sentimental sphere. A synagogue is needed "to worship the God of our forefathers"; "many Jews are lost in this country from not being in the neighborhood of a congregation"; and "we have no further

[1] *Publications of the American Jewish Historical Society*, X, 98–99.

claim on you than that of children of the same faith and family, requesting your pious and laudable assistance to promote the decrees of our holy Religion." The synagogue was a tribal institution, a family affair; it was a device for preserving a connection in which the Jew had a status which was something more than sufferance. It was a religious duty, a *mitzvah*, an honor, to contribute to its founding. And finally, there was the cemetery. They had a burying ground, in which they had "already interred four persons." The body of one "poor stranger was brought to be interred from Louisville, a distance of near 200 miles."

It may be pertinent to remark here on this unusual interest in the dead and in burial. No material reason could possibly account for this extraordinary attention to the death rites. Students of Jewish life generally stop in their analysis of this custom when they have attributed it to the religious motive. This religious motive, when analyzed further, turns out to be the motive of security. Through the funereal rites the continuity of the group is preserved and the individual lives on in the memories of the group; gains immortality. The profound interest in burial seems to be explained finally in terms of those innumerable strong ties of sentiment that bind the individual to the tribal organization, and, like a great share of all the strange actions of human beings, in terms of their imagination, in terms of the fact that men live in their memories of the past and their dreams of the future.

Returning to the subject of the German immigration of the early nineteenth century, it should be noted that the stream of straggling newcomers was on the whole provincial. They came mostly from the smaller towns of South Germany—Baden, Württemberg, and Bavaria—or from similar localities in the Northeast—Pommern, Schlesien, Posen, and East Prussia. The peculiarities of custom and ritual which they had developed there absorbed most of their religious life. They clung to their particularistic point of view. Besides the religious bond, they were tied by the fellowship of their *Landsmannschaften*, or Old World local community organizations. They led an indigenous life, isolated by differences in status from their superior Sephardic predecessors, by religious and social customs from their Christian neighbors, and by physical distances from each other.

Not until 1848 was this situation materially changed. In that year, impelled by the revolutionary movements that were disturbing Europe, Jews from Germany, Austria-Hungary, and Poland came to the United States in such numbers that they soon outstripped the older settlements in influence. These newer immigrants, unlike their immediate predecessors, were a sophisticated city people. Having participated in a political revolutionary movement side by side with their Christian neighbors, and having fled mainly from the political reaction which this revolutionary movement incited, they were less inclined to stress the religious, and more the social and political, issues of the time.

In contrast to the Jewish immigrants of the earlier period, this group included a number of personalities who had played an outstanding rôle in the economic and political life of their native country, men who had tasted of the life outside the ghetto, who had a modern *Weltanschauung*, and who were already infused with the spirit of the reform movement that was making headway at that time in Germany. These Jews found most of their political ambitions realized in this country. But on the religious side they found their co-religionists still engulfed in the orthodox ritualism of the Old World. Orthodox Judaism in America possessed a strength which it has never possessed in Germany since the beginning of the nineteenth century. As a result the Jewish communities of America divided into two opposing camps: the orthodox, to which belonged the older "American," English, and Polish Jews, and the Reformed, which had the adherence not only of the newly arrived Germans but gradually gained support from the more rebellious sections of the older groups.

The immigrants of this period found the older settlers intrenched in the most advantageous positions in commerce and in finance. A large proportion of the newcomers settled in the important cities of the East: New York, Philadelphia, Baltimore, and Charleston, and opened small business establishments. Others went West, as peddlers and small merchants. Not infrequently a recently arrived Jewish immigrant, carrying his pack on his back, struck, in his peregrinations, a village or small town that seemed to offer opportunities, and settled there. Several great fortunes have had their humble beginnings in this fashion. The Jewish peddler was generally a welcome visitor at the isolated farmhouses. The arrival of a Jew in town became a matter of interest to the whole community. This was the case with Joseph Jonas, a watchmaker by trade, who was the first Jew to settle in Cincinnati. This was in the year 1817.

He was a curiosity at first, as many in that part of the country had never seen a Jew before. Numbers of people came from the country round about to see him, and he related in his old age of an old Quakeress who said to him: "Art thou a Jew? Thou art one of God's chosen people. Wilt thou let me examine thee?" She turned him round and round, and at last exclaimed: "Well, thou art no different to other people."[1]

When news of the discovery of gold in California reached them, in 1849, the Jews were not slow to move westward. On the Day of Atonement of that same year, a *minyan* (assembly of ten men for prayer) was held in a tent in San Francisco. During this period it was not an uncommon practice for an Eastern group of Jews to send an agent West to explore the country and gather information on the prospects of founding a Jewish settlement. This was the procedure followed in the case of the first Jewish settlement of Chicago.

The first occasion that arose indicating a nation-wide solidarity among the Jews of the United States was during the agitation and protests against the persecution of the Jews of Turkey, in the so-called Damascus incident in 1840.[2] Another occasion was the proposed treaty of the United States with Switzerland. This treaty did not guarantee the Jews equal treatment with other citizens of the United States. The Jews protested vigorously, and brought pressure to bear upon the United States Senate and the President to prevent ratification. From 1850 to 1874, when the new Swiss constitution was adopted, this question continued to agitate the American Jews. Subsequent emergencies which have mobilized American Jewry for collective action have served to make it a memorable period.

The Jewish communities in the United States around the middle of the nineteenth century were fairly autonomous organizations. The heads of the religious institutions settled

[1] Wiernik, *op. cit.*, pp. 137–38.

[2] See Cyrus Adler, "Jews in American Diplomatic Correspondence," *Publications of the American Jewish Historical Society*, Vol. XV.

religious issues according to their own independent judgment, not bowing, as did most European communities, to the decisions of officially or unofficially recognized rabbinical authorities of wide jurisdiction. The ritual also was becoming "Americanized." As members of the various congregations rose in wealth and social position, intermarriages with Christians were not infrequent, and some conversions to Christianity took place.

The newer immigrants from Germany were even more radical in their religious beliefs than the earlier settlers or so-called "Americans." Had it not been for the influx of a new element, the character of the Jewish settlements might have lost its distinctiveness and a separate Jewish community in America might have been improbable. Not that there were no orthodox Jews left in the United States at that time, for there were numbers of important orthodox congregations, but they were swamped, not only in numbers, but in wealth and in influence, by the reformed groups.

For the most part the German Jews took their Reform Judaism seriously and were aggressive fighters in its behalf. They published a number of influential journals to propagate their notions, which they had discovered applied even more to the American milieu than to the European situation in which they had originated. The advocates of reform stressed the argument that unless the ritual was thoroughly adapted to American conditions, and unless the realm of the secular be widened, and that of the strictly religious be narrowed, there could be no hope for the survival of Judaism at all. They predicted that the next generation would be lost entirely to the Jewish faith unless the synagogue kept pace with social change. They insisted that their movement was in no wise injurious to the solidarity of Judaism, but was the only means of preventing wholesale conversion, intermarriage, and desertion.

Among the leaders of this movement, which was a direct offshoot of the German school calling itself Wissenschaft des Judenthums, were Max Lilienthal, Isaac Mayer Wise, David Einhorn, Samuel Adler (the father of Felix Adler, founder of the Society for Ethical Culture), and Bernhard Felsenthal and Samuel Hirsch (father of Emil G. Hirsch, of Chicago).

THE RUSSIAN INVASION

Around 1845, when the Jews of Poland were first conscripted into the army, the immigration from Russian Poland increased considerably. These *Hinter-Berliner*, as they were derisively called by the German Jews of America, were even poorer than those who had preceded them. Moreover, they brought with them a set of traditions that were strangely different from the cultural baggage of the German Jews, and were, as a result, farther removed from the general current of life and thought of America. They were a closely knit, self-contained body having little in common with the rest of the established Jewish communities. They drifted into the occupations that the German Jews had outgrown, and, since a good many of them were craftsmen, they remained in the larger industrial centers instead of scattering, as the German Jews had done, into the growing towns in various sections of the country. In many cases they became the employees of the German and Spanish-Portuguese Jews who were already established in manufacturing and commercial enterprises.

These newcomers served, however, as a leaven that rekindled the dying embers of religious enthusiasm in the communities in the centers of population. They drew their rabbis and leaders from the orthodox seats of learning in Eastern Europe. If these immigrants were not themselves scholars or versed in rabbinical lore, they were at least able to appreciate the older type of Jewish learning, and they proceeded to establish, in connection with their synagogues, the old-fashioned *cheders* and *Talmud Toras* for the perpetuation of their religious traditions. Their close communal organization, which had developed through centuries of life in the pale, which excluded them more effectually from secular life in the world about them than had been the case in the West, was transferred bodily to the New World.

These immigrants spoke a common household language, Yiddish, and retained the warmth and intimacy of their *Landsmannschaft* (local village organization) and their *Chevra* (religious community). They retained their European customs and continued in strict adherence to the ritual. They kept the Sabbath and the holidays. They married only within the faith, and duplicated in the slums of New York, Philadelphia, and other large cities the tenements of the ghetto and the pale. What is more, they brought with them problems of poverty which aroused the consciousness of the older settlers. They reminded the Portuguese, the Spanish, and the German Jews of the fact that they themselves were Jews, and they reconciled many wavering spirits within these groups to the basic tenets of orthodoxy.

But these early Russian immigrants were after all but the vanguard of the throngs that arrived in the eighties. The pogroms in Russia at that time aroused the Jewish communities in all of the Western countries to united action. Not only were numerous protest meetings held, but organizations were formed to assist the survivors and welcome and care for the refugees. The older and more prosperous Jewish settlers foresaw that the tremendous influx of impoverished immigrants would soon swamp the slums of the large cities, and the effect would be to produce a reaction on the public and lower the status of the Jews generally in the United States. They took steps, therefore, to colonize the new-comers in the agricultural and less densely settled regions of the country. These enterprises generally failed, and the Jews drifted back to the sweatshops of the larger cities, or became independent shopkeepers, peddlers, and trades-men.

The Russian immigrants soon formed numerous self-education societies, lodges, and trade unions, mutual aid organizations, and synagogues of their own. In New York alone the number of congregations in 1872 was twenty-nine. In sixteen years it multiplied tenfold. These immigrants, haunted by memories of exclusion from the schools of Russia, and finding the educational institutions here open to them, were not slow to take advantage of their newly discovered opportunities. They entered the night schools and sought places in the professions. Nor did they suddenly forget their political activities of old. Soon they began to build up a press of their own, in their own language, Yiddish. These papers were a powerful factor in the organization of socialist circles and in giving full expression to the organizing tendencies of the masses.

By the end of the nineteenth century the Russian and Polish Jews vastly outnumbered those from Western Europe. The differences in life habits, in cultural back-ground, in religious belief and practice, in social and eco-nomic status between the two groups, divided American

Jewry into two opposing camps, isolated from each other not only through physical barriers, since each dwelt in a separate area of settlement, but isolated even more completely through profound differences in religious and secular attitudes and customs, supported as these differences were by deep-seated prejudices and distinct forms of communal organization.

The increase in numbers of American Jews created a "Jewish problem." Of this problem the earlier Jewish immigrants, who stood on the brink of assimilation, were keenly conscious. The anti-immigration agitation and the Dreyfus affair in France served to intensify this consciousness. Efforts on a national scale were undertaken by the Jews to care for their own people. But the old leaders were gradually pushed into the background. The *Maskilim*, or Germanized Hebrew scholars, were superseded by the more aggressive Zionists and the organized Jewish masses of workingmen under socialist banners.

At present the Jewish population of the world numbers around fifteen million.[1] Of these, approximately 3,600,800 live in the United States.[2] The government of the United States, in its census reports, takes no account of religious

[1] *American Jewish Yearbook* (1927-28), p. 232. The number is given as 14,780,000. The *American Israelite* gives the number as 15,430,000, with 3,100,000 in the United States. "According to David Trietsch, a German-Jewish statistician, there are now 18,080,000 Jews in the world. He estimates the number of Jews in the United States at 4,400,000 of whom 2,000,000 are in New York City." (*Chicago Daily News Almanac and Yearbook* for 1928, p. 559.) According to the United States Census of Religious Bodies, Summary of More Important Statistics By Denomination, 1926, taken from the *World Almanac*, and republished by Arthur E. Holt in the *American Journal of Sociology*, May, 1929, p. 1120, there were in 1916 1,615 Jewish churches in the U.S. and in 1926 there were 2,953. The Jewish church members in 1916 numbered 357,135; in 1926 they numbered 4,087,357. These figures obviously are open to serious objection.

[2] Bureau of Jewish Social Research, estimate, 1920.

affiliation. As a result, no official figures are available. There are a number of national Jewish agencies, however, who have credible sources for the determination of the approximate statistics on Jewish population. The great proportion of the Jewish population in this country lives in the following cities:[1]

New York City	1,643,012	Baltimore	67,500
Chicago	285,000	Newark	55,000
Philadelphia	240,000	St. Louis	55,000
Cleveland	78,996	Los Angeles	43,000
Boston	77,500	Pittsburgh	42,450

The following table indicates the influx of Jewish immigrants since the beginning of the large-scale Russian immigration:

Years	Number
1881–98	533,478
1899–1907	829,244
1908–26	976,219

Net increase since 1881 .... 2,338,941[2]

Two-thirds of the Jewish immigration of 1924 was from Poland, Russia, and Roumania, the strongholds of orthodox Judaism. In view of the new immigration restrictions, estimates of orthodox accretions to American Jewry are likely to be inaccurate, since many immigrants now have to seek admission under the quota of countries other than their own. The influx of Reformed Jews from Germany and other western countries is, therefore, probably less than one-third of the total indicated by statistics. In spite of immigration

[1] *American Jewish Yearbook* (1927–28), pp. 243-46.
[2] *Ibid.*, p. 250.

barriers, therefore, the tendency for the Jewish immigration from the East vastly to outnumber that from central and western Europe persists. The future composition of the Jewish population of the United States promises to change at a rate and in a direction not far different from that shown during the last fifty years. Similarly the regions in which the new arrivals tend to settle remain about the same. The statistics on the destination of the Jewish immigrants show that they continue to prefer the large urban centers, New York alone being the destination of 55.6 per cent of all Jewish new arrivals, during the year ending June 30, 1926, while it was the destination of only 23.3 per cent of non-Jewish immigrants.[1]

[1] *Ibid.*, p. 255.

Street Musicians

CHAPTER IX

ORIGINS OF THE JEWISH COMMUNITY
IN CHICAGO

THE PIONEERS[1]

Of the three thousand Jews in the United States about the year 1818, when Illinois was admitted into the union, only one apparently had ventured as far west as Illinois. The principal Jewish settlements of that time were those along the Atlantic seaboard. The first Jew to arrive in the swampy region around Lake Michigan known as Chicago was a peddler, J. Gottlieb, in 1838. Little is known about him, but it is believed that he found California even more attractive than the thriving settlement at Chicago, and went west during the gold rush of 1849. By 1841 we find evidence of at least four or five Jewish residents in the city, which then had a little over five thousand inhabitants. These early arrivals were mainly Bavarian Jews, who had come to America just a few years before, and had first settled in eastern communities.

At this time one feature of governmental restriction in Europe proved particularly irritating to the members of the expanding Jewish communities. In the German principalities families were limited in number by law, and before mar-

---

[1] For further details of this account, see H. L. Meites, *History of the Jews of Chicago*, Chicago, 1924, one of the most detailed and comprehensive works of its kind of any Jewish community in the United States. Also A. T. Andreas, *History of Chicago*, Chicago, 1877; H. Eliassof, "The History of the Jews of Illinois," and "The History of the Jews of Chicago," in *Reform Advocate*, May 4, 1901, and January 30, 1909; also article, "Chicago," in *Jewish Encyclopedia*.

riage licenses were issued, "vacancies" were supposed to exist in the community for the establishment of another family. This right to marry and settle in a community was called *Familiantenrecht*, and existed in certain parts of Europe until quite recently. Many efforts were made to evade it, and emigration was one of the paths open to a young couple contemplating marriage.

The settlers of this period were for the most part very young men engaged in peddling or merchandising. An interesting and representative account of these pioneers is furnished by one of them:

It was on the first of September, in the year 1840, just at a time when great excitement prevailed in New York, in fact, all over the country, on account of the election between Harrison and Van Buren, that I landed in New York, a stranger in a strange land. There were no steamers at that time, and people came from Europe in sailing vessels; all were dumped in New York and kept together as near as possible.

Now began the problem of how to proceed to make a living, for the majority of the immigrants were poor, and strangers to the language and customs of the country. Upon the advice of those who were here before them, the greater part of the Jewish young men went peddling. There were two or three Jewish merchants who supplied Jewish peddlers with "Yankee notions," which they called *Kuttle Muttle*. The principal merchant was dubbed *Hershel Ganef* (Hirsch, the thief); he trusted them all, instructed them what to call things, and how to offer them for sale.

There was a synagogue in New York called the "India Rubber *shul*" because it was principally upheld by peddlers whose stock in trade was mostly suspenders. . . . . All those absent from home hurried to the city on a holiday, in order to be there for the service. . . . .

The families had all brought with them their old-country piety, and also their *Shabboth* lamps with six or seven arms, filled with stearic oil, made cotton wicks by hand, and on Friday evening before the beginning of the Sabbath, would light them, then offer a consecrative prayer, and after that would not touch fire and, of course, had to have a fire woman, *Shabboth goye*, whenever a light or fire was needed on the Sabbath. They had a congregational oven to which all who belonged brought their pots and kettles on Friday afternoon. The oven was heated, the pots placed in, and the oven doors sealed with clay in order to retain their heat, and kept closed until Saturday noon, when they came to get them. The coffee for the Sabbath morning was kept hot on ashes on top of this oven. At one time I was honored with an invitation by an acquaintance of mine to participate in eating a genuine German *Shabboth Kugel* (pudding). When seated at the table the fire woman came in and wanted her money for her services, when the wife said, "We don't pay money on *Shabboth*. You come to-night, and my husband will pay you."[1]

As a rule, relatives came together to a given community and co-operated in establishing themselves and maintaining their religious and family life, but there were a number of lone wolves who lived in boarding houses or "temperance hotels" and attached themselves to the rest of the community.

Among the early settlers were several merchant tailors and dry goods dealers, a tobacco dealer, a grocer, and several peddlers who made Chicago their headquarters. Most of the Jews established themselves on Lake Street, which was then the principal business section of Chicago. They lived behind or above their stores. The early newspapers and directories of the city indicate that they advertised their wares widely and became active participants in the economic and political life of the community. The first brick house in Chicago was built for Benedict Shubert, in the business district, on West Lake Street. This was an undertaking which in those days was an unmistakable sign of prosperity. Others fared not so well. Among them was a peddler, Isaac Ziegler, whose lack of traditional Jewish business enterprise is attested to by the fact that "it is said of him that he spent much of his time

[1] Mayer Klein, quoted from Meites, *op. cit.*, p. 40.

helping to extricate teams that had sunk into the mud on Madison and Clark streets, in front of his place of business, and finally, in an effort to divert traffic, caused signs to be put up in the middle of the road reading 'Bottomless' and 'Road to China.'"[1]

Early in the forties the tide of immigration from Germany became so great that the older settlers in the East began to look for ways and means of establishing the newcomers in the outlying regions. While this might have been a self-defense measure, they regarded it as one of their religious obligations. A Jewish philanthropist, Renau, of New York, sent an agent to Chicago to investigate the possibilities of founding a Jewish settlement there. A colonization project was started near Chicago in Schaumburg, Cook County. The agent reported to the colonization society under whose auspices he was sent at Mr. Renau's instance, that "this part of the land, especially the town of Chicago, opens a vista into a large commercial future." A number of Jews came, but left after a short stay, either taking up a plot of land of their own as a farm (land sold then at about one dollar an acre) or else settling in Chicago to engage in business. Characteristically enough, Meyer, the agent, himself finally left the Schaumburg project to engage in the real estate business in Chicago. In comparison with the thriving business life that was developing in the near-by metropolis, farming in Schaumburg seemed altogether too prosaic for the enterprising Jewish settlers.

Between 1840 and 1844 the Chicago Jewish community was increased by about twenty new immigrants. This influx continued until 1849, when a strong tide of new settlers was brought in following the completion of the Galena & Chicago

[1] Meites, op. cit., p. 38.

Railway to Elgin, and the great wave of emigration following the European reaction after the abortive revolutions of 1848. By this time the Jewish element had come to include, besides the Bavarians, an increasing number from the Rhenish Palatinate, and from Posen and East Prussia. Although the Jewish community had grown, the various families lived within a few blocks of each other, within the area that now constitutes the Loop, or central business district. Only one family lived on the West Side: Henry Horner, a grocer, who established himself on Randolph and Canal streets. These settlers, most of them coming from localities in Europe very close to each other, maintained intimate relations with one another. They visited frequently at one another's homes, and especially on Friday evenings and on Saturdays, when their places of business were closed, they took advantage of the opportunity for comradeship and the mutual interchange of news from the Old World and their relatives in the East. Newcomers in the community generally found the older settlers helpful, not only in important material respects, but in getting accustomed to the new conditions of life and maintaining their morale.

As in the communities from which they came, so in Chicago, the Jewish settlers soon felt the need of establishing those immediately essential institutions of communal life such as the synagogue and the burial society. The first religious services were held on the Day of Atonement, 1845, in a room above the store of one of the members, on what is now Wells Street, at the corner of Lake. For the first time in their history they were able to bring together ten adult males to constitute a *minyun*. The next year, it seems, the attendance was no larger. Before a congregation could be formally organized, the need for a communal cemetery was felt. An acre of ground was purchased from the city in 1846, for forty-six dollars, in what is now Lincoln Park, in the heart of the residential section, but what was then outside the city limits.

The organization of a burial society was the first overt act toward the organization of a Jewish community in Chicago. Because of the presence of certain pious members in the community who attempted to subsist on a limited diet rather than violate the prescribed ritual, a congregation was organized in 1847, and a *shochet* and reader procured from New York. The burial-ground society turned over its property to the newly organized congregation, which assumed the name Kehilath Anshe Ma'ariv (Community of the Men of the West). The orthodox Ashkenazic ritual was introduced and the members strictly observed the Sabbath. Signs appeared in the windows of the places of business owned by Jews, on Sabbath, reading "Closed on account of Holiday." The first place of worship was in a room above a store on Wells and Lake streets but as the community grew and became more prosperous a frame synagogue was constructed on the site of the present post-office at Clark and Quincy streets. The dedication of this synagogue aroused the interest of the Chicagoans of that day. The *Daily Democrat* of June 14, 1851, reported it as follows:

DEDICATION OF THE JEWISH SYNAGOGUE

The ceremonies at the dedication of the first Jewish synagogue in Illinois, yesterday, were very interesting indeed. An immense number had to go away, from inability to gain admittance. There were persons of all denominations present. We noticed several clergymen of different religious denominations.

The Jewish ladies cannot be beaten in decorating a church. The flowers, leaves, and bushes were woven into the most beautiful drapery

that Chicago ever saw before. The choir, consisting of a large number
of ladies and gentlemen, did honor to the occasion and the denomination. . . . .

No person that has made up his mind to be prejudiced against the
Jews ought to hear such a sermon preached. It was very captivating
and contained as much real religion as any sermon we ever heard
preached. We never could have believed that one of those old Jews
we heard denounced so much could have taught so much liberality
towards other denominations and so earnestly recommended a thorough study of the Old Testament (each one for himself) and entire
freedom of opinion and discussion.

We would sooner have taken him for one of the independent order
of free thinkers, than a Jew. Mr. Isaacs is an Englishman and is
settled in New York City. There are Jewish synagogues as far west
as Buffalo and Cleveland.

The Jews in our city are not numerous, but are wealthy, very re-
spectable and public spirited.

The Jewish Sabbath is on Saturday, and a very interesting service
takes place today. The whole Mosaic law written on parchment (they
never have it printed for church services) will be unrolled from a large
scroll and read from. Rev. Mr. Isaacs will again preach. The service
will commence at 8 A.M. and last until 11 A.M. The earlier part of the
service will be most interesting.

Gentlemen are requested to keep their hats on, and to take seats
below. The ladies will take seats upstairs, according to the Jewish
custom of separating the sexes.

During the cholera epidemic of 1849, the Jewish community ranks were somewhat thinned. But the stream of
incoming settlers, among them some who had intended to
seek their fortune in the gold fields of California, but felt
that Chicago was a promising stopping place, soon replenished the ranks. The community was closely knit, and each
shared the fortunes of every other member. Weddings and
funerals were communal affairs, and every Sabbath and holiday brought the Jews from the neighboring regions together

in the temporary synagogue, which, in spite of its liberal rabbi, retained most of its Old World familial and communal character. As newcomers arrived they were introduced to the older settlers in the synagogue, and the homes of the established families were thrown open to them.

The first Jewish settlers of Chicago, as has already been indicated, were Bavarian Jews. The congregation which they had formed was coming to be known as the Bayerische Shul, in contradistinction to the Polische Shul, the Kehilath B'nai Sholom (Congregation of the Men of Peace), which was organized in 1852 by the growing *Landsmannschaft* of German-Polish Jews who were also known as *Herzogtümer*, because they hailed from the *Herzogtum* of Prussian Poland. The Bavarians considered themselves the earliest settlers, and looked down upon the Poles as an inferior caste. Most of the German Jews had by this time acquired considerable means, and could afford to maintain a higher standard of living. Some of them were men of education. On religious questions they were influenced by the modernist movement in vogue among German Jewry. Some of the Bavarians even thought the Bayerische Shul's ritual too orthodox, and agitated for greater reforms. A small group of the members of this congregation organized a Hebrew Benevolent Society in 1851, with the following object: "To provide in time of health for each other; for times of need and sickness to which the human frame is liable; and also to pay the last duty and homage in what must fall to all living; and ....while we are able, to do good and to assist our brethren and fellow-men while life is granted to us."[1] They organized a second ceme-

[1] Meites, *op. cit.*, p. 52.

tery association and bought three acres of ground in Lake View, near Graceland, as a burial ground. The meetings of this society, says the historian, "were marked by commendable decorum, as the meetings of other Jewish organizations in the early days unfortunately were not."[1]

A similar organization was formed by the members of Congregation B'nai Sholom. Meanwhile this congregation and the burial organization had each bought an acre from Kehilath Anshe Ma'ariv, so that there were now four Jewish cemeteries, three of them side by side. But this was merely an outward manifestation of the division that was beginning to characterize the Jewish community. Old World class distinctions and intertribal prejudices were reasserting themselves even in the small pioneer community of Chicago. The pioneer congregation found it necessary to revise and modernize its ritual to satisfy the growing elements who were dissatisfied with the rigid, orthodox procedure. In this group intermarriage with Christians was not unusual, but conversion to Judaism of the non-Jewish mate was insisted upon. No one could be a member of even as liberal a group as the Hebrew Benevolent Society who, if he had married a Gentile, did not insist that conversion to Judaism take place, or who failed to observe the Day of Atonement.

During this period the Jews began to play an active part in the local life. Henry Greenebaum, who, with his brother Elias, had established a bank in Chicago, was elected alderman from the sixth ward, and his brother became school agent. The local Jews began to participate in the national Jewish movements. A local lodge of the Independent Order of B'nai B'rith was established in 1857. This organization made active efforts to heal the breach between

[1] *Ibid.*, p. 53.

the various dissenting elements in the Jewish community. After two years it was able to unite the Polish and German elements in the consolidated United Hebrew Relief Association. The Jews of Chicago also took an active part in the campaign to defeat the treaty with Switzerland, which discriminated against Jews, referred to in the previous chapter. They sent a delegate to a national convention of Jews in Baltimore in 1857 to protest against the treaty and present a memorial to the President of the United States. Reverberation of the American Reform movement began to reach Chicago from its center in Cincinnati, largely through its organ, the *Israelite*.

In 1857 about forty members of the oldest congregation organized themselves as a secessionist party into the Israelite Reform Society. They wrote to the *Israelite:* "We will have service in the style of Temple Emanu El in New York. . . . . A nice organ and a good organist are already provided." In true ghetto style, one of the main bones of contention within the congregation was the prayerbook to be used. The "Polish" congregation had already adopted its own Polish *Siddur* (prayerbook). The Reform element insisted that Kehilath Anshe Ma'ariv adopt the version used in the Reform Temple of Hamburg, but the conservative element insisted that the *Roedelheimer Siddur* (in use in Frankfort and printed in Roedelheim, near Frankfort) be continued. The controversy assumed violent proportions, all the contentiousness of older established communities being duplicated in the young settlement of Chicago. Had the community remained stable, it is probable that great divisions would not have occurred. But there was a constant influx of new members and of religious leaders who were enthusiastic about the new doctrines, in which they saw the

only successful method of continuing as Jews and yet over-
coming the medievalism and separatism of the orthodox
creed. The Reform movement had assumed all the characteristics of a sect. When an election was held in Kehilath
Anshe Ma'ariv in 1857, a member who signed himself
"Observer" wrote to the *Israelite* the following report:

The Congregation Kehilath Anshe Ma'ariv has just closed its
meeting, having passed through a most spirited and closely contested
election for their officers for the ensuing year. There were two formal
organizations supporting their respective nominees, and upon distinct
platforms.

"Equality, Reform, and Education," was the motto of the successful party; equality among members to be inaugurated in lieu of a
self-constituted privileged class (of but few), who have from time im-
memorial contrived to manage the congregational affairs in accordance
with their own out-of-place ideas; reform in the divine service; devotion and harmony in prayer; introduction of a choir; the maintenance of decorum by the members, which has been most sadly neglected; education by procuring able and competent men to fill the
places of preacher, teacher, and reader. . . . .

The Congregation numbers 98 members. At the first ballot there
were 83 votes cast, with the following results, viz., for the reform
candidate for President, Elias Greenebaum, 51 votes; opposition,
32 votes.

Oh! what a fall was there, my countrymen!

Upon indication of the state of facts, after the first ballot, the
present chairman, Mr. S. Cole, declared the meeting adjourned, but
had to yield his temper to the calm, stern, and just indignation of the
meeting, and re-opened. . . . .

Such a glorious triumph on the one hand, and complete defeat
on the other was anticipated by none!

Chicago at last has spoken for progress, and you may put her down
as a sound pillar in the beautiful temple of the God of Israel.[1]

No such violent storms struck the more homogeneous
and conservative Polish group represented by congregation

[1] Quoted from Meites, *op. cit.*

B'nai Sholom. The slow accretions in the membership of this organization merely served to strengthen the religious and communal ties.

Meanwhile, even in the local distribution of the Jewish community of Chicago, there had taken place a definite crystallization of social and religious strata. By 1858 the Jewish community, which had grown substantially, was no longer centered on Lake and Wells streets. Numerous Jewish firms were to be found on Randolph, on Clark, and on La Salle Street. Some were north of the river. But the older and more prosperous members of the community were now to be found predominantly on Edina Place (Plymouth Court) and Buffalo Street (Federal Street). A few lived north and northwest of the present Loop; one lived "out in the country on Wabash Avenue, corner New Street, seven blocks south of Twelfth, where the houses were not yet numbered." There was only one Jew living close to the neighborhood west of the Chicago River that was later to develop into Chicago's Ghetto, and that was a butcher, Moses Goodman, who lived on Harrison Street, between Clinton and Jefferson.

While it is difficult to trace substantial migrations from one part of the city to another during this period, it is apparent that by 1860 there were definite areas of settlement to which one could point in Chicago: one area containing the older settlers, who had already adjusted themselves fairly well to their new surroundings, toward the south of the Loop, and another on the western fringe of the Loop, made up largely of later arrivals. The new settlers drifted into the area abandoned by the older ones, since it was in process of becoming a business area.

COMMUNITY PROBLEMS

Before the outbreak of the Civil War the most important question before the Jews of Chicago was still the question of reform in the religious ritual. By this time, however, under the influence of outstanding local leaders and with the moral support from the older Jewish communities in the Eastern United States, particularly New York, Baltimore, and Cincinnati, the Reform section in Chicago had crystallized into a separate congregation which later became one of the outstanding bodies in American Jewry—Sinai congregation. The new congregation bought a Christian church at Monroe and Clark streets and converted it into Chicago's first "temple."[1] In the "Polish" group there also occurred a split, which, in the spirit of Civil War days, was called a "Secesh" movement. The basis of this division, however, unlike that in the German camp, was not programistic, but purely personal and factional. The synagogue to which it gave rise was known until recently as the Secesh Shul. Minor organizations such as Jewish young men's, young women's, and ladies' societies sprang up around the congregations then in existence and added strength and solidarity to the communal organization.

During the Civil War the Chicago Jews were numerous enough to organize a company of their own and finance it themselves. They had no difficulty, although the Jewish population did not exceed a thousand, in raising one hundred men and over $11,000. Meanwhile the factional conflicts within the community smoldered. The end of the war brought a renewed interest on the part of the Jews in the

[1] The term "synagogue" is applied to orthodox and conservative houses of worship, while the Reform congregations have "temples."

political life of Chicago. More than ever before, Jews were elected and appointed to local public office.

In 1863 the Sinai congregation built a new temple at Plymouth Court and Van Buren Street. They had paid $7,000 for the property, attesting to the growing strength and prosperity of the membership. For the first time in a Jewish service in Chicago the men removed their hats in the temple, a radical innovation for the time. The rabbi of the congregation, Bernard Felsenthal, who by this time had achieved a national reputation in Jewish Reform circles, declined re-election when the congregation refused to elect him for more than one year at a time, and a number of his followers organized a new congregation, known as Zion, but based on practically the same principles as Sinai. The former held services in a Baptist church on the West Side, but soon thereafter erected a building on Desplaines Street, between Madison and Washington—the first Jewish house of worship on the West Side. The Polish congregation meanwhile had grown and its membership could afford a new synagogue of its own, which was erected on Harrison Street, south of the Loop, at a cost of $20,000. The most important undertaking of the Jewish community as a whole, however, was the building of the first Jewish hospital, which was opened in 1868. It was located on the North Side, on La Salle Street, between Schiller and Goethe, although the center of the Jewish community at that time was along Van Buren, Clark, and Wells streets. The Chicago Jews, particularly the B'nai Brith lodges, of which there were two at that time, contributed generously to the establishment of the first Jewish orphan asylum in Cleveland. This was indicative of the beginning of Jewish philanthropic activities on a national scale.

The sixties represent a period of expansion, not only for
Chicago, but for its Jewish community. A Jewish settlement on the near North Side had grown to such proportions
that a new synagogue was established on Superior Street,
near Wells. The expansion of the area of the city, magnified
by the poor transportation facilities, seems to have been the
motive for the new organization. In this, as in most of the
other Jewish congregations of that time, German was the
current language.

Dr. Chronic, the enterprising and scholarly rabbi whom
Sinai had imported from Germany, established the first
Jewish publication in Chicago which was printed in German,
called *Zeichen der Zeit*. The Bavarian congregation was still
the leading Jewish organization in the city, and, in keeping
with the standing of its members, bought a church in the
then fashionable district of Wabash Avenue and Peck Court
for $50,000.

Two new national elements had meanwhile been added
to the Jewish settlement: a small group of Holland Jews who
linked up with the "Polish" congregation of B'nai Sholom,
and a more important group both from the standpoint of
numbers and their subsequent rôle—the Latvian Jews. Unlike their predecessors, this latter group spoke Yiddish.
They were ultraorthodox, and had behind them a tradition
of rabbinical scholarship. They, like the Germans before
them in the early days, engaged in peddling, taking up the
occupation abandoned by the earlier immigrants. Finding
all the Chicago congregations too radical, they organized a
minyun of their own in 1865. A rival *minyun* was formed
the next year, when David Zemansky, who had sent most of
the "Litvish" peddlers West with packs which he sold them,
arrived in Chicago from New York. These two groups

united in 1867 and formed the Beth Hamedrash Hagodol (the great synagogue), located on Pacific Avenue, south of Van Buren Street. This orthodox group proceeded immediately to establish a *cheder* for the religious instruction of the young. New immigrants came in such numbers that other synagogues were established in rapid succession. Among them was the Ohave Emuno congregation, nicknamed *die halbe Emuno* (the half-faith) because it was noticed that some of its members who peddled were accustomed to driving up with their horses and wagons on the Sabbath to attend services, which was contrary to the orthodox practice. Several members of the old "Polish" congregation united with this group, thus adding strength to this new faction whose ritual they found more akin to their own.

The new element, however, was torn by all sorts of strife. They were considerably more provincial than their Bavarian and *Hinter-Berliner* predecessors. They settled by small town or village groups, and rigidly maintained their lines of distinction. Thus, the Mariampol group seceded from the Beth Hamedrash Hagodol in 1870, because, the story goes, one of the attendants at the synagogue was seen saying *Kaddish* (memorial prayer for the dead) while wearing a straw hat, which violated the strict commands of the faith. Unlike the Germans and the "Poles," this group did not enter actively into the secular life about them. They lived in a village world, and within that village they were concerned mainly with their fellow-Jews who came from Mariampol, Suwalk, Litvinova, and similar localities. The affairs of their synagogue were the only public life they knew, and as a consequence, whenever a quarrel occurred about a *chazan* (cantor), a *shochet* (slaughterer), and a *mohel* (circumciser), they were ready to gather up the members of their *Landsmannschaft* and organize a store-front congregation of their own.

Just before the great Chicago fire another congregation was organized in what was then known as the "South West Side," around Halsted and Fourteenth streets, where a German and Bohemian settlement had been established in the midst of a neighborhood of substantial residences where some of the most important Chicagoans then lived. This was the B'nai Abraham congregation, organized in 1870, composed mainly of German-speaking Bohemian Jews.

The center of Jewish population about 1870 was in the area bounded by Van Buren Street on the north, Polk Street on the south, the river on the west, and Clark Street on the east, in the immediate vicinity of the city's business area. The location of the B'nai Abraham congregation on the Southwest, Zion on the Northwest, North Chicago Hebrew congregation on the near North Side, and the Bavarian congregation on the South Side, mark the outposts of the Jewish settlements before the great fire.

One other aspect of Jewish life of this period is worth mentioning. During the three decades between the time of the first Jewish arrivals in the city and the great conflagration, the Jewish settlers, coming as they did from German communities that had sent great numbers of non-Jewish pioneers to the West, were on friendly terms with the growing German population of the city. They spoke the same language, and many of them shared the same political views, especially since the revolution of 1848 was the incentive to emigration for a large number. During the Civil War a number of Jews who were not in the "Jewish Companies" had served in the ranks predominantly made up of Germans. It was therefore not unusual for the German Jews to be found often in company with their German acquaintances at Turner Hall or at the Concordia Club. Most of the Jewish meetings and social functions since the beginning of the Civil War had been held in the Concordia Club. The prosperous element among the German Jews in 1869 organized the "Standard Club," which became the center of the social life of the Jewish aristocracy of Chicago. The club built a home in the most fashionable district of South Michigan Avenue. Even more than the separate religious institutions that characterized the Jewish community and divided off the various strata from one another, this club was indicative of the great chasm which separated the Bavarians from the *Hinter-Berliner*, and especially the latest arrivals, the Russians.

CHAPTER X
THE JEWISH COMMUNITY AND THE GHETTO

THE GROWTH OF THE COMMUNITY

The great Chicago fire of 1871 marks not only a turning-point in the history of the city of Chicago, but also in the development of the Jewish community. The Jews, being in most instances dependent upon their businesses for their livelihood, found themselves especially hard hit by the catastrophe, for most of the business establishments were located in the area that was swept by the fire and reduced to ashes. The core of the Jewish area in and around the Loop was completely destroyed. Hundreds were homeless and helpless who had formerly been affluent and active in the philanthropic enterprises of the community. The Jewish lodges and relief organizations, with the assistance that came from many other Jewish communities in various parts of the country, mobilized for relief and reconstruction. Many communal institutions were wiped out by the fire, and great parts of the population were dislodged from their neighborhoods.

Besides bringing important changes in the economic position of many members of the community, the fire brought about a complete realignment of areas of residence. While the fire was still burning, a group of Jews organized the German-speaking congregation Rodfe Sholom, later called Beth El, on the Northwest Side, in the neighborhood of Milwaukee Avenue, on May and Huron streets. Numerous new lodges and associations were organized immediately after the fire, among them the Chicago Rabbinical Association, which did much to foster co-operation between the various elements and factions of the Jewish population represented by different congregations.

Scarcely had the community recovered from the first fire when another broke out in 1874, which swept over the near South Side, and did its greatest damage among the Russo-Polish settlers, who had been spared by the first. The United Hebrew Relief Association responded to their need, since most of the afflicted section of the population was poor. It was difficult, however, to raise the necessary funds. This was due in part to the fact that the community had not yet fully recovered from the earlier catastrophe, but it was due also to the criticism by the German Jews that the Russians had not contributed their share during the former crisis, and were therefore *schnorrers*. In order to counteract the narrow sectional spirit to which the community suddenly had returned, the Relief Association asked Dr. Liebman Adler, the former rabbi of Bavarian congregation, who was a respected member of the community at large, to draw up an appeal for funds. His appeal read as follows:

Scarce two decades have elapsed since all the Israelites of this city were living as in the bonds of one family and circle. Each knew the other. All worshipped harmoniously in one temple and shared others' woes and joys.

How great is the change! Thousands scattered over a space of nearly thirty miles, in hundreds of streets, divided by pecuniary, intellectual, and social distinctions, provincial jealousies, and even religious distinctions and differences. Separation, division, dissolution, estrangement, repeated and continual, are the words which characterize the history of our brothers in faith until now. Dissolved in the mass of our population, we are losing the consciousness of our homogeneity and the strength gained for each individual by concerted action.

Let us also consider the oft-heard complaint that Poles and Russians absorb a disproportional large share of the means of this Association.

Brothers and sisters, are these poor ones less to be pitied, are they less poor, are they less Israelites because Poland or Russia is the land in which they first saw the light, or rather the darkness, of this world? The poor of those countries are doubly poor. These unfortunates come to us from a country which is the European headquarters for barbarism, ignorance, and uncleanliness. In those countries, thousands of Israelites are densely crowded into small towns and villages, and they become singular and peculiar in their customs, manners, and ideas. In conferring charity it is the duty of the Israelite first to look to the needs and then to the deserts of the recipient.[1]

This appeal brought the desired help. Coming as it did from a spokesman of the German Jews, it was the first formal acknowledgment after the fire of the disintegrating forces within the community. It showed clearly that the German Jews took their superior status for granted, and looked down with pity—benevolently, to be sure, but with a certain contempt—upon their Russian and Polish co-religionists. The physical distance over which Chicago Jewry had spread was, as Rabbi Adler noted, an indication of the social distance that separated the two camps in the Jewish community from each other.

The realignment that followed the second fire clearly showed the lines of division that had by this time become firmly imbedded in the community structure. The East European Jews, who had lost their homes and synagogues east of the river, now crossed to the West Side. The Mariampol congregation was the first to take that step which marked the beginning of Chicago's real ghetto district. The full consequences of this movement did not become ap-

[1] Meites, *op. cit.*, p. 133.

parent, however, until the great Russian influx of the next decade.

Meanwhile, efforts to achieve a reintegration of the divergent elements in the community continued. A committee from Sinai and Kehilath Anshe Ma'ariv congregations made efforts to reunite their respective groups, especially since both congregations had lost their synagogues. By this time the Reform movement had already progressed to a point where Sinai had substituted Sunday for Saturday services, in an effort to bring the religious life of the members more in harmony with that of the community at large, and also to obtain better attendance, since a large part of the congregation was employed on Saturdays and the Saturday attendance was confined mainly to women and the older and more conservative men of the congregation. Sinai was even willing to compromise by holding services on Saturdays and Sundays, but Kehilath Anshe Ma'ariv was unalterably opposed to Sunday services, and the attempted *rapprochement* failed. Sinai thereupon built a synagogue near the fashionable Prairie Avenue district on Indiana Avenue and Twenty-first Street, while Kehilath Anshe Ma'ariv bought the building of Plymouth Church, on Indiana Avenue and Twenty-sixth Street. These new locations indicate the extent of the southward movement of the more prosperous German element of the Jewish population by 1875. To these structures there was added, in 1880, the new Michael Reese Hospital, on Twenty-ninth Street and the Lake, which was the most ambitious institutional undertaking of the Jewish community.

The cultural life in the Jewish community during this period, while it showed many evidences of adaptation to the temper of the city, was by no means independent of the sources from which it had sprung. The orthodox groups always imported their rabbis from the East European centers of rabbinical learning, and even the reformed groups, who in many respects had gone farther in the introduction of innovations in ritual and belief than the reformed congregations in Germany, were still a cultural dependency of the Old World to a much greater degree than the intellectual life of America at large was compelled to lean on European scholarship. This is indicated by the call for a rabbi issued by Sinai in 1879. It read:

> With a view of securing to this congregation a minister whose name will be an honor to Judaism, and of whom we may have reason to expect that by word and deed he will teach the tenets of our faith in full accord with the convictions shared by all members of this congregation; and thereby inspire young and old with that love for our holy cause which is essential to the preservation of our religion, be it
>
> *Resolved,* That the Executive Board be herewith requested to invite and receive applications for the position of minister of this congregation from Jewish theologians of modern reform principles and of good repute who have graduated at a German university, with honor, are excellent also in all those branches of study which characterize the learned rabbis of our day, and who are good orators, able to preach in the German and English vernacular.[1]

Sinai's rabbi had to be not merely learned in religious lore; he had to be, above all, *ein moderner Mensch* who could speak to the public at large in the name of the Jewish congregation. The man whose response to this call was accepted was Rabbi Emil G. Hirsch, who held the outstanding position in the Jewish community of Chicago for over forty years.

Some years before the reform and semi-reform groups in the city had become conscious of the fact that there were in

[1] Meites, *op. cit.*, p. 138.

the community no unifying cultural forces, and that its life was not of such a character as to be self-perpetuating. The orthodox sections of the Jewish population, and particularly the Russian and Polish groups, were in a different position. They were less absorbed into the larger life of the city; they continued to speak their familiar Yiddish; they lived close together; they gathered round their synagogues in daily prayer; they had their *cheders* that transmitted the heritage to the younger generation, and what numbers deserted the group were more than compensated for by the constant influx of orthodox and pious immigrants from Europe.

A futile attempt was made by the reformed and semi-reformed groups to introduce new vitality into the communal life by the organization of the Jewish Educational Society of Chicago, which followed the parochial pattern set by other denominations, but which attempted to combine some of the principles of the orthodox traditions. The following appeal was issued in 1876:

Israelites of Chicago:

What have you done for preserving our faith and transmitting the noble bequest of ages to posterity? True, you have in the different parts of this city formed congregations and erected beautiful houses of worship, redounding to the honor of the God of our Fathers. You have ministers preaching to you every Sabbath and Festival Day, well accredited by the surrounding world. You have Sabbath schools and teachers, besides, to imbue the youth with all elements of Jewish religion and history. But are you satisfied that thereby you have done all in your power to maintain the religion of our Fathers in its pristine glory and purity? True, you have raised your children as Jews, but do you believe that they, after having attended the Sabbath school up to the time of their confirmation, will be able to expound and to defend Judaism before the world? Or do you know of any one of them desirous of pursuing the study of Jewish lore and history, in order to know what Judaism is, and what it has accomplished in its wonderful march? And suppose there are such people, what opportunities have they of studying Hebrew and acquiring the knowledge indispensable for a thorough understanding of Judaism? Where are the schools from which you expect your future rabbis and teachers and the well-read laymen to come? The latter can certainly not be imported from the old country for the purpose of upholding our Jewish institutions.

Indeed, indifference and dissension, ignorance and shallowness have long enough eaten the very marrow and root of our sacred inheritance. Compare the zeal and devotion, the generosity and sympathy manifested in Christian churches by young and old, with the indolence and lethargy which have estranged the young, particularly, to our holy cause, so as to make every attempt of enlisting their interest fail at the very outset. Christian mission societies send forth their soul-hunting agents to ensnare Jewish young men and tear them away from the breast of their religion, while the Jewish community, for want of religious education and protection, leaves them to spiritual starvation.

You are no doubt aware of the call issued both in the east and west, for establishing a Jewish theological seminary, in response to which several congregations of this city have joined either the one or the other movement. Yet this undertaking must be regarded premature as long as in the various centers of American Judaism there are neither pupils imbued with the spirit of Jewish lore, so as to feel induced to enter upon a theological career, nor high schools where talented youths could prepare themselves for such a course. We must have a Jewish high school in every large community, where especially gifted young people from their eleventh or twelfth year are to be advantageously taught in Hebrew literature and Jewish history, in addition to the various branches of a general high school, the Hebrew forming an organic part of the entire school system; where, moreover, lessons in Jewish religion, history, and literature are given twice or thrice during the week to such young people who are anxious to receive information about Judaism, while pursuing their mercantile or scientific course during the day. . . . .[1]

[1] Pamphlet, *Jewish Educational Society of Chicago*, September 15, 1876.

What suddenly began to concern the older generation of Jews, who had been brought up in the spirit here outlined, was the growing generation of Jewish children in the Chicago community. They were aware that the European rabbis and teachers who had been imported into the community hitherto had not been able to enlist the respect and arouse the enthusiasm of the rising generation. What was needed, they thought, was a type of leadership that was adapted to the new conditions—a native leadership—which the community thus far had not produced. The solution they sought again in the traditions of the ghetto of the Old World, but apparently the community itself was neither fully convinced of the need nor of the suitability of the remedy. In spite of the vision of "soul-hunting Christian missionaries," presented by this appeal, they were not aroused to action. The interests and attitudes of the various elements within the community itself were so divergent as to make collective action on a program of internal organization of the whole Jewish community impossible.

It was, as it has always been, only in defending itself from without that the Jewish community has been able to act with any unanimity. The older generation did try, however, to preserve its cultural traditions in various ways. Under the auspices of the Zion Literary Society, educational and musical programs were given from 1877 on, and a weekly newspaper was issued which appealed to the communal interests of the more liberal section of the German faction. Other papers were established in English and German, but on the whole, during the seventies, the field for these journalistic enterprises was very limited. The community was still too small and lacked the cultural unity to make any of these sectional enterprises a success. It is important to note, however, that as early as 1879 a weekly Yiddish paper appeared in Chicago, the *Israelitische Presse*, but survived for only a few months. While local papers encountered difficulty, the Jews of the various classes did read the papers published in New York and Cincinnati, which gave space to local items.

By 1880 the Jews of Chicago, in a total population of 500,000, were estimated to number 10,000.[1] The Jewish population was now increasing and spreading out over wider areas of the city. Two new synagogues were organized by the German-speaking group: Anshe Emeth, in 1878, by the Jews who lived on what was then the far North Side, on Division Street; and Emanuel congregation, on Blackhawk and Sedgwick streets, in 1880. The Russian group in 1875 organized another *minyun* known as the Russische Shul, familiarly spoken of as "Shileler," since it was organized by a group coming from the village of Shilel, Russia. With the growth of the Russian population this became one of the most substantial groups on the West Side, and built a synagogue on Clinton and Judd streets.

THE TIDE FROM THE EAST

The so-called "May Laws" of 1882, which virtually expelled great masses of Jews from their homes in the villages and towns of Russia, inaugurated a tide of immigration to America which was destined to change the whole complexion of American Jewry within a decade. The years preceding this final governmental action were marked by intermittent pogroms and violent persecution which had already brought Jews in considerable numbers to the United States. But

[1] "Union of American Hebrew Congregations," *Statistics of Jews of the United States*, 1880.

these earlier immigrants settled mainly in New York and the larger cities of the East. Only a small proportion came as far west as Chicago. A report of the United Hebrew Relief Association for 1881, however, already speaks of "Russian refugees," and a year later we read in the report of that organization, "....Our office is constantly crowded by refugees." These newcomers had few friends or relatives to welcome them here. They were pioneers, as were the Germans before them. Most of them had, however, lived at least for a short time in the tenements on the East Side of New York, and were sent West by friends, *Landsleute*, and immigrant aid organizations, where they hoped to find competition less keen and opportunities for establishing themselves greater.

In Chicago these immigrants of course sought the area where rents were cheapest and where the surroundings made their own cultural life possible. This they found in the area west of the river and south of Harrison Street, close to the business section, or "Loop," in the vicinity of the markets and the light manufacturing district, where they could save carfare in going to and from work.

One of these newcomers tells of arriving in Chicago and asking a stranger where the Jews lived:

He was directed west, where he was told the "greenhorns" were to be found. He had no idea then that Jews were to be found elsewhere in Chicago. . . . . He tells us: "Chicago, especially the West Side, then was a place of filth, infested with the worst element any city could produce. Crime was rampant. No one was safe. Jews were treated on the streets in the most abhorrent and shameful manner, stones being thrown at them and their beards being pulled by street thugs. Most earned their living peddling from house to house. They carried packs on their backs consisting of notions and light dry goods, and it was not an unusual sight to see hundreds of them who lived in the Canal Street district, in the early morning, spreading throughout the city. There was hardly a streetcar where there were not to be found some Jewish peddlers with their packs riding to or from their business. Peddling junk and vegetables, and selling various articles on the street corners also engaged numbers of our people. Being out on the streets most of the time in these obnoxious occupations, and ignorant of the English language, they were subjected to the ridicule, annoyance and attacks of all kinds.[1]

The Jews of this period, unlike their predecessors in the city, spoke Yiddish, and their dress and their demeanor constituted easily recognizable marks. Most of them wore beards, and the long coats and boots of the Russian pale. They never ventured outside of their streets and houses unless necessity compelled them. They brought with them the hunted look of the pale, which had become fixed through constant dread of pogroms and attacks. They lacked self-confidence and poise, a lack intensified by the inability to communicate with strangers; and often they were unable to communicate even with the Jews whom they met, who did not speak Yiddish.

The area into which they came was occupied mainly by Germans and Bohemians, although a small German-speaking group of Bohemian Jews had already established itself there, and another German group bordered their settlement on the north and the northwest.

Very few among the immigrants of the eighties had any skilled occupations, as in the villages and towns from which they came they were mostly petty merchants and tradesmen. Only a few were prevailed upon by the colonization agencies to go on farms, and still fewer remained on the farms. They had no capital with which to open business establishments. Unskilled labor and peddling were the only

[1] Account of Bernard Horwich, quoted by Meites, *op. cit.*, pp. 150–51.

occupations that seemed at all adapted to them. Often they
took to the former only long enough to enable them to get
into some small business of their own, even if it were only
selling stationery or notions on the street corners. Unlike
the typical Jewish immigrants that preceded them, they had
not come to improve their economic or social position, but
rather they had fled from conditions that threatened life
itself.

Of the thousands that came to America in the first years
of the eighties, approximately two thousand came to Chicago
during 1881–82. The entire Jewish community, which numbered little more than 10,000, organized to meet this tide of
impoverished and panic-stricken people. A Russian Refugee
Aid Committee was organized. "Families were separated
into groups of ten, each group being installed in a temporary
home, with one family at the head. The privileges of such
a home were ordinarily granted for three weeks. At the end
of that time a family was expected to be in a position to
take quarters on its own responsibility."[1]

Many of the heads of families found employment in the
establishments of the German and Polish Jews, particularly
those engaged in the manufacture of clothing. The immigrants were suffering from additional industrial handicaps
because their orthodoxy prevented them from working on
Saturdays. A free employment bureau was established to
care for their vocational needs. The fund-raising appeals of
the Chicago Jewish community for this period emphasize
that it is the duty of the established members of the community to help their co-religionists in less fortunate circumstances to become self-supporting. Allusion is often made to

[1] Minnie F. Low, "Jewish Philanthropy in Chicago," in Charles S.
Bernheimer: *The Russian Jew in the United States,* p. 87.

the probability that unless these numerous immigrants with their peculiar appearance and strange customs are adequately cared for they are likely, not only to become a burden to the community at large, but also to reflect on the character of the Jewish community.

The Jews on the South and the North Side were becoming conscious of the growth of a ghetto on the West Side, which, though removed from their own residential districts by considerable distance, would be regarded by Gentiles as an integral part of the Jewish community. They considered themselves even farther removed in social distance than in miles from these poor, benighted peddlers with long beards, with side-locks, and long black coats. They sensed that all the progress they had made in breaking down barriers, in preventing the development of a ghetto, and in gaining recognition for themselves, as persons rather than as Jews, with their Christian neighbors might now, with the new connotation that was attached to the word Jew, come to a sudden halt.

And yet they did not wish to have these Jews too close to them. These Russians were all right—of that they were quite certain—but, like the southern Negro, they had to keep their place. All sorts of philanthropic enterprises were undertaken in their behalf, but in the management of these enterprises the beneficiaries were given no voice. Charity balls by the débutantes of the German-Jewish élite in behalf of the wretched West Side Jews were held at the splendid clubs of the German Jews, which by this time had increased to four, and charitably inclined young Jewish men and ladies-bountiful spent their leisure hours in alleviating the hardships of the Jewish slum dwellers.

But the Russians did not take altogether willingly to the

American ways of dispensing *zdoko* (charity). They were accustomed to assisting one another in the Old Country in much more informal style. The Jewish communities they had known in Russia were self-sufficient large families. These German Jews of the "societies" asked all sorts of embarrassing questions before they dispensed their financial and other aid. They made investigations and kept records. Most of all, they did not understand—they did not know— their own people; in fact, they were only halfway Jews; they did not even understand *mama loshon* (the mother-tongue), or Yiddish.

The Russian Jews were not slow in building up their own separate community life. Numbers of new small congregations were formed, some of them with barely a *minyun*. But these *shuls*, most of which were merely private rooms or store-front synagogues, were places that glowed with the familiar, intense religious enthusiasm of old. They were not pretentious structures in which hundreds were gathered once a week or on holidays, with organs and choirs, but they were family or village gatherings in the side-streets of the ghetto. Each of these congregations constituted a little world by itself, but a full world, in which were gathered all the interests of the people, religious, educational, social.

In addition to these *shuls* there were *cheders* with bearded teachers, where the young boys learned to *daven* (pray), to lay *tphillin* (philacteries) and read the Torah. In October, 1884, there took place a notable celebration which for the first time brought the West Side Ghetto dwellers and the rest of the Jews in the city together on a large scale. The occasion was the celebration of the one-hundredth anniversary of the birth of the Jewish philanthropist, Sir Moses Montefiore. The most distinguished citizens of Chicago and the leaders of the Jewish community took part in the gathering, which was held in the finest hall in Chicago, the Central Music Hall. It gave the new arrivals their first dramatic view of the New World, the Jewish world beyond the pale.

Among the spectators in the gallery were some of the more recent Russian arrivals who did not understand a word of the proceedings, but came away with impressions that they did not soon forget, of how dignified a Jewish celebration could be made. They carried this impression back with them, and from that time felt prouder than ever before that they were Jews. It gave them their bearings in Chicago and America. The first immediate result was agitation on the West Side and throughout Chicago for the establishment of a Talmud Torah to bear the name of Moses Montefiore. In this work all "sides" of Chicago took a hand. . . . .[1]

As the number of "refugees" continued to increase, literary societies and mutual aid organizations came into existence, in which the members of the Russian group who had accumulated some wealth took the lead. In 1887 Leon Zolotkoff established the first successful Yiddish newspaper in Chicago. This organ, at first a weekly, but soon a daily, exercised a tremendous pressure in welding the orthodox, Yiddish-speaking group together, and in stimulating their communal life. It gave local Yiddish writers an opportunity to exercise their talents, and brought to the Yiddish group the movements that were stirring the ghetto of New York.

In an effort to divert the younger generation of Russian immigrants into other vocational channels than peddling, two efforts were made by the Jewish community at large. One of these was the founding of the Jewish Agriculturists' Aid Society, with the object of establishing immigrants on farms, and the other was the Jewish Training School, to encourage the learning of the crafts and manual arts among the

[1] Meites, *op. cit.*, p. 154.

younger generation. As was the case in similar efforts here and in other cities, these devices did not stem the tide of Jews who flocked to the night schools to study for the professions, or those who went to peddling and entered the sweat-shops of the developing clothing industry.

EXPANSION AND DIVERSIFICATION

While the West Side was developing institutions of its own, which were organized along orthodox lines, and thus was giving form to its cultural heritage by building up a ghetto, the Jews on the South and the North Side were merging their interests more and more with those of the city at large. The members of the Standard Club had taken an active interest in the fund-raising campaign of the newly organized University of Chicago. Dr. Hirsch, of Sinai, had by this time become the outstanding spokesman of the Jewry of the city. By 1887 he was receiving a salary of $12,000 a year. He was the highest-paid rabbi in the world. That was one way the community had of measuring its greatness. It is interesting to note, in this connection, the tremendous difference in the salaries paid by the orthodox synagogues and the Reform temples. The first Reform congregation in America, Emanuel of New York, paid its first rabbi-preacher the then munificent salary of $200 per year, while the first Russian congregation, Beth Ha-Midrash of New York, ten years later, i.e., in 1855, paid its rabbi two dollars a week.[1] Apparently the Reform Jews were willing to pay to be represented by a *Weltmensch* as rabbi. In 1891 Rabbi Hirsch began to publish his weekly *Reform Advocate*, which gave Reform Jewry in Chicago a unifying organ and an intellectual program.

[1] Wiernik, *op. cit.*, pp. 177, 190.

In the late eighties the Chicago community began to take on new characteristics. The lines of division between the various groups became more fixed and clearly defined. The status of each group was rigidly set, and the objectives of each were made articulate through separate organizations, institutions, leadership, and press. In 1888 the presence of a new element in the community is witnessed by the organization of a Hungarian synagogue on the West Side, on Maxwell Street. A more significant symptom of impending change, however, is indicated by the formation of the first Russian congregation on the South Side, and the further southward migration of Kehilath Anshe Ma'ariv. Apparently the overflow from the ghetto was drifting in the beaten path of the older settlers. The impetus which the World's Fair gave to the growth of Chicago is indicated by the growth of the South Side congregations during the nineties and the establishment of several new institutions, especially the Orphans' Home and the Home for Aged Jews, in Woodlawn, a residential section on the far South Side. By 1895 Zion congregation, the first German congregation on the West Side, found that its members had for the most part joined their *Landsleute* on the South Side, and the congregation was reorganized and moved its temple to Forty-fifth Street and Vincennes Avenue, in the neighborhood of the growing Jewish settlement on the South Side.

The continuous stream of Russian immigrants resulted in the expansion of the West Side community. New synagogues were formed on Paulina and Taylor streets, one of these, Mishna Ugmoro, "barring from membership all who were not well versed in Jewish lore and scrupulously observant of every tradition."[1] At the other extreme was Sinai,

[1] Meites, *op. cit.*, p. 190.

with its Sunday services, its hatless congregation, whose leader, Dr. Hirsch, was one of the outstanding figures in the World's Parliament of Religions during the World's Fair.

The Chicago ghetto, with its centers at Maxwell Street and Jefferson Street, had by this time developed its colorful atmosphere of tenement houses and street markets, its *kosher* shops, its basement sweat-shops, and, last but not least, its Christian missions. A local missionary society made active efforts and spent considerable sums to convert Jews to Christianity, but the converts were few in number. Hull House had by this time become the center of immigrant life on the West Side, and numbers of Jews flocked to its concerts, lectures, and library. The need for a Jewish settlement began to be felt by the more intellectual members of the Jewish community, and in 1893 a small group opened the Maxwell Street Settlement, at 183 Maxwell Street. The more independent groups in the ghetto itself rather resented the philanthropic interest of the South Side Germans, and organized a people's institute, which they hoped to keep free from the spirit of "uplift," in the form of the Self-Education Club.

Before the nineteenth century closed, Chicago Jewry underwent a number of crises. The World's Fair had focused attention on organization within the community and had given great impetus to the formation of religious bodies on a national scale. A number of Jewish national organizations were called into being at about that period. One incident which did much to unite the Jewish community in concerted action was the agitation against the attempted extradition of political prisoners to Russia in 1893, in which the whole community took an active part. Within the community itself, institutions and organizations had become so numerous that the need for centralization was manifest. In 1900 the philanthropic agencies were united into a single collecting and disbursing agency, which in 1901 developed into the Associated Jewish Charities, with 1,700 subscribers and a fund of $135,000.

The influence of the Zionist movement was also beginning to make itself felt, and the Dreyfus case rekindled the self-consciousness of the community, as evidenced by the numerous protest meetings held. In 1900 a Chicago Jew had been nominated for governor of Illinois and had polled over half a million votes, a symptom of the active participation, at least on the part of the older settlers, in the civic life of the community. By the opening of the new century the Jews of Chicago numbered approximately 75,000, in a population of 1,600,000.[1] The Russian Jews were by far in the majority, with 50,000; the Germans came second, with 20,000; the rest made up the other 5,000. The community then consisted of fifty congregations, thirty-nine charitable societies, sixty Jewish lodges, thirteen loan associations, eleven social clubs, four Zionist societies, and a number of other organizations.[2]

Although the growth of the professional spirit in social work and community organization tended, ever since the beginning of the twentieth century, especially within the Jewish communal body, to discourage the formation of small independent organizations, these organizations constantly reappeared. In spite of well-laid plans for a unified community, the separate parts of that community tended always to split into sections and get out of hand. A dramatic instance will indicate the readiness on the part of the Jews to form an organization to meet a real or supposed need:

[1] H. Eliassof, "The Jews of Illinois," *Reform Advocate*, May 4, 1901.
[2] *American Jewish Yearbook*, Vol. 5662.

A Jewish infant had died, and the mother was too poor to pay for its burial. She did not want it to be buried otherwise than in Jewish surroundings and with Jewish rites. There was no one to help her, and in her desperation the poor woman decided upon a bold step. Taking the dead child in her arms during the night, she carried it to the Mariampol *Shul*, then on Canal Street, and left it on the steps. In the morning the members of the synagogue arrived and found it there. One may imagine the horror of the sight which met their eyes. Their pity and sympathy were excited, the mother of the infant was found, and a decent burial in a Jewish cemetery was arranged.[1]

This incident, with its attending publicity, led to the formation, in 1892, of a free burial society on the West Side. In similar fashion, nurseries, charitable associations, and societies of various kinds are constantly being created, only to be merged into others or to pass out of existence. And if one is not fortunate enough to organize a philanthropic organization, one must at least support those that are already in existence. The fashionable ladies of the Gold Coast are not alone in their enthusiasm for "pet charities"; the humblest ghetto home has at least one or two collection boxes for some holy cause, and the collectors who make their rounds in the ghetto streets bent on fund-raising for institutions and movements far and near are seldom turned away empty handed. To give is still a *mitzvah* (a good deed, a religious duty) in the ghetto.

From 1900 on it becomes difficult to trace all the varied developments in the diverse sections of the Chicago Jewish community. The Kishinev pogroms in 1905 marked another period of crisis when the community locally, and the Jews nationally, organized themselves into various bodies to protest against the outrages and to receive the great waves of "refugees." The scenes of 1881–82 were repeated in Chicago,

[1] Meites, *op. cit.*, p. 191.

with the important difference that this time the Russian Jews were able to take the initiative, and that the community was much larger and therefore able to absorb the newcomers with less difficulty.

The expansion of the community due to this large influx, to which was added a substantial Roumanian element, showed itself topographically in the migration of the more prosperous West-Siders to the Northwest Side and to Lawndale. The latter area was derisively called *Deutschland* by the residents of the ghetto, and its new residents, *Deitchuks*, because the orthodox Jews saw in this movement from the ghetto area also a desertion of the old customs and religious belief, and the aspiration to emulate the German Jews with their *goyishe* ways.

The period of the first decade of the twentieth century marks also the growth in the prosperity of a substantial number of members of the Jewish community. This is strikingly indicated by the large individual subscriptions to philanthropic enterprises. The founding of the Chicago Hebrew Institute, a recreational and educational center on the West Side, on Taylor and Lytle streets, preceded by a smaller institution on Blue Island Avenue, again brought together the diverse sections of the Jewish population in a large-scale communal undertaking. By this time (1908) the name of Julius Rosenwald figures as the outstanding contributor to the educational and charitable enterprises of the Jews of Chicago.

The large increase in orthodox members becomes manifest also through the founding of new synagogues in Lawndale, and especially on the Northwest Side. The smaller synagogues on the West Side are abandoned largely to the new arrivals, and the movement west, northwest, and south on the part of the older settlers assumes vast proportions. The question as to whether the older institutions are to be conducted on an orthodox or a reformed basis appears in the foreground as an important issue. Separate orthodox orphan homes, homes for the aged, and hospitals organized during this period indicate the emergence of a definite dual organization within the community.

The outbreak of the European War, and particularly the organization of Jewish relief work in Europe after its conclusion, and the political activities of the Jews in the organization of the American Jewish Congress to promote the interests of the Jews in the peace conferences, together with the new developments in Zionism, lent to the most recent period of Chicago Jewish history the atmosphere of stirring activity, of practical politics, and business-like methods of large-scale fund raising. A number of million-dollar campaigns, of "drives" for various causes, local and national and international, were carried through. The Zionists in the community had won over a large part of the Jewish population, even of the German and Reform Jews. The issues of immigration laws and anti-Semitism were met by the organization of "anti-defamation" societies. Locally this latest period is marked by the growth of the Jewish community to approximately 300,000 members. The diminution of the European influx, however, became noticeable through the gradual transition of the near West Side into a predominantly non-Jewish area, and the establishment of new Jewish frontiers on the South Shore, in Hyde Park, North Shore, Ravenswood, Albany Park, Humboldt Park, and Columbus Park, all of them high-grade residential neighborhoods on the outskirts of the city. By 1926 the Jewish community of Chicago had come to be the third largest in the world, exceeded only by New York and possibly Warsaw, but with a more diversified set of characteristics in its various parts than either of the other two. From the standpoint of organization the recent period shows increasing centralization and consolidation of communal effort on the one hand, and an increasing rate of mobility and cultural transformation of the various Jewish settlements on the other.

The story of the founding and development of the Jewish community of Chicago is fairly typical of what happened in the last one hundred years in every urban center in the United States. In its initial stages the Jewish community is scarcely distinguishable from the rest of the city. As the numbers increase, however, the typical communal organization of the European ghetto gradually emerges. The addition of diverse elements to the population results in diversification and differentiation, and finally in disintegration.

Maxwell Street

CHAPTER XI
THE CHICAGO GHETTO
THE NEAR WEST SIDE

West of the Chicago River, in the shadow of the Loop, lies a densely populated rectangle of three- and four-story buildings, containing the greater part of Chicago's immigrant colonies, among them the area called "the ghetto." This area, two miles wide and three miles long, is hemmed in on all sides by acres of railroad tracks. A wide fringe of factories, warehouses, and commercial establishments of all sorts incloses it. It is the most densely populated district of Chicago,[1] and contains what is probably the most varied assortment of people to be found in any similar area of the world.

Along the northern edge of this area we find the city's "main stem" of the migratory workers, Hobohemia. This is paralleled on the south by the Italian and Greek settlements, interspersed by Turks, Gypsies, Mexicans, and a host of lesser groups. On the west there still linger the Irish and Germans who at one time had this whole area for themselves. In the remaining area, bounded by Roosevelt Road, Robey Street, Clinton Street, and the railroad embankment south of Fifteenth Street, live most of Chicago's first generation immigrant Jews.

A description of the so-called "river wards," which correspond closely to the near West Side, centering around Halsted Street, is furnished by Jane Addams in her early

[1] In 1900 the population per square mile was 39,600; in 1910, it was 50,900; and in 1920, 39,100 (United States Census reports).

195

impressions in Hull House, located in the heart of this district. In 1910 she wrote:

Halsted Street has grown so familiar during twenty years of residence, that it is difficult to recall its gradual changes—the withdrawal of the more prosperous Irish and Germans, and the slow substitution of Russian Jews, Italians, and Greeks. A description of the street such as I gave in those early addresses still stands in my mind as sympathetic and correct.

Halsted Street is thirty-two miles long, and one of the great thoroughfares of Chicago; Polk Street crosses it midway between the stockyards to the south, and the ship-building yards on the north branch of the Chicago River. For the six miles between these two industries the street is lined with shops of butchers and grocers, with dingy and gorgeous saloons, and pretentious establishments for the sale of readymade clothing. Polk Street, running west from Halsted Street, grows rapidly more prosperous; running a mile east to State Street, it grows steadily worse, and crosses a network of vice on the corners of Clark Street and Fifth Avenue. Hull House once stood in the suburbs, but the city has steadily grown up around it and its site now has corners on three or four foreign colonies. Between Halsted Street and the river live about ten thousand Italians—Neapolitans, Sicilians, and Calabrians with an occasional Lombard or Venetian. To the south on Twelfth Street are many Germans, and side streets are given over almost entirely to Polish and Russian Jews. Still farther south, these Jewish colonies merge into a huge Bohemian colony, so vast that Chicago ranks as the third Bohemian city in the world. To the northwest are many Canadian-French, clannish in spite of their long residence in America, and to the north are Irish and first-generation Americans. On the streets directly west and farther north are well-to-do English-speaking families, many of whom own their houses and have lived in the neighborhood for years; one man is still living in his old farm house.

The policy of the public authorities of never taking an initiative, and always waiting to be urged to do their duty, is obviously fatal in a neighborhood where there is little initiative among the citizens. The idea underlying self-government breaks down in such a ward. The streets are inexpressibly dirty, the number of schools inadequate, sanitary legislation unenforced, the street lighting bad, the paving miserable, and altogether lacking in the alleys and smaller streets, and the stables foul beyond description. Hundreds of houses are unconnected with the street sewer. The older and richer inhabitants seem anxious to move away as rapidly as they can afford it. They make room for newly arrived immigrants who are densely ignorant of civic duties. This substitution of the older inhabitants is accomplished industrially also, in the south and east quarters of the ward. The Jews and Italians do the finishing for the great clothing manufacturers, formerly done by Americans, Irish, and Germans, who refused to submit to the extremely low prices to which the sweating system has reduced their successors. As the design of the sweating system is the elimination of rent from the manufacture of clothing, the "outside work" is begun after the clothing leaves the cutter. An unscrupulous contractor regards no basement as too dark, no stable loft too foul, no rear shanty too provisional, no tenement room too small for his work-room, as these conditions imply low rental. Hence these shops abound in the worst of the foreign districts where the sweater easily finds his cheap basement and his home finishers.

The houses of the ward, for the most part wooden, were originally built for one family, and are now occupied by several. They are after the type of the inconvenient frame cottages found in the poorer suburbs twenty years ago. Many of them were built where they now stand; others were brought thither on rollers, because their previous sites had been taken for factories. The fewer brick tenement buildings which are three or four stories high are comparatively new, and there are few large tenements. The little wooden houses have a temporary aspect, and for this reason, perhaps, the tenement-house legislation in Chicago is totally inadequate. Rear tenements flourish; many houses have no water supply save the faucet in the back yard; there are no fire escapes; the garbage and ashes are placed in wooden boxes, which are fastened to the street pavements. . . . .[1]

This description—and there are others that corroborate it— brings out the fact, which holds good for the slum districts of most American cities, namely, that the slum is the out-growth of the transition from a village to an urban com-

[1] Jane Addams, *Twenty Years at Hull-House* (New York, 1916), pp. 97-100.

munity. In Chicago this transition took place in a single generation. Land values rose from the level of farm land to centrally located urban real-estate levels. The streets and the buildings soon became inadequate, and the neighborhood rapidly deteriorated. Property owners saw no reason for undertaking improvements, for the rent they could squeeze out of their holdings did not warrant costly repairs, especially since their property was located on the very edge of the central business district, and would therefore, within a few years, be more valuable for industrial sites than residential purposes. Meanwhile, however, several generations of immigrants found this area their temporary living quarter.

The immigrants drifted to the slum because here rents were lowest—a primary consideration. In addition, they found themselves within walking distance of their employment. Finally, here, in neighborhoods owned by absentee landlords, there was very little resistance to the invasion of people with a lower standard of living and an alien culture. The immigrants themselves, being for the most part disfranchised through non-citizenship, like the hobos, were politically impotent to improve their condition even had they the desire to do so, which generally was not the case, since most of them regarded the slum as merely their temporary dwelling place.

During the nineties of the last century writers on this district referred to a larger and a smaller ghetto. The greater ghetto included an area of about a square mile, comprising parts of the old Nineteenth, Seventh, and Eighth wards, bounded by Polk Street on the north, Blue Island Avenue on the west, Fifteenth Street on the south, and Stewart Avenue on the east. Of the 70,000 people then living in this area, 20,000 were estimated to be Jews. This area was practically co-extensive with the "slum district" as defined in the seventh special report of the Commissioner of Labor, on the *Slums of Great Cities*. The lesser ghetto was found in the Seventh Ward, bounded by Twelfth, Halsted, Fifteenth, and Stewart. Nine-tenths of the population of about sixteen thousand in this area were Jews.[1] In 1895 Charles Zeublin described this area as follows:

The physical characteristics of the ghetto do not differ materially from the surrounding districts. The streets may be a trifle narrower; the alleys are no filthier. There is only one saloon to ten in other districts, but the screens, side-doors, and loafers are of the ubiquitous type; the theatre bills a higher grade of performance than other cheap theatres, but checks are given between the acts, whose users find their way to the bar beneath. The dry-goods stores have, of course, the same Jewish names over them which may be found elsewhere, and the same "cheap and nasty" goods within.

The race differences are subtle; they are not too apparent to the casual observer. It is the religious distinction which everyone notices; the synagogues, the Talmud schools, the "Kosher" signs on the meat markets. Among the dwelling-houses of the ghetto are found the three types which curse the Chicago workingman: the small, low, one or two story "pioneer" wooden shanty, erected probably before the street was graded, and hence several feet below the street level; the brick tenement of three or four stories, with insufficient light, bad drainage, no bath, built to obtain the highest possible rent for the smallest possible cubic space; and the third type, the deadly rear tenement, with no light in front, and with the frightful odors of the dirty alley in the rear, too often the workshop of the "sweater" as well as the home of an excessive population. On the narrow pavement of the narrow street in front is found the omnipresent garbage-box, with full measure, pressed down and running over. In all but the severest weather the streets swarm with children, day and night. On bright days groups of adults join the multitude, especially on Saturday and

[1] See Philip Davis, "General Aspects of the Population of the Chicago Ghetto," in Bernheimer, *op. cit.*, pp. 57–60.

Sunday, or on the Jewish holidays. In bad weather the steaming windows show the overcrowded rooms within. A morning walk impresses one with the density of the population, but an evening visit reveals a hive.[1]

In the thirty years since this description was written, the ghetto has probably changed less than any other part of the city. Here and there the Jewish settlement has been dented in by the invasion of subsequent immigrant groups, railroads, warehouses, and industries, and in a few directions it has spilled over into neighboring territory. But on the whole its outlines and characteristics remain as described.

The present area of the Chicago ghetto may be defined by the following boundaries: the railroad tracks and terminals on the east, the railroad viaduct on the south, the street-car line at Robey Street on the west, and the main traffic artery of the West Side—Roosevelt Road—on the north. These boundaries are the rough natural barriers that definitely mark off the ghetto from the surrounding natural and cultural areas. The center of this area is located at Maxwell and Halsted streets. Four street-car lines divide the area further into distinct neighborhoods—the Halsted, Fourteenth, Blue Island, and Racine Avenue lines. Roosevelt Road, Halsted, Maxwell, and to some extent Jefferson Street, are the important business thoroughfares. But there is not a street in the whole area that does not have a number of stores and business or industrial establishments.

Along the business streets building improvements in recent years are noticeable, but there has not been a new residence built in the whole area for the last fifteen years.

[1] Charles Zeublin, "The Chicago Ghetto," in *Hull House Papers and Maps* (Chicago, 1895), pp. 94–95.

The land values of the area have risen phenomenally during this period in the business section, though not so much as in the city generally. In the zoning regulations of the city the area is designated for light manufacturing. A number of large factories are already operating in the area, among them a piano factory, a picture-frame factory, and a number of clothing and machine shops. Junk yards abound in the ghetto, in Chicago as in every other city of America. In recent years the transfer of the South Water Street fruit and vegetable market, Chicago's large produce center, to the southwestern edge of the ghetto has considerably affected the complexion of the whole area. Considerable land is held for speculative purposes, with a view to the impending invasion of the district by other industrial establishments.

As a residential area the near West Side generally, and the ghetto in particular, has declined in recent years. In spite of the immigrant population, whose families may be expected to be large, the number of children has decreased to a point necessitating the closing of several public schools in the last few years. Numbers of buildings are being condemned for dwelling purposes by the authorities, and since repairs do not offer advantage to the owners, they are allowed to go to ruin. The ghetto is a striking instance of a deteriorated neighborhood. Within thirty years the district has been transformed from a substantial residential neighborhood into a slum, and finally into a semi-industrial area.

THE GHETTO AS A CULTURAL COMMUNITY

Difficult as it is to set forth adequately the physical characteristics of the ghetto as a natural area, its cultural characteristics are unmistakable. The ghetto is pre-eminently a cultural community. Into its teeming, crowded, narrow streets the main outlines of life of the European ghetto and the Russian pale have been transplanted almost in their entirety. The very location of the ghetto is not merely determined by accessibility and low rents, but by tradition. The Jews who have lived in ghettos know the value of nearness to the market place or the commercial center of the city in which they live. The ghetto of Prague was located near the Tandelmarkt; the ghetto of Frankfort, in the immediate vicinity of the fair grounds; and so with every important ghetto in Europe. The New York ghetto, bordering on the East River, the Bowery, and Broadway, and the Philadelphia ghetto, between the Delaware River and the business section, are notable examples of other American ghettos, similarly situated. Just as the Gypsies generally settle on the outskirts of a town, so the immigrant Jews settle near the business section or on the river and railroad fronts.

Similarly the population density of the ghetto is to be accounted for, not only by the poverty of the immigrants and their inability to pay high rents, but also by the traditions of close community life of crowded ghetto quarters in the Old World. Probably no other people has been able to live under the crowded conditions that the ghetto and the slum impose with a lower mortality rate than the Jews.[1] Whether this be due to acquired immunity, or to the ritualistically prescribed diet and hygiene, or to the attitude on the part of parents toward children and the nature of Jewish family life, it is certain that the Jews have made some sort of accommodation to urban conditions as presented by the typical slum district.

No matter from which side one enters this ghetto, one

[1] See Kate Levy, "Health and Sanitation of the Jews in Chicago," in Bernheimer, op. cit., pp. 318 ff.

cannot fail to be struck by the suddenness of the transition. In describing the New York ghetto, one writer has said: "No walls shut in this ghetto, but once within the Jewish quarter, one is as conscious of having entered a distinct section of the city, as one would be if the passage had been through massive portals separating this portion of the Lower East Side from the non-Jewish districts of New York."[1] Chicago's ghetto is younger than that of New York, just as the New York ghetto is a mere upstart compared with that of Frankfort; but the characteristics of the ghetto are not to be measured by the years that a given area has been inhabited by Jews. The ghetto, no matter where it is located, has a long history, and is based upon old traditions of which the American ghetto is a mere continuation—a last scene of the final act. The Jewish ghetto, at any rate, is rooted in the habits and sentiments of the people who inhabit it, and in all those experiences that go with the ghetto as a historical institution.

The New York ghetto, of course, has a considerable history independent of its European background. In that separate history are to be sought its distinguishing characteristics when it is contrasted with the European institution. The Chicago ghetto can boast only of a much shorter independent life, but most of its inhabitants, before arriving in the West, have had a considerable experience on the East Side of New York, which they have brought with them to Chicago.

There is also the great weight of numbers. The one and a half million Jews in the city of New York, through their very numbers, constitute more of an independent commun-

[1] Milton Reizenstein, "General Aspects of the New York Ghetto," in Bernheimer, *op. cit.*, p. 44.

ity than do the Jews of Chicago. The active and autonomous life of a community of such size is bound to result in the greater persistence of its cultural traits in the midst of disintegrating influences. The ghetto of New York has been more or less a model for all American Jewish communities. It still exercises a dominating influence over all other cities. It sets the pace through its outstanding personalities and institutions. It is the undisputed center of American Jewry, as the city of New York is the center of the cultural life of America.

New York has been the first stop for most Jewish immigrants; Chicago, a second landing. But since the beginning of the twentieth century the Chicago community has been the source of a great deal of independent, creative life among the Jews. As numbers increased, more and more immigrants, relatives and *Landsleute* of those who had settled here, were brought directly to this city without a preliminary initiation into American ghetto existence in another city. With the growth of local institutions and organizations a number of movements of national significance have centered here.

There is one important difference between the ghettos of the Old World and those of the New. The former are on the whole homogeneous bodies concentrated in a single section of a city, with a common city-wide, if not regional, cultural life. The American ghetto, on the other hand, is, as a rule, split up into various sections, containing various national groups of Jews and reflecting the influences of heterogeneous waves of immigration, as well as of successive generations of the same groups.

In the ghetto proper we find only the first generation of immigrants, and generally those coming from Russia, Poland, and Roumania. The earlier groups of immigrants, the Spanish-Portuguese, the Germans, and the Austrians, having come from countries in which they had to some extent been out of the ghetto for two or three generations, and having acquired some of the outward characteristics of their neighbors, have, as a rule, scattered over wider areas and never attained the cohesion and solidarity of the Russian and Polish Jewish masses. Moreover, the early German immigrants came from Jewish communities which to the extent that they had a separate existence were not decreed by formal laws and regulations, while the Russians came directly from the compulsory ghetto. Finally, the German immigrants were predominantly an urban people, while the Russians and Poles hailed from the villages and small towns, and were not far removed in their social world from the peasants from whom they kept strictly aloof.

Although they were technically free to settle where they pleased, they crowded close together in the area of deterioration, where they carried on their life much as they had done in Europe. They felt themselves no more akin to the more prosperous and partially assimilated German Jews than they did to the Gentiles. As one of them put it:

When I first put my feet on the soil of Chicago, I was so disgusted that I wished I had stayed at home in Russia. I left the Old Country because you couldn't be a Jew over there and still live, but I would rather be dead than be the kind of German Jew that brings the Jewish name into disgrace by being a Goy. That's what hurts: They parade around as Jews, and down deep in their hearts they are worse than Goyim, they are *meshumeds* [apostates].[1]

The center of life, in the new ghetto as in the old, was the synagogue. The synagogues of the Polish and Russian Jews were from the beginning of their settlement in Chicago

[1] "Autobiography of an Immigrant," manuscript.

separate from those of the Germans. In January, 1926, there were forty-three orthodox synagogues on the near West Side. Most of these are small, only a few having over one hundred members. They are made up largely of immigrants who originate from the same community in Europe. They are open daily, and are frequented by a small group of elderly people who gather for prayer and for a discussion of the Talmud under the leadership either of the regularly appointed rabbi or of one of their most learned members. For the most part these synagogues are either converted Christian churches, or buildings that were once used by congregations that have moved to other parts of the city. No new synagogue has been built in the ghetto in recent years, and few of those now there have been kept in repair. As a rule their deterioration proceeds at a pace parallel to that of the neighborhood in which they are located. They are equipped with a basement, which is used for the daily services and meetings, while the main floor is occupied only on the Sabbath and on holidays. The services consist partly of silent prayer and partly of chanted responsive readings. Scarcely a detail is left to the whim or desire of the worshipers. The *siddur*, or prayerbook, but more often the age-old law of custom, regulates even the minutest items of the ritual. Although a cantor or reader is the nominal leader, the members of the congregation take an active part in the proceedings, sometimes following their own tempo. As a result there is often a noticeable lack of unison. Those who are engaged in business often finish their daily prayers before the rest, and leave feeling that at least they have done their duty. A Jewish peddler said:

I drive my horse and wagon up to the *shul* every day except on Shabboth, and come back in time for Ma'ariv [evening prayer]. I have done it for years, and expect to do it for the rest of my life. I couldn't sleep at night nor work during the day if I hadn't *davvened* [prayed] and layed *tphillin* [put on the philacteries]. It only takes a little while, but then when you come out you feel you are a man. A half-a-Jew is no Jew at all.[1]

Next to his family, the main link of the newly arrived immigrant with the community is his synagogue. There he becomes oriented to the new surroundings and finds the familiar scenes and experiences that bridge the gap between the Old World and the New. A middle-aged Maxwell Street merchant tells of bringing his aged father over from Southern Russia:

The first chance I had to get a ticket over to him, I did it. While he was on the way I got a little worried. I thought, what will he do when he gets here? I am at work and he will know nobody and he will be very lonesome. And I want to make his last days happy. But when he came he solved the whole problem for me. The first thing he asked was, "Where is the Odessaer Shul?" When he got there he was as happy as a baby. He met a lot of *Landsleut*, and America and Chicago didn't seem so bad. He went to shul morning and night until a week before he died, and he knew more about every *chevraman's* [member of the congregation] business than I did.[2]

The synagogue is the central institution in the whole community. It usually has its rabbi, who visits the homes of the members and advises them in their domestic and business problems. It generally has a religious school, or *cheder*, which the children attend after school hours. It has a circumcisor. In most cases it has various mutual aid societies, including a burial society, connected with it. The *rov*, or rabbi, is an honored person of some learning, who sometimes is called upon to decide issues which ordinarily in America

[1] "The Experiences of a Maxwell-Street Chicken Dealer," manuscript.

[2] "From Odessa to Chicago: An account of the Migration and Settlement of a Jewish Family," manuscript.

are considered secular in nature, but which according to Old World ghetto practice come under the jurisdiction of the rabbi. The following instance shows the extent to which the synagogue is a control organization:

Sam, a sixteen-year-old boy, had attacked a little girl and raped her. The father of the girl went to the father of Sam, asking what he would do. Sam's father in turn came to a social agency for advice about the matter. When the social worker called at the home of the girl he was informed that the case was settled. He had taken the matter to the *rov*, and Sam's father had agreed to abide by the *rov's* decision, which was to pay fifteen hundred dollars damages to the family of the girl.[1]

Through the synagogue the members come into touch with the important events of concern to them, and the synagogue still remains the most effective organ of approach to the ghetto community.

The synagogue has throughout the ages been the heart of the Jewish community, and it still is today. In spite of anything which may be said to the contrary, everything of importance in Jewish life is still nurtured and fostered, directly and indirectly, by the synagogue. Very often we hear dirges and lamentations about the dying influence of the synagogue, about the insignificant rôle which it is playing in modern Jewish life. Yet whenever anything goes wrong with us, the blame is almost instinctively placed at the door of the synagogue.

The order of the day in American Jewish life is the drive. This institution is our inheritance from the war days; but while other groups in the community are slowly forgetting about the drives, the American Jew continues to drive faster and faster. . . . . Of course the purpose of all these drives is to obtain money, which, it seems to be commonly agreed, can no longer be obtained without "thunderings and lightning." We do not know how successful these drives are, nor do we know how much money is being wasted in staging them; but at all events we know that the "drivers" come to the synagogue for aid in their work—to that old and decrepit synagogue with which many

[1] From a record of the Jewish Social Service Bureau, Chicago.

of our leaders have much profound sympathy. A certain national Jewish institution, for example, decides to have a drive in order to raise, let us say, fifty thousand dollars in Chicago. This figure, the drivers maintain, is a very small one, in view of the importance of the cause, and in view of the fact that there are at least two hundred fifty thousand Jews in Chicago. To get fifty thousand dollars out of two hundred fifty thousand Jews should be a very simple affair, our "drivers" argue, since this makes only one dollar for every five heads. Now, the easiest way of reaching Jews is through the synagogue, since the house of worship is the only place where Jews still gather for the cultivation of the things of the spirit, and where they are still ready to listen to appeals of mercy. In fact, there are very few other places where Jews can be reached outside the synagogue. There are of course Jewish lodges; but here people get together for mutual benefit purposes only, and they are not ready to pay attention to anything which does not concern their own "good and welfare." If, then, after the two hundred fifty thousand Jews are approached through the various synagogues, and the money is not raised, then our "drivers" hasten to proclaim from the housetops that the synagogue Jew is stingy, that he is dead to everything Jewish and humane, and that the religion for which the synagogue stands is outworn and antiquated.

Our "drivers," however, in their heated criticism of the synagogue, overlook one minor but very significant detail. They forget that the very large majority of Chicago Jews even do not step into a synagogue, and that those who do frequent synagogues are the only ones who continue to support Jewish causes. If Chicago Jewry had a directory of synagogue members, and if lists of contributors to important Jewish causes would be regularly compiled in this city, it could be easily proved that the most liberal Jews in our midst are synagogue members. Besides, we must remember that after all is said and done, synagogue members are essentially doing the most significant piece of work in the community, even if they should refuse to become interested in anything else. What is keeping the Jewish community alive is the spirit of Judaism generated by the synagogue and disseminated among posterity. The work of the synagogue itself is of greater importance than anything else undertaken in behalf of any movement or institution, for without the synagogue all those institutions and movements could not even come into existence.[1]

The synagogue, as has been felt by its leaders, has been fast losing ground with the rising generation, who have been bored by its ritual and restricted by its regulation of the affairs of everyday life. But since it is based upon the iron laws of medieval rabbinism and since it flourishes almost exclusively in the circumscribed world of the ghetto, the synagogue has resisted innovation. The synagogue has been especially hostile to Reformism; it has taken the stand that nothing shall be changed, lest all perish. Even if the synagogue Jew has had contact with the secular world he will cling to the ritual if he wishes to remain within the community. An editorial in a local orthodox paper reads:

Religion and politics: God is the Maker and Lord of the Universe, from the milky way down to Loomis Street in Chicago. . . . . You will agree with me that this omnipotent and omniscient God has plenty to do, ... without looking into my, our, your, chicken soup pot. You will admit with me that such a God cannot be worried over the fact that a knife used for butter is finding its way into a chicken soup pot. Nor can he be worried over the fact that there is no eirev in town, or that the one has his beard clipped, and the other shaved. I think that all that is not God's business, and whoever says it is, is ignorant and blasphemous.

But still the question whether a knife used to cut cheese finds its way in a soup-kitchen pot is of importance nevertheless. It is not of importance to the omnipotent God, but is of importance to us Jews. The question of Kosher and Trefa is not a religious question, has nothing to do with God, because he is not a kitchen God, but the God of the Universe. Though seventy years may be like one day in his eyes, he must be so busy with the management of this Universe that he cannot possibly look into a soup-kitchen pot for lack of time. Nor can he be concerned with the question whether you and I take a close

[1] S. Felix Mendelsohn, Sentinel, January 16, 1925.

shave or clip our beards; whether we have our shoes shined on Sabbath; whether we carry a walking cane on holidays or not. From
the point of view of Jewish life and its forms, however, these questions
are all important. They do not concern God in the least, but they may
disturb our traffic here, downstairs; may affect our lives and our very
existence as a people.

All these Rabbinic ordinances, laws, and decrees have been promulgated by our Rabbis with the only object of creating a wall between ourselves and the nations sheltering us, so that we remain a
national entity and do not disappear from among the nations of the
earth.

Orthodoxy thus is not religion, but state, politics, forms of social
and political life of the Jewish people. . . . .

If a Jew in the *Diaspora* ceases to observe the Rabbinical laws and
ordinances, he is likely to intermarry; is likely to assimilate with Gentiles and to disappear as a Jew. . . . .

Orthodoxy is motivated by the desire to preserve the forms of
Jewish life as a means to an end. The end is the preservation of the
Jewish nation in the *Diaspora*. Reform is a political proposition because it abolishes and destroys the forms of Jewish life with the object of bringing about the destruction of the Jewish people by ultimate
assimilation. . . . .

Orthodoxy means, in the final analysis, the will to live as a Jew,
while Reform means the will to die as a *Goy*.[1]

The emphasis that is put upon "form" is central in the continuity of any sect, and orthodox Judaism, in the American
milieu, has been reduced to the position of a sect. It is in
sharp conflict with all those groups who would deviate from
the sanctioned form. It is this sentimental attachment to
traditions and sacred values that makes the control on the
part of the synagogue over the lives of the individuals so
binding and so absolute. The fact that the Chicago Jewish
community spends approximately one million dollars a year
for Kosher meats, over and above the cost of ordinary meats,

[1] S. M. Melamed, *Chicago Chronicle*, February 20, 1925.

in order to have them slaughtered according to the approved method of cutting their throats by a regularly appointed *shochet*, or slaughterer; the fact that hundreds of old men and young refuse to work on the Sabbath and thereby disqualify themselves for a great many vocational opportunities; the fact that orthodox Jews will refuse to shave, and that young rabbinical students would rather use a depilatory powder than allow a razor to touch their faces—these and countless other details of ritualistic observance are matters of form, rooted in sentiment and sanctioned by tradition.

It is these forms, too, that have given rise to some of the most picturesque ghetto types. The Chassidic Jew with flowing beard and long side-locks and his long black coat is still seen occasionally in the ghetto streets. At funerals one may watch an old lady in front of the undertaking rooms collecting alms in her handkerchief from the mourners and bystanders. This *Fatchelyudene*, as she is called, is capitalizing the ritualistic form appropriate to the occasion. In and out of the synagogue there is to be found the ubiquitous *Kleikodeshnik*, or professional pious individual, to whom piousness is merely a form. And there is the *Schönerjüd*, or idle, learned individual, and the *Zaddik*, whose virtue is held up as a model to the young, and the *Gottskossak*, whose task it is to supervise the conduct of the community, much against the members' own will. These and other types flourish in the ghetto because of the emphasis put on form, because they are tolerated and developed by the sentiments and practices of old.

The orthodox community resents and reacts violently to any attempt to alter or to mock these forms, for they constitute the very fabric of its social life. Thus, when the question as to whether a butcher who professes to sell Kosher meat must really live up to the approved religious ritual came before the courts because a Jewish butcher had been selling to his customers as Kosher, meat which really had not been approved by the rabbi, there was an outburst of indignation which resulted in protracted litigation. A Jewish writer made the following comment on the Supreme Court's decision in the matter:

The decision of the United States Supreme Court upholding the constitutionality of the New York State Kosher Law was expected; common sense and legal technicality in this case dictated such a decision.

Those who fought the law on the ground that it is contarry to the Constitution to involve religion in law did not have a leg to stand on. The Kosher law does not compel anybody to eat or sell kosher meat; the law deals only with honesty in commerce and prohibits a certain form of misrepresentation which affects many people. When a butcher says that he is selling kosher meat, it should be kosher, and he should not mix the product with non-kosher meat, for that is contrary to the Jewish laws.

Similar laws exist for quite some time. The pure food laws that were enacted about twenty years ago have abolished another type of misrepresentation. It is prohibited to label margerine as butter, etc. Only recently a law was adopted prohibiting misrepresentation in stamping metals. When gold is stamped 14 k, it must be 14 k. These regulations are framed to maintain honesty in commerce. They are the functions of government, and the kosher law is a legitimate part of such regulations, though it was adopted only a few years ago.

The claim of the opponents that it will be difficult to find out what is kosher is ridiculous. There is only one sort of koshruth, that which is guaranteed by orthodox rabbis in accordance with the ancient Jewish law. The reformers have given up koshruth long ago, and have no pretense to it. They admit openly that they do not believe in it; but the hundreds of thousands of Jews who do believe in it should not be defrauded. The fact that the fight against the kosher law was conducted by Jewish merchants of non-kosher products for their personal profit is our eternal shame.[1]

[1] J. Fishman, *Jewish Morning Journal*, January 6, 1925.

The observance of the dietary regulations, in the form of the exclusive use of Kosher foods, is so universal a mark of orthodoxy among Jews that in some Jewish communities the plan has been considered, and employed, of placing a tax on Kosher meat to raise the necessary funds for the upkeep of the communal institutions.

It is easy to understand why nothing arouses the resentment of the orthodox Jew quite so much as the mockery of his hallowed forms of worship by the Reform rabbis. In an editorial entitled "The Rabbinic Menace" we read:

> The modern rabbi who is aping the Christian pastor is a real menace to the existence and continuation of Judaism in America. . . . . The modern rabbi, be he conservative or reform, is attempting to Christianize the synagogue or the temple by introducing the so-called religious services on Friday evening or Sunday morning. These religious services are neither religious nor services, but burlesque shows. Whenever I attended such services, I felt that the Americanized Jews are developing into a bunch of hypocrites. These religious services are often attended by Jews who know better, but still they participate in the hokus pokus, and tolerate the reading of a portion of the Bible in English in that oily and priestly tone so strange to the Jewish mind and the Jewish traditions, and tolerate a rabbi who is just aping the Christian pastor, and making a monkey of Judaism, and tolerating a so-called religious performance that is comedy pure and simple.
>
> Either one is a religious Jew and attends religious services in the same way as our ancestors did, or as all pious Jews still do, or one does not attend services at all. The so-called "after supper" services are a mockery, and there is as much religion in them as in the Sunday services of the reform rabbis. Aesthetically, they are disgraceful, and religiously they are contemptible. Only Jews with full pockets and empty minds can participate in such services and be parties to such performances.[1]

There are occasions, however, when the orthodox Jew, in taking stock of his ghetto organization, finds that he lives

---

[1] S. M. Melamed, *Chicago Chronicle*, Vol. VIII, No. 11.

after all in a puny world. This is particularly true when he compares his humble synagogue with the pretentious temple, and his poverty with the wealth of the "half-goyim," or reformed element.

It is no wonder that some of the orthodox rabbis are obliged to deal with "sacramental wine," much as most of them dislike it; they cannot make a decent living on the pitiful salary they receive. The Congregation Knesseth Israel, the biggest and richest orthodox congregation in Chicago, with property worth a half million dollars, and a large sum of cash in the treasury, pays its rabbi only $2,500 a year! How can a man raise a family on such a salary? Sinai pays its rabbi $20,000 a year, and he has not one-tenth the responsibility that Rabbi Ephraim Epstein has. Moses Salk, president of Knesseth Israel, who is a prominent business man, should know that a rabbi must not have financial worries, that he must be provided to make a living and be able to raise a family in an honorable fashion. If the rabbi is not satisfactory there is a way to release him and secure the services of one who will be satisfactory. But to pay a rabbi a starving wage is not only sacrilegious but criminal, and all those who permit such an outrage are guilty of both crimes.[1]

But the invidious comparisons between the ghetto and the Jewish community outside are rare. More often the only standard of eminence that the groups within the ghetto apply is that which is found in their own restricted world. Congregations are ranked, not only according to their size, but also on the basis of their reputation for piety and charity.[2]

[1] *Chicago Chronicle*, January 16, 1925.

[2] "An appeal was made on the Sabbath of Chanuka in the various synagogues for the Denver Consumptive Relief Sanitorium New Building Fund. Anshe Makarev, the smallest congregation, with a membership of about 30, contributed $90, while Congregation Anshe Knesseth Israel Nusach Sfard, of Independence and Douglas Boulevard, whose president, A. Friedman, *claims* that it is the biggest congregation in Chicago, where Alderman Jacob Arvey made a fervent appeal, contributed the munificent sum of $12!...." (*Chicago Chronicle*, February 6, 1926).

The synagogue and the rabbi, as we find them in the ghetto, leave scarcely a single phase of the life of the congregation free from their control. This is particularly true of family life. Marriage and divorce, and the adjustment of quarrels between husband and wife and parents and children, all are legitimate relations for communal control. Recently Rabbi Ezekiel Lipschitz, dean of the orthodox rabbis of Poland, came to the United States and Chicago for the expressed purpose of locating the husbands of 18,000 Russian and Polish Jewish women who had been deserted during the last twenty years. He received the hearty coöperation of the local synagogues and rabbis. The family is one of the chief concerns of the community as a whole. A national organization with headquarters in New York and branches in almost every city in the United States and Canada, the National Desertion Bureau, has the expressed function of locating deserting husbands and wives. In its work this bureau makes full use of the publicity that the Jewish press affords. Some Yiddish newspapers contain a regular column entitled "Gallery of Deserting Husbands," in which pictures and descriptions of the culprits appear.

Even in the most private affairs of the membership the community takes an active interest. Its criticisms, especially when voiced through the press, generally are a corrective for the vices of the community. A leading politician of the ghetto is scored in the following item:

"Sanitary District Trustee Morris Eller Wins Great Victory for Chicago Water Supply," reads a screaming headline in Tuesday's *Jewish Courier*. And we thought that Michael Rosenberg was also a Trustee of the Sanitary District, and that he, too, had something to do with the water situation. But Morris Eller puts his picture in the paper and claims all the credit for himself. Talk about *chutzpah!* [nerve].[1]

[1] *Chicago Chronicle*, January 16, 1925.

The injudicious private act of philanthropy of a member
is made the object of an attack in the following item:

Herman Iglowitz, who was entrusted to distribute $1,000 to
charitable institutions, should take lessons in fairness. Mr. Morris
Cohen, of 3841 Adams Street, celebrated his silver wedding anniversary at Gold's last Sunday evening, and in consideration of that
joyful event, he contributed $1,000 to charity. Not being familiar
with the existing institutions and their needs, Mr. Cohen delegated his
friend Iglowitz to make the distribution. We are convinced that had
Mr. Cohen known how unfair Iglowitz would be he would not have entrusted him with such a delicate mission. Iglowitz gave to the Jewish
Charities, $150, which means that the Marks Nathan Orphan Home,
the B.M.Z., the Mount Sinai Hospital, and the other affiliated institutions—30 in all— will receive the munificent sum of $5 each, while
to the Hachnosas Orchim [an immigrant sheltering home], on Sawyer
Avenue, known at best as a superfluous, unworthy, and makeshift
institution, Iglowitz gave $100! The Daughters of Zion and Douglas
Park Day Nurseries, the Beth Hamedrosh L' Torah [orthodox rabbinical college], Denver Sanitorium, and the Haddassah [a Zionistic
women's organization] receive only $75 each, and the Keren Hayesod
(Palestine Fund), Grenshaw Street Talmud Torah, and Ladies' Aid
for Consumptives, receive each $50, but the Sawyer Avenue Hachno-
sas Orchim, where "booze" was for a time part of their income, and
which certain officers peddled on the streets, to the disgrace of the
community, to them Iglowitz gives $100! Gosh, what unfairness rests
in the heart of ignorance. . . . .[1]

The well-known type of the *Staatsbalbos*, or the patriarchal leader, to whom questions of final judgment on religious and secular matters (however small the realm of the
secular is in the ghetto community) are deferred, arises out
of this closeness of personal relationships of the members of
the community to each other, and the surveillance that the
community exercises over the conduct of each of its members. For instance, the keeping of the Sabbath and the

[1] *Ibid.*, February 6, 1926.

holidays on the part of each individual is a matter of great concern to the community. A local Jewish organ recently wrote:

We are pleased to note that our suggestion to the Rabbinical Association to enlist the services of the local Jewish press to refuse to publish items of social affairs taking place on Friday evenings brought the desired result. The following letter was sent out by the Chicago Rabbinical Association to the Jewish press:

"In its desire to impress upon the Jewish people the sanctity of the Sabbath and its importance in Jewish life, the Chicago Rabbinical Association desires to enlist the co-operation of the Jewish press. We would, therefore, appreciate it most sincerely if you would refuse to publish in your paper any announcements of affairs taking place on the Sabbath. Such a stand on the part of the Rabbinate receiving the co-operation of the Jewish press may, it is hoped, encourage a deeper appreciation of the sacredness of the Sabbath and discourage its desecration."[1]

While the community is of course concerned with the religious observance of its members as a whole, it is particularly anxious about the younger generation. The wild behavior of the young people and their frequent violation of the religious taboos, especially non-attendance at the synagogue, violation of the dietary laws, failure to put on the philacteries in the mornings, and, most important of all, the occasional instances of intermarriage, are regarded as serious symptoms of community disintegration. Jewish parents frequently will deny themselves the essentials of life in order to send their boys to a religious school. The family's status in the Jewish community depends in considerable measure upon the learning of their children. In the Old World this training is mainly religious, such as the *cheder* and the *yeshiba* offer. But in America secular learning may

[1] *Ibid.*, February 13, 1925.

in part compensate for deficiency in religious knowledge. The main concern of the orthodox father, however, is to have a *Kaddish*, i.e., a son, or other relative, who will mourn for him after his death. A Jewish father appealed to a settlement worker for aid in persuading his son to go to *cheder*, with the plea: "He is no son of mine. Why, when his mother died he wouldn't even say Kaddish for her. I suppose when I die it will be the same way. What good is a son like that? I wish he had never been born."[1] An aged Jewish peddler came to the office of a social agency asking to be taken to the hospital for the insane, where his only son was confined. He said: "I am getting old, and I feel that I am going to die pretty soon, and when I die I want somebody to say Kaddish for me. If my son Isidor can't do it, I have the trouble and the shame of having to hire somebody else. I want to see if he can say Kaddish."[2] The father felt considerably relieved when he had assured himself that his son was able to repeat the prayer after him.

The violation of the Sabbath and of other sacred traditions of orthodoxy has increased to such proportions that the organized community is stirred to action. Since the younger generation will not as a rule even attend the Friday evening service, which is held at sundown, many congregations have attempted to adapt themselves to the changed conditions of employment in American cities and have postponed this service till after supper. These congregations, while professing to be orthodox, are generally called "conservative," to distinguish them from the strictly orthodox on

[1] "Culture Conflicts in the Immigrant Family " manuscript.

[2] From a social case history in the files of the Jewish Social Service Bureau.

the one hand, and from the reformed congregations on the other.

The recent editorial which appeared on this page on the frequent and flagrant violations of the Sabbath, by Chicago individuals and organizations, has, we are happy to say, done some good. Many well known members of our faith have applauded our unmistakable stand, admitting that things have gone altogether too far in this direction. The Chicago Rabbinical Association . . . . has begun to take a decided stand on the matter, since it is from the spiritual leaders that the community expects light and counsel in religious matters.

In the meantime, however, we wish to point out that our ultra-orthodox brethren are creating conditions which make it conducive to their children to violate the Sabbath. Our good and pious brethren, of course, know very well the significance and importance of the Sabbath in Jewish life, and they themselves are careful to observe it by taking in an early service Friday evening, and by having a good meal after the service. Their children, however, do not go to services, but they naturally participate in the excellent meal. Services after supper these members of the young generation do not care to attend, because their pious parents convinced them that the late services are conducted by the "trafah" reform and conservative rabbis who are not builders, but destroyers of Judaism. Nevertheless, on Friday evening these young folks do feel in a holiday mood, and they therefore spend their energy of their "extra Sabbath soul" on card playing and similar entertainments of frivolity and joviality, and when some one in the Jewish young people's club says something about the impropriety of desecrating the holy day of Israel, these ladies and gentlemen know immediately that this protest must come from the influence of reform, or conservative rabbis, who have introduced such an un-Jewish idea of holding services Friday evenings after eight o'clock! Why, their very parents and grandparents warned them against listening to the sermons of these rabbis, which are given on Friday evenings! It is this form of reasoning which, we are convinced, is contributing materially towards the open violation of the Sabbath, for when one should take the time to analyze the constituency of those organizations which are advertising their public affairs given on the Sabbath, he would easily discover that it is most frequently made up of children of orthodox parents who are opposed to modern Jewish congregations and their teachings. It is this tragic situation which reminds one of the ancient biblical proverb: "The fathers have eaten sour grapes, and the children's teeth are set on edge."[1]

One movement recently inaugurated in an attempt to keep orthodoxy intact, by the Jewish Education Committee, was the organization of a sort of "Jewish Boy Scout" movement. The *Tzofim Handbook*, the manual of these Jewish Boy Scouts, has this to say:

The Tzofim are those pupils who look upon the Hebrew school as upon . . . . a small sanctuary, and upon themselves as its Priests and Levites. Just as the Priests and Levites served the Temple and the people, so are the Tzofim at the service of the Hebrew school and of the Jewish people.

Tzofim is a Hebrew word meaning vanguards, watchers or scouts. The Tzofim are the vanguards who lead the way for the rest of the pupils. The Tzofim are scouts ready to serve their people.

The Tzofim, like the Boy Scouts, do a good deed a day, have a pledge, and a sign, and a handshake. They have Hebrew songs, and have their daily tasks. Their pledge reads:

1. I promise to be true to the God of Israel, to learn his Torah, and to try to live according to its commands.

2. I promise to be loyal to the Jewish people, and to help my fellow Jews everywhere. "For all Jews are responsible for each other."

3. I promise to be true to our ancient ideal of rebuilding the Jewish homeland in Palestine.

4. I promise to be loyal to America and its ideals of religious liberty to all.

5. I promise to be a good pupil and a good comrade to my fellow students.[2]

The public appearance of these Tzofim was recently greeted with communal approval. An editorial reads:

[1] *Sentinel*, February 6, 1925.

[2] *Tzofim Handbook*, published by the Board of Jewish Education, Chicago.

An event of communal importance was the celebration held last Sunday afternoon at the Kehilath Jacob Hebrew School. Representatives of eight of the largest Hebrew schools in the city came together to observe *Chamishoh Osor Sishevat*, and they did it in fine style. Hebrew speeches and songs and Palestine movies made up the entertainment. But the significant feature of the evening was the celebrants themselves: They were not presidents or directors of the schools; they were not even grown persons, but Tzofim, members of the organization comprised of pupils of the local Hebrew schools.

Hatzofim, as the organization is known, had two hundred and fifty of its members at the celebration. Perhaps the most impressive part of the occasion came when, after the powerful address by Dr. Alexander M. Dushkin, wherewith he initiated new Tzofim, the youngsters recited their pledge—a pledge of loyalty to the Jewish people and its ideals, ending with the words the Jews uttered when they received the Ten Commandments: Na-Aseh V'Nishma, "We will do and we will obey."

Hatzofim has a splendid idea back of it, that should attract every Jewish lad who is intelligent and devoted to his people. . . . .[1]

The ghetto community is so closely knit, and its members are so directly under the control of the community, that the attempts of Christian missions which have established themselves in the ghetto have made no appreciable progress in converting any Jews in the ghetto itself.

The ghetto is a complete world, but it is a small and a narrow world. It has its intellectuals, but their intellectuality is of a circumscribed sort. What it lacks in breadth of horizon, the ghetto life makes up in depth of emotion, in strength of familial and communal ties, and in attachment to tradition, form, and sentiment.

The ties of family, of village-community, and of *Landsmannschaft* that bind the ghetto inhabitants into little nuclei of more or less autonomous units are only partially apparent

[1] *Chicago Chronicle*, February 13, 1925.

to the outsider. The ghetto family will survive crises that would tear an ordinary family asunder, and a stranger who is able to call himself a *Landsmann*, not only loosens the purse-strings of the first individual he meets, but also has access to his home. Not only do the *Landsleute* belong to the same synagogue, but as a rule they engage in similar vocations, become partners in business, live in the same neighborhood, and intermarry within their own group. A *Landsmannschaft* has its own patriarchal leaders, its lodges and mutual aid associations, and its celebrations and festivities. It has its burial plot in the cemetery. It keeps the memories of the group alive through frequent visits, and maintains a steady liaison with the remnants of the Jewish community in the Old World.

Occasionally these organizations join forces with other local clusters of Jews from the same general region in Europe. In the case of Jews who come from the same country, but who are few in number in comparison to the dominant groups, such as the Oriental Jews, the Spanish-Portuguese Jews, the Roumanian Jews, and to some extent the Hungarian Jews, the *Landsmannschaft* organization may cover a larger territory. The provincial or national ties are generally strengthened by a common dialect, peculiarities in diet, and local customs. In critical situations, particularly crises in the Old Country involving the whole group, they act as a body. Sometimes this requires financial assistance to the community abroad; at others, lodging a protest against the government; or, again, enlisting the support of other Jewish groups locally and nationally to bring about desired results. Hand in hand with the ties of sympathy between the members of a *Landsmannschaft* go also the antagonisms and prejudices between these groups which have been brought over from the Old World. The social distances between Roumanian Jews and Hungarian Jews, between Lithuanians and Poles, between Poles and Russians, and between Russians and Galicians are sometimes so great as to make corporate action within the ghetto impossible. Intermarriage between some of these groups is almost as rare as intermarriage between ghetto Jews and Gentiles.

The description of the ghetto would be incomplete without mention of the great number of other characteristic institutions that give it its own peculiar atmosphere and mark it as a distinct culture area. Among them are the Kosher butcher shops, where fresh meats and a variety of sausages are a specialty, and where, besides the butcher, there is to be found a special functionary, the *shochet*, who kills fresh poultry to order, mumbling a prayer as he cuts the throat of each chicken, duck, or goose with his *chalef* (ritually approved butcher-knife). There is the basement fish store to gratify the tastes of the connoisseur with a variety of herrings, pike, and carp, which Jewish housewives purchase on Thursday in order to serve the famous national dish of *gefüllte fish* at the sumptuous Friday evening meal. On the sidewalks in front of butcher shops and fish stores throughout the ghetto, especially on Thursdays and Fridays, there sits the bowed and bearded form of the horse-radish grinder. Often he turns out to be a religious teacher or talmudical scholar from the Old World, who, on account of his years, finds other avenues of making a living closed. There are Kosher bake-shops with rye bread, poppy-seed bread, and pumpernickel daily, and a kind of doughnut known as *beigel* for *Shabboth*. And finally there is the bath-house, which contains facilities for Turkish and Russian, plain and fancy, baths, besides being the modern counterpart of the ritual bath, or *mikveh*, which is patronized by the women at certain prescribed occasions. The Russian and Turkish bath serves the ghetto as a hotel, since it is the custom to stay overnight, and since there are no hotels in the ghetto.

The ghetto has its own theater, where plays of the Russian dramatists are given in Yiddish, and where Sholom Asch and Peretz Hirschbein appear in the repertoire side by side, with translations from Shakespeare, Ibsen, Shaw, and *risqué* Broadway comedies. But the Chicago Yiddish theater, like the Yiddish press, is for the most part but a sideshow of the New York ghetto. The Yiddish newspapers and the Yiddish theater draw their talent from New York. And if there happens to be discovered a literary genius or an *actorke* on the local scene, the wider and more appreciative audience of Second Avenue—the Yiddish Broadway of New York—soon snatches them off.

Native to the ghetto are also the basement and second-story bookstores, cafés, and restaurants where the intellectuals hold forth on the latest developments in Zionism, socialism, philosophy, art, and politics, while they play a game of chess or pinochle. The Maxwell Street police station, the cigar stores, and the curtained gambling houses are the haunts of the loafers and gangsters of the district. Finally, at the offices of the shyster lawyers, the *realestateniks*, and sacramental wine dealers, one finds the fixers, the ward heelers, and petty politicians of the ghetto.

But with all these varied activities and personality types, the ghetto nevertheless is a small world. The life with which it throbs is a provincial and sectarian one. Its successes are after all measured on a small scale, and its range of expression is limited. Not until the Jew gets out of the ghetto does he really live a full life. The ghetto community is not capable of collective action on a larger scale. It has its tragedies and its comedies, and what it possesses in depth and intensity it lacks in breadth and in substance. It is the slave of forms hallowed by tradition and sentiment, but is shallow in content and out of touch with the world. It is the product of sectarianism and isolation, of prejudices and taboos. The ghetto is a closed community, perpetuating itself and renewing itself with a minimum of infusion of influences from without, biologically as well as culturally. It is almost as completely cut off from the world as if it were still surrounded by a wall and its inhabitants were still locked nightly behind ghetto gates.

THE JEWS AND THEIR NEIGHBORS

The near West Side has been the stamping-ground of virtually every immigrant group that has come to Chicago. The occupation of this area by the Jews is, it seems, merely a passing phase of a long process of succession in which one population group has been crowded out by another. There seems to be more regularity in this process, however, than at first sight appears. In describing the foreign quarter of New York City, one writer has pointed out the constancy of the association of certain racial and cultural groups in the transition of the community from one stage to the next. In every great city there is going on a constant sifting process in the course of which each racial, national, and cultural group tends to find its habitat in the various natural areas that the city affords. Moreover, it has been pointed out that the various immigrant colonies in New York City seem to assume the same geographical pattern that the mother-

countries of the immigrants assume on the map of Europe.[1]
While not quite the same can be said for Chicago, there is an
unmistakable regularity in the association between local immigrant groups, and particularly between the Jews and their
neighbors.

The first Jewish settlers on the near West Side were
mostly Bohemian Jews. As was to be expected, they settled
in that part of the city which was open to immigrants from
the point of view of rent, accessibility, and tolerance. But
these early Jewish settlers drifted to that particular portion
of the city lying beyond the central business district which
was occupied by Bohemian immigrants, most likely because
they were accustomed in the Old World to live side by side
with that people, knew their language, and had developed a
modus vivendi, including the attitude of mutual tolerance,
and, most important of all, trade relationships. The Jews
opened their stores and began to peddle in this Bohemian
neighborhood, and prospered. The elevation of the railroad
tracks on Fifteenth Street cut this area in two, and the
Bohemians moved southwestward as the city expanded and
industrial plants arose in that direction, while the Jews remained behind and expanded their area of occupation westward and northward.

In the course of the extension of the Jewish settlement
they encountered the Irish and the Germans. As these
groups moved on, the Jews followed, only to be succeeded
by the Italians, the Poles and Lithuanians, the Greeks and
Turks, and finally by the Negroes. Such observations as
have been made in other large American cities, notably New
York and Philadelphia, indicate that a similar order of suc-

[1] Konrad Berkovici, *Around the World in New York*. New York, 1924.

cession is to be seen there.[1] This phenomenon seems to be due, not merely to the chronological order of immigration of these various groups, but also to the relation of the standards of living of the various nationalities to one another, and to the attraction and tolerance of the successor by the predecessor. In the course of this transition the area has become converted from a pioneer residential section into a deteriorated neighborhood, from the outskirts of an overgrown village to the slum of a great city.

One may also note a certain degree of regularity in the economic relations between the inhabitants of the ghetto. In the early days of Chicago the clothing manufacturing establishments of the city employed largely Irish and German girls. These girls refused to work side by side with the Russian and Polish immigrants when they began to make their presence felt in the eighties. In part as a result of this, the sweatshop system arose. Work was given out to the Jewish immigrants to be done at home. It required but little capital to set up a tailoring establishment. The enterprising Jewish immigrants soon realized the possibilities of contracting for the performance of most of the operations required in the needle industry outside of cutting. This in turn relieved the manufacturer of the responsibility for factory maintenance, and, besides, lowered the cost of production. In less than two decades the Irish and the Germans had been largely replaced by Jewish labor in the tailoring trades, only to be succeeded in turn by the Italians and Poles, as the changing membership of the trade unions in the needle trades indicates.

The immigrants drift to the lowest economic level in the division of labor, and rise to the next rung in the ladder as a

[1] Bernheimer, *op. cit.*

new wave of immigrants succeeds them. The Jews took to peddling when they came here. This occupation had hitherto been beneath the dignity of any immigrant group. They made it profitable, and in turn were to some extent, especially in the fruit and vegetable branch, displaced by the Italians.

The relationship between the Poles and the Jews in Chicago is of especial interest. These two groups detest each other thoroughly, but they live side by side on the West Side, and even more generally on the Northwest Side. They have a profound feeling of disrespect and contempt for each other, bred by their contiguity and by historical friction in the pale; but they trade with each other on Milwaukee Avenue and on Maxwell Street. A study of numerous cases shows that not only do many Jews open their businesses on Milwaukee Avenue and Division Street because they know that the Poles are the predominant population in these neighborhoods, but the Poles come from all over the city to trade on Maxwell Street because they know that there they can find the familiar street-stands owned by Jews. These two immigrant groups, having lived side by side in Poland and Galicia, are used to each other's business methods. They have accommodated themselves one to another, and this accommodation persists in America. The Pole is not accustomed to a "one-price store." When he goes shopping it is not a satisfactory experience unless he can haggle with the seller and "Jew him down" on prices.

One of the most significant signs of the relationship between the Jews and their neighbors in the ghetto is found in the contacts between the members of the younger generation. They mingle not only in school but they are members of the same gangs. The recent outbreaks of gang warfare in

Chicago show that in many instances the Jews, the Irish, and the Italians are engaged in joint illicit liquor enterprises, or combine their forces in "hi-jacking." In politics, too, while the tendency on the part of Jews has recently been to put their own men into office, it is not uncommon to find the Jews supporting an Italian for alderman, or to find the Italians supporting a Jew for a judgeship or a place on the Sanitary Board. Partnerships in peddling between Jewish and Italian boys on the West Side are frequently formed, and on the whole they seem to be very successful. Each has a special gift to contribute toward the success of the business.

The latest invasion of the ghetto by the Negroes is of more than passing interest. The Negro, like the immigrant, is segregated in the city into a racial colony. Economic considerations, race prejudice, and cultural differences combine to set him apart. The Negro has drifted to the near West Side for precisely the same reason that the Jews and the Italians came there. Unlike the white landlords and residents in other sections of the city, the Jews have offered no appreciable resistence to the invasion by the Negroes. As one clothing merchant on Maxwell Street put it, "A dollar is just as good whether a white hand or a black hand hands it over. Anyway, their hands are white on the inside."[1] Many of the immigrants in the ghetto have as yet not heard of the color line. The prevailing opinion of the merchants on the near West Side is that the Negro spends his money freely, and usually has some to spend, and therefore is a desirable neighbor. The attitude of a great many Jewish property owners in the district is typified by the following statement by one of them:

[1] "Reflections of a Maxwell-Street Merchant," manuscript.

When I rented my two story frame building to a colored family, some fellows came to see me, to tell me that I oughtn't to rent to niggers because they brought the value of the property down. I told them it was none of their business whom I rented to. The property in the neighborhood is in such poor shape that if you didn't rent to anybody that comes along, you would have it stand empty and pay your taxes out of your pocket. I asked those fellows whether they would pay my taxes or rent the building themselves, and they took to their heels.

We Jews ought to be the last ones to hold a prejudice against another race, after all that we have been through.[1]

In the ghetto the Negro seems to have found another haven of refuge in a city where the areas that he occupies are already overcrowded. In this connection it may be noted that the spread of the Negro settlement along fashionable Grand Boulevard on the South Side has also displaced the center of the German-Jewish settlement in that area.

The transition and deterioration of the ghetto community has been proceeding at such a speed that the complexion of the area changes from day to day. Dilapidated structures that a decade ago were Christian churches have since become synagogues and have now been turned into African Methodist Episcopal or colored Baptist churches. Under the latest coat of paint of a store-front colored mission there are vestiges of signs reading "Kosher Butchershop" and "Deutsche Apotheke."

MAXWELL STREET

The heart of the ghetto is marked by two great thoroughfares: Halsted Street and Maxwell Street. The former is lined on both sides with imposing emporiums: furniture stores, sausage stores, fur stores, cloak and suit, silk and dry goods, shoe, hat and cap, tobacco, and department stores.

[1] "Interviews with a Marooned West-Side Family," manuscript.

On Halsted Street business goes on as it would in the Loop. The stores advertise and have one price. Not so with Maxwell Street. Maxwell Street is as native to the ghetto as Halsted Street is now foreign to it. On Maxwell Street there is life; on Halsted Street, decorum. Maxwell Street is the Halsted Street of a generation ago. The proprietors of the substantial establishments on Halsted are the graduates of Maxwell, for the most part. The modern business man on Halsted Street represents the ideal of the sons of the push-cart owners on Maxwell Street.

Maxwell Street, the ghetto's great outdoor market, is full of color, action, shouts, odors, and dirt. It resembles a medieval European fair more than the market of a great city of today. Its origins are to be sought in the traditions of the Jews, whose occupations in the Old World differed little from what they are here. To these traditions correspond also the traditions of the other national groups who form their clientèle.

It has been said that the Poles and Galicians seldom patronize a modern department store, but that they prefer the thrill which comes with shopping on Maxwell Street. Buying is an adventure in which one matches his wits against those of an opponent, a Jew. The Jews are versatile; they speak Yiddish among themselves, and Polish, Russian, Lithuanian, Hungarian, Bohemian, and what not, to their customers. They know their tastes and their prejudices. They have on hand ginghams in loud, gay colors for one group, and for one occasion; and drab and black mourning wear for others.

The noises of crowing roosters and geese, the cooing of pigeons, the barking of dogs, the twittering of canary birds, the smell of garlic and of cheeses, the aroma of onions, apples, and oranges, and the shouts and curses of sellers and buyers fill the air. Anything can be bought and sold on Maxwell Street. On one stand, piled high, are odd sizes of shoes long out of style; on another are copper kettles for brewing beer; on a third are second-hand pants; and one merchant even sells odd, broken pieces of spectacles, watches, and jewelry, together with pocket knives and household tools salvaged from the collections of junk peddlers. Everything has value on Maxwell Street, but the price is not fixed. It is the fixing of the price around which turns the whole plot of the drama enacted daily at the perpetual bazaar of Maxwell Street.

The sellers know how to ask ten times the amount that their wares will eventually sell for, and the buyers know how to offer a twentieth. Everybody who pushes his way through the crowd is a potential customer, everybody except sight-seers, and they are spotted immediately by the discerning eyes of the "pullers," who are engaged in perpetual conversation with the shifting mass of human beings that pass continuously between the rows of street-stands piled high with wares.

The "puller" is a specialist. He has developed a fine technique of blocking the way of passers-by. Before he is aware of it, the unwitting and unsuspecting customer is trying on a suit that is many sizes too large and of a vintage of a decade ago. The seller swears by all that is holy that it fits like a glove, that it is the latest model put out by Hart Schaffner & Marx, and that he needs money so badly that he is willing to sell it at a loss of ten dollars. If the customer is skeptical and is inclined to ask how the dealer can stay in business and lose ten dollars on a suit, he is told confidentially, "You see, we sell so many of 'em."

On the sidewalk a puller shouts, "Caps, fifty cents!" In a moment he has a victim by the arm, and the salesman is trying on caps. "Yes, they are fifty cents apiece." He finds one that fits. "Seventy-five cents for that one."

"But I thought you said they were fifty cents?"

"Yes, but this one fits you!"

On a trunk wedged in between a herring stand and a stall piled high with neckties, a middle-aged man with a trim Van Dyke beard, who still goes to *Shul* on *Shabboth* while his son runs the stand, is seated, engaged in familiar conversation with his *Landsfrau* from Lodz, who runs the hardware stand across the row, when he spots a likely customer some ten paces distant. He interrupts his conversation long enough to shout, "Genuine Solinger razors!" When the customer approaches his stand he grabs him by the arm. "A genuine Solinger razor, worth six dollars, for two and a half!" The customer registers lack of interest, but he is held tightly by the coat-sleeve. "Let me show how it cuts." In a moment the merchant has pulled a straggling lock of hair from his head, and with a deft swish of the razor is demonstrating its superb quality. "How much will you give me? Make me an offer." The customer shakes his head. "Make me an offer; you can't insult me. What will you give me?" The customer offers a quarter. "Do you want to insult me? Do you think I steal them?" The customer tries to get away, but is held tight. The razor merchant, with an air of disgust, makes a gesture of putting the article away.

"Now, make me a decent offer; and remember, be a gentleman."

"A quarter is all I'll give you."

"Well, give me the quarter." The razor is pushed into

the pocket of the customer, who promptly pulls it out and says, "I haven't got my money with me."

"Well, of all the *chutzpah* (nerve)! Why do you bother me, and you let me pull out my hair for you. If I weren't a gentleman, I'd have you arrested." The razor transaction has failed, and the conversation with the *Landsfrau* is resumed.

Up until ten years ago all the life and color that is now Maxwell Street was to be found around the corner, on Jefferson Street; but the city has grown and the market has been pushed farther west, until now it extends to Sangamon Street, five blocks distant. Many of the owners of street-stands and shops have grown rich and no longer live in the district, but they still own the property. The attics and basements in which they once lived with their families have now been turned into storerooms and warehouses. The sons and daughters of these former push-cart owners are now conducting fashionable shops in other parts of the city, or are lawyers or doctors, but their parents in many cases still stick to the gold mine on Maxwell Street.

Competition is keen. The original Maxwell Street population closed up shop and went to the synagogue every Friday afternoon and Saturday morning, but today the market is deserted only on the Day of Atonement and the Jewish New Year. As one veteran put it: "Things aren't as they used to be around here fifteen years ago. We had a better class of Jews then. Everybody was gone on *Shabboth*. But now everybody is after the money, and you got to get out of business or stay here every day, because Saturday is one of our busiest days.[1]

In accordance with the tradition of the pale, where the

[1] "Observations of a 'Puller,'" manuscript.

women conducted the stores while the men spent their time in pious devotion and learning, a number of Jewish women are among the most successful merchants of Maxwell Street. They almost monopolize the fish, herring, and poultry stands.

Some years ago the street stands were permanent fixtures, but recently the city ordinances have prohibited them. At present all the stands are on wheels, and are removed nightly. At five-thirty every morning a mob of men, women, and children may be seen flocking to an empty lot on Thirteenth and Union streets, where an old man rents push-carts for twenty-five cents per day. He knows each of his carts individually, and whenever anyone hastens away with one of his three-hundred-odd vehicles without paying, the owner of the push-carts comes to the market later and collects. He has no difficulty in finding the culprit, for he can identify every one of his vehicles. By six o'clock in the morning the best and largest push-carts have been hauled away. Everyone tries to maneuver for the most favorable position on the street. A corner location, especially on Maxwell and Halsted streets, is worth fighting for.

Frequently the policeman who patrols the street has to decide who came first and is entitled to squatter rights for the day. After "Charlie the Policeman" has settled all the quarrels, fraternization ensues.

When they are all set for business, around ten-thirty in the morning, Mr. Cohen, who sells pop, says to Mr. Goldberg, who sells roasted chestnuts and sunflower seeds, "I'll bet you a dollar it's going to rain." Mr. Goldberg says it won't, and the bet is on. They go to Charlie, and what he says goes. And as the dull morning business goes on, there is a voice yelling every once in a while, "Charley, is it going to rain today?"[1]

[1] *Ibid.*

The prosperity of the ghetto fluctuates with the employ-ment and the earnings of the immigrant and Negro laborers in the industries of Chicago. It has its weekly routine, cor-responding to the habits of that population. Thursday is "chicken day," when the Jewish customers lay in their sup-plies for the Friday evening meal. Most of the purchasing is done by the men, who take a much more active part in the conduct of the household and the kitchen than is the case among non-Jewish immigrant groups. The man sees that the chicken is properly killed, for if something should go wrong, he, as the responsible head of the household, would have to bear the sin. In front of the butcher shops hang signs: "The *shochet* will kill your chickens for ten cents apiece." But there are also a number of butcher shops where hams and non-Kosher meats are sold. The keeper of one of these shops expressed himself as follows: "If they want to eat *chasser* [pork], I should worry. I can sell it to 'em as well as anybody else. When you are in business you can't be too particular. Don't the Kosher meat markets have to sell the *trefah* (non-Kosher) parts of their meat to the goyim?"[1] This same butcher, however, buys his Kosher meat from another shop, and would not allow his own family to eat *trefah*.

Friday is "fish day" on Maxwell Street. The turnover of some of these street-stands and stores is enormous. Sunday is the busiest day of all. Poles, Russians, Lithu-anians, Bohemians, and Negroes, with a scattering minority of old German and Irish purchasers who in former days lived next to the Jews on the near West Side but now are scattered all over the city, come to supply their wants on Maxwell Street. Many of the stands and stores have their permanent clientèle, and are known for the cheapness of their wares.

[1] "Reflections of a Maxwell-Street Merchant," manuscript.

On Sundays there is bedlam on Maxwell Street. The customers are in a holiday mood. Shouts and curses in many languages mingle with polite and familiar conversation in Yiddish.

The Maxwell Street market has been a hotbed of local politics and graft. Rival political leaders vie with each other for control of the administration of the market. The street venders frequently complain of extortion by politicians. Since it is very difficult to organize the Maxwell Street merchants because of the many feuds and factions and the extreme individualism of the community and their village attitudes, it has been easy for politicians to build up a system of private patronage and "protection."

Special police patrolled the Maxwell Street market yesterday, following an assault upon Max Janowsky, new market master, by a score of angry peddlers, who are said to have resented his attempt to eject a woman huckster from her stand.

It is alleged that Janowsky, who was recently appointed by Mayor Dever to replace Harry Lapping after a graft scandal, tried to punish the woman for refusing to contribute to the $250,000 jackpot, said to be collected annually by overlords of Maxwell Street.

When he started to yank the woman's cart away from the curb, according to Alderman Henry L. Fick (20th), his sponsor, a score of neighboring venders showered him with rocks and other missiles. As a result he is now on crutches, with his head wreathed in bandages. The woman disappeared during the mêlée.

Considerable pressure is being brought to bear upon the mayor and city council to close the market, on the ground that graft is too widespread to check.[1]

The latest feud developed ten days ago, when the banana cart of Edward Schatz and his son Benjamin was literally "kicked off the street." Among the venders it was whispered that Alderman Fick was squaring accounts with the Schatzes for carrying a "shakedown"

[1] *Chicago Tribune*, July 15, 1926.

complaint to the mayor, which ended in the firing of Lapping. In sworn affidavits the Schatzes charged that for several years they had been compelled to contribute $300 annually, in addition to the dime a day collected by the city, in order to remain undisturbed in business on the street.

The money, it was charged, was paid to Victor Cohen, who masqueraded with Fick's consent as assistant market master. Cohen, it was alleged, represented "certain politicians having influence over market affairs."

Another motive for the ousting of Schatz and his son was said to be a desire on the part of these same politicians to remove the principal obstacle to their overlord system of illegal taxation. Pay-day on the market with the Schatzes present could only mean one thing—trouble. It was also felt that their stay on the market, in the face of an open break with the bosses, could not have a healthy financial reaction, as other merchants, who paid because they felt they must, might try to follow the example of the Schatzes.

With the mayor absent from the city, Alderman Fick has maintained a defiant attitude.

"No one can come into my ward and defy me," the alderman is quoted as saying. The Schatzes have made their bowl, now they're through peddling bananas on the West Side.

And so Maxwell Street awaits the mayor.[1]

The ghetto, in the opinion of some, has not passed after all. The Jews are still paying tribute to their lords for their right to live and bargain in the ghetto. One of them said: "America isn't so different from Russia. Of course we haven't any pogroms, but we have *rishes* [prejudice] just the same, and we have to buy our right to make a living from the grafters and the politicians, instead of the Tsar and the bureaucrats."[2]

The ghetto inhabitants, particularly the most recent arrivals take it more or less for granted that they do not pos-

[1] *Chicago Daily News*, July 15, 1926.

[2] "Reflections of a Maxwell-Street Merchant," manuscript.

sess equal rights before the law. They feel that they must rely to a large extent upon political pull and fixers to obtain "favors" and achieve their ends, and consequently the ghetto of Chicago, like the East Side of New York, has become the cradle of powerful political machines. The older settlers soon become conscious of their rights, however, and assert themselves effectively against the oppressions of petty politicians.

In spite of its prosperity, the Rialto of the ghetto—Maxwell Street—is fast passing away. As the immigrants get into closer touch with the outside world, they see that after all the ghetto offers but limited opportunities for success. They establish themselves in stores and offices in other parts of the city and become large-scale merchants, real estate dealers, manufacturers, and building contractors. Compared again with the world beyond the ghetto, the ghetto world shrinks to a vanishing-point. Not only do the Jewish merchants move away from Maxwell Street to more reputable quarters, but in recent years there have been few recruits to fill the vacancies. A few recent immigrants still drift to the push-carts, but generally only for a short time, until they have accumulated sufficient wealth to move elsewhere. Maxwell Street is declining, and is being left to the rats that haunt its streets at night.

CHAPTER XII
THE VANISHING GHETTO
THE FLIGHT FROM THE GHETTO

"Let us go to America," said a Jew from Kiev to his wife, after he had lost his fortune in a pogrom, "let us leave this hellish place where men are beasts, and let us go to America, where there is no ghetto and no pale, where there are no pogroms, and where even Jews are men."[1]

He came, but he landed in the ghetto. It took him some time to find out that it was a ghetto; it took him twenty years to discover that the place on Jefferson Street near Roosevelt Road, where he lived a third of his lifetime, was near the very heart of the ghetto. He had become a citizen, and he had voted at elections; he had a business on Jefferson Street, and he had accumulated a comfortable fortune. He had allowed his beard to grow, and he went to *Shul* as he did in Kiev. His wife kept a Kosher house, and he had brought up his boy to play chess and to discuss the Talmud. It had never occurred to him that there was a ghetto in America and in Chicago.

He discovered the ghetto quite accidentally, and the discovery shocked him beyond description. His whole world collapsed one evening when his oldest son, after the Friday evening meal, said to him that now, since he was going to law school and the family was pretty well fixed, and as he had acquired some friends whom he would like to invite to his house, they ought to move out of the ghetto. "The

[1] "An Immigrant Autobiography," manuscript.

ghetto!" said the father, "Are you dreaming? What do other
people have that we haven't got? Don't you like this flat?
Isn't the furniture good enough? Isn't this home swell
enough for you?"

That night the old man could not sleep, and the next
morning in *Shul* he was a little bewildered by the services.
His mind was wandering. A month later they moved to
Central Park Avenue, in Lawndale. The son felt happier,
but the father didn't go down to his store on Roosevelt
Road and Jefferson Street on the street car with quite the
same zest mornings as he used to when they lived upstairs
over the business. Nor did he feel the same way when he
went to the synagogue. His *Landsleute*, he noticed, looked at
him with a rather quizzical air; they didn't shake hands with
the warmth of days gone by, and they weren't quite as
familiar as they used to be.

Two years later, when the son had opened a law office,
the father sold his store and began to dabble in real estate,
using his son's office as his headquarters. He had found
that the synagogue on the near West Side was too far away,
and had joined a congregation on Douglas Boulevard, three
miles farther west. He had trimmed his beard a little, too.
He still played chess with his son, but instead of discussing
the Talmud they discussed the real estate boom on Craw-
ford Avenue. Once in a while he soliloquized, "And I
thought I was rich; why, I have made more money in the
last year or two than I made during the twenty years before. Yes, I lived in the ghetto and didn't know it."

What happened in this family is fairly typical of what
has happened in hundreds—yes, thousands—of Jewish families on the West Side. Their life in the ghetto was so circumscribed, and they were so integrally a part of it, that they

were unaware of its existence. They discovered the ghetto through chance contacts with the world outside; and then they fled. In most instances it is the children who discover the ghetto for their parents. They go to school; they work in the stores and offices in the loop; they make friends; they go to dances, and the girls are seen home by escorts; they are mobile, and the world of the ghetto begins to shrink, then to bore, and finally to disgust. In contrast with the sweep of Michigan Boulevard, the gaudy splendor of the Trianon Ballroom, and the grandeur of the Oriental Theater, the ghetto streets look narrow, dark, and filthy.

Sometimes parents, who feel at home because they have never been outside, resist for a time, but then family conflicts arise that make life intolerable. They eventually yield, and the exodus begins. What ten years ago was a slow westward movement has now developed into a veritable stampede to get out of the ghetto.

There are no accurate statistics available on the number of Jews in any part of the city, since the United States census regards Jews as a religious group and therefore does not enumerate them separately. Since most of the Jews on the West Side are Russian born, and since a fair proportion of them give Yiddish or Hebrew as their mother-tongue, the census reports on these classes may be of significance in indicating the size of the Jewish population in various areas of the city, and of the movement of the population from one district to another. Comparisons for different census periods are made doubly difficult by the fact that Chicago has undergone a change in its ward boundaries.[1] The school census of the city of Chicago for 1914, for wards 10, 11, 19, and 20,

[1] Details for census tracts have been compiled by the Social Research Laboratory of the University of Chicago.

when compared with the United States census for 1920, reveals changes in the proportion of Russian-born persons as shown in Table I. It is not an unfair assumption that the majority of the Russian-born persons in these wards were Jews.

The emigration of the Jews from the West Side is further indicated by the school principals' reports on the relative proportion of Jewish children enrolled in the public schools of the area. The comparisons for the years 1914 and 1923 are given in Table II.[1]

TABLE I

Ward	1914	1920	No. Decreased	Per Cent Decreased
10...........	13,016	7,557	5,459	42
11...........	5,831	3,628	2,203	37.7
19...........	7,309	2,850	4,459	61
20...........	16,775	6,779	9,996	60
Total....	42,931	20,814	22,117	50.2 (Average)

In addition to these, the Jewish Training School, with 650 pupils, 547 of whom were Jewish, located in the heart of the ghetto, has been closed. The flight of the Jewish population from the district has been considerably more noticeable than the general exodus of the population from the near West Side.[2]

The Michael Reese Dispensary and the Jewish Peoples'

[1] Report of "A Study of the Social and Recreational Needs of the Jewish Community of Chicago," manuscript in files of Jewish Peoples' Institute of Chicago, Chicago, 1923.

[2] The decrease in total number of pupils from 1914 to 1923 was 5,493, or 48 per cent, while the decrease in Jewish pupils was 4,975, or 63 per cent. See *ibid.*, p. 29. A sample study made in connection with our present study in 1925 seems to indicate that the decrease in Jewish pupils has continued steadily during the intervening years.

Institute, two of the leading institutions of the Jewish community of Chicago, which were but a decade ago in the midst of the Jewish community, are now drawing an increasing number of their clients from Lawndale and the Northwest Side.[1] The old plant of the Jewish Peoples' Institute is now in the heart of the Italian district. It has a branch on the Northwest Side to accommodate its increasing number of Jewish patrons there, and has just erected a large com-

TABLE II

School	Total Pupils		Jewish Pupils		Per Cent Jewish	
	1914	1923	1914	1923	1914	1923
Washburne.....	1,575	Closed	1,465	Closed	93	Closed
Garfield........	1,525	1,351	1,400	1,079	92	30
Foster..........	2,075	1,360	1,640	775	80	57
Smythe.........	1,225	1,176	1,078	1,052	88	89
Goodrich.......	1,200	1,200	736	23	65	2
Dore...........	1,093	850	329	25	30	3
Medill (grade)...	837	Closed	335	Closed	40	Closed
Polk...........	1,250	Closed	250	Closed	20	Closed

munity center in Lawndale, on the assumption that the center of the Jewish population will be in that area for some time to come.

The mass migration out of the ghetto is not to be explained merely on the basis of the deterioration of the area and its conversion into an industrial zone. Nor is it accurate to say that the Jews are being pressed out by succeeding immigrant groups and Negroes. A study of the motives of migration reveals that the Jews are not merely

[1] From the private files of Mr. Philip L. Seman, general director, Jewish Peoples' Institute. For the Michael Reese Dispensary an investigation made in the course of our study revealed a constantly and rapidly declining number of Jewish patients from the near West Side.

fleeing *from* the ghetto, but that they are also drifting *to* other areas. The physical deterioration of the near West Side as a residential area and the decay of local culture have gone on *pari passu*, of course, and have made the area undesirable as a living quarter for those who have acquired sufficient wealth to afford something better. But as a rule the Jew is not so much running away from the area because it is a slum, nor is he fleeing from the Negroes; but he is fleeing from his fellow-Jews who remain in the ghetto. From the ghetto he drifts to Lawndale, where he hopes to acquire status, or where at least his status as a ghetto Jew will be forgotten.

DEUTSCHLAND

If the near West Side is the home of the first generation immigrant and of the ghetto, then Lawndale is pre-eminently the area of second settlement, of *Deutschland*. One of the important adjustments that any immigrant group has to make, it has been observed, is that of finding a suitable habitat corresponding to the habits and attitudes of the individuals. This adjustment to the areas of a large city tends to take the form of distinct areas of settlement. When he first arrives, the immigrant settles in the slum, which is called the area of first settlement. But if the immigrant himself continues to live in this area for his whole lifetime, his children seldom do. In a fast-growing city a neighborhood has a life of no more than one generation. It changes its local color with the turnover of its inhabitants.

The Jews are seldom permanent inmates of the Western ghetto. The influences from without penetrate subtly and slowly, and lure at least the children into the more spacious world around them. In the last stages of his ghetto life the Jew becomes conscious of the narrowness of his world, and when he has definitely entered into the full realization of his status he migrates to the area of second settlement. In the concentric zones that surround the core of the city or the central business district, this is generally the second ring—the zone of workingmen's homes.[1] The Jews of the ghetto began to migrate toward this region during the first decade of this century. The current in this direction became strong when the wave of Russian immigration following the revolution and pogroms of 1905–6 set in and flooded the ghetto. The settlers who arrived during the eighties and the nineties of the last century were gradually displaced by the newcomers. In Lawndale the Jews again came into contact with the Germans and the Irish, whom they had dislodged from the ghetto a generation before.

Lawndale, when the Jewish settlers arrived, was a quiet residential zone of lower middle-class standards. It had spacious streets, yards, and parks, many wide open spaces, and substantial duplex apartments. The Germans and the Irish who inhabited it had had some experience with the Jews previously on the near West Side. They had given up Halsted Street without much of a struggle; but on Kedzie Avenue and on Douglas Park Boulevard, where they had built new homes, they determined to make a stand. A few Jewish families got a foothold in the area by buying a home here and there, but when the tide from the ghetto set in, it met determined opposition. As they could not rent, they had to buy—and buy they did. They bought Lawndale in blocks, and by 1915 Lawndale was Jewish. Jews have done to Lawndale in Chicago what they have done to the Bronx in New York:

[1] See Ernest W. Burgess: "The Growth of the City," in Robert E. Park, *The City*, chap. ii, Chicago, 1925.

Crowded northward, the Jews discovered the wilds of the Bronx. The doctors advised them to go and live there when they had a "touch of consumption." It was "the country." What they did with these wilds is history. They destroyed beautiful forest estates and built ugly tenement houses, created a new Hester Street where there was a park. But they also created a town where there were only rocks and marshes. Theaters, synagogues, institutions, hospitals, factories, gambling houses, other houses. There is now a generation of Bronx Jews, quite distinct from the East Side Jew. It's the second-generation Jew, with all the outward characteristics minus beard and mustache, playing baseball, great fight fans, commercial travelers, clean-shirted, white-collared, derby-hatted, creased-trousered. The women are stylish and stout, white-skinned, long-nosed, bediamonded; social workers, actresses, stump speakers, jazz dancers, with none of the color and the virtues of their erstwhile bearded, bewigged parents, and a few vices of their own acquisition. But they bathe frequently.[1]

There is a generation of Lawndale Jews. In the ghetto they are called *Deitchuks* because they affect German ways, aren't quite so particular about Kosher food, don't go to the synagogue quite so often, patronize the Loop for their entertainment, and speak Yiddish at home only. That is why the ghetto Jews refer to Lawndale as *Deutschland*. Everything beyond the pale is either the world of *goyim* or the world of *Deitchuks*. There is only a step between the one and the other. The *Deitchuk* is considered as something worse than the *goy*. He is a poor imitation of a Jew, and he is not a *goy* only because the *goyim* won't have him.

The outstanding vocational type of the ghetto is the *Schacherjude*, the push-cart peddler and small-scale merchant. *Deutschland* is inhabited by *Menschen*, or more often, the *Allrightnicks*. Both are persons keenly conscious of their superior status, at least economically; but while the former

[1] Konrad Bercovici, "The Greatest Jewish City in the World," *Nation* (September 12, 1923), p. 261.

has achieved his success without sacrificing much of his identity as a Jew, the latter, in his opportunism, has thrown overboard most of the cultural baggage of his group, and as a consequence is treated with the disdain befitting an apostate or *meshumed*. The *Allrightnick* offends the group because he is no respector of its values. In the ghetto, wealth is inconspicuous; in *Deutschland* it is displayed. The *realestatenick* makes hundreds of dollars for every dollar of the peddler, but the former flaunts his wealth before the world as if it were millions. He is self-satisfied, and in his community he becomes a *Macher*, a man of affairs. The business traditions of the Jews are so ancient that we should indeed be surprised to find that this vocational type lacked status; but the *Allrightnick* represents the type of business man to whom success is everything.

The transformation in the personality types that is wrought by these distinct culture areas is nowhere more apparent than in the contrast between the intellectuals in the ghetto and in *Deutschland*. The ideal of learning which in the ghetto produced the type of student known as the *Yeshiba Bochar*, or talmudical student, and the *Melammed*, or rabbinical teacher, persists, though in a somewhat altered form. In Europe, and to a large extent in the modern ghetto, learning was religious. In the area of second settlement it is likely to be of a secular sort. In the ghetto a poor but learned talmudical student is a desirable candidate for son-in-law of a prosperous merchant, but in *Deutschland* the young doctors, lawyers, and politicians push him into the background. Probably nothing has done more to alter the attitude toward the intellectual, and to change the conception of intelligence itself, than popular secular education; but the main outlines of the old pattern persist. Intellectuals can flourish only in a community that supports them and gives them status. If the community consists only of ignoramuses, if it is narrow and confining, the intellectuals leave it and seek a more congenial and more cosmopolitan habitat.

In the area of second settlement we find a set of distinct social types, the outgrowth of the changed social organization. There is the *Lodgenik*, or joiner; the *Radikalke*, or the emancipated woman; the society lady or the philanthropic woman who goes back to the ghetto "to do something for these poor people," of whom she was recently one; and the *Ototot*, or the almost emancipated person who clings to a little beard.[1]

These types indicate that the culture area represented by Lawndale is an area of transition in which the character of the ghetto is being remolded under the influences of wider contacts and a larger world. Social types range themselves in constellations, each stellar figure with its little circle of satellites seeking its place in the life of the group and changing its position and character as the culture of the area is transformed. Together they constitute a sort of galaxy of personalities in which the culture of the group finds every expression.

An analysis of the outstanding personality types in any given area shows that they depend for their existence on, and are a direct expression of, characteristic attitudes and sentiments in the group. As the life of the group changes, new types appear, but they are on the whole outgrowths and transformations of earlier types. They are at the same time

[1] For the identification of a number of these types I am indebted to Mr. John Landesco.

indexes of assimilation of the members of a social group to another, and represent, therefore, various stages in the assimilative process.

These types may also be conceived of as the effect of mobility upon personal behavior. They express the range of contacts of the individuals with other cultures. The isolated person is merely a person of few and superficial contacts. The ghetto Jew is provincial and has a dwarfed personality because he seldom penetrates beyond the pale. His daily routine is confined largely to the narrow area of his immediate vicinity. Even when he drives his wagon through the other sections of the city, he does so with his eyes closed to the life that goes on, and open only, as the saying goes, "to business."

There is a striking difference between the migrations of the families within and those without the ghetto. Of two hundred families studied, one hundred lived in the ghetto and the other one hundred in Lawndale and on the North-west Side. Of the one hundred ghetto families, forty-five moved in one year (1924). The average distance between their old and their new homes was three blocks. Of the one hundred families on the Northwest Side and in Lawndale, sixty moved in the same year, but the average distance between their old and their new homes was a mile and one-half.[1] Mobility seems to be cumulative, gaining momentum in the case of the Jews as they leave the ghetto and move to the area of second settlement. The movement becomes more frequent and covers a wider range as the confines of the ghetto are left behind. This movement is a measure of the

[1] "A Study of Migration on the West and Northwest Sides of Chicago," manuscript.

restlessness which shows itself on the subjective side in the speed and the degree of the transformation of the attitudes of the group.[1]

Instead of the small, ramshackle synagogues of the ghetto, we find that *Deutschland* has its modern, pretentious structures. In place of the strictly orthodox ritual of the ghetto, *Deutschland* has its "conservative" synagogues, midway between orthodoxy and reform. Instead of the dingy and crowded dwellings of the near West Side, Lawndale and the Northwest Side have their modern apartment buildings with sun parlors, garages, and baths.

As he emerges from the ghetto, the Jew loses his distinctive personal appearance. This change in facial expression and in bearing is most apparent in the young people. The second generation becomes self-assertive, straightens out its spine, and lifts its head. The number of athletes whose parents were ghetto Jews has in recent years been increasing at an amazing rate:

The gloved fists of Benny Leonard and the rest of the Jewish fighting fraternity should forever put an end to the vicious notion that our race is devoid of physical stamina. Was there ever a pluckier, gamer, astuter lightweight in the entire history of the American ring than Leonard? Joe Gans was a wonderful fighting machine, and Battling Nelson was a marvel; Wolgast, Ritchie, Freddie Walsh, and

---

[1] A study is now in progress of the Jewish community of New York, by the Bureau of Jewish Social Research, New York City, which in a preliminary report seems to indicate a similar situation. This study gives the Jewish population of New York City as 1,728,000 (for 1925) or one third of the total population of the city. In one decade (1916–25) Manhattan lost 200,000 Jews. Washington Heights was the only part of the city-proper showing an increase in Jewish population, while Coney Island has become 96.7% Jewish. (*Jewish Communal Survey of Greater New York*. First Section: Studies in the New York Jewish population. New York, 1928.) See also "Jews of New York," *Survey*, 60: 93.

Kid Lavigne were worthy lightweight champions; but the Jew Benjamin Liner, son of a Warsaw immigrant, is the greatest of them all!

And there is nothing at all the matter with our new Jewish Featherweight "Champ," Louis "Kid" Kaplan, late from Bialystok, and now a resident of Meriden, Connecticut.

Abe Goldstein, until recently the bantam champion of the world, lost only on points to Eddie Martin in a 15-round bout at Madison Square Garden. There were plenty of fans in the Garden that evening who felt that Goldstein deserved the decision. Have no fear, he will stage a "come-back."

As soon as Leonard really lays down his crown a worthy successor will be found in Sid Terris, an East Side boy. He is the sensation of the town. Sid was born twenty-one years ago, on Clinton Street. None of Sid's Gentile antagonists has as yet suggested that the little fellow with the Jewish physiognomy is a physical coward.

Old-timers needn't be told about Joe Choynski, who fought the best of the heavyweights twenty-five years ago; Abe Attell, featherweight champion 1911–22; Leach Cross, a great lightweight in his day; Battling Levinsky, Soldier Bartfield, and Charlie White. These men have made fistic history in this country.

When one turns to the younger fellows in the fighting game, there's no dearth of Jewish talent. There's Lew Tendler, still the idol of the Quaker City; Jack Bernstein, Corporal Izzy Schwartz, Charley Rosenberg, and a host of others.

But a lie dies hard. Sometimes I think we shouldn't be annoyed by this sort of loose talk. After all, the people who are certain about the alleged congenital cowardice of the Jewish race are the selfsame upholders of law and order and defenders of the constitution that pass laws to banish Darwin from college textbooks. We can afford to be in the same boat with the author of *Origin of Species*.[1]

The area of second settlement is also pre-eminently an area of conflict—conflict within the family and the community. Families tend to disintegrate under the stress of contradictions between behavior patterns which result from

[1] *Jewish Daily Forward*, February 25, 1925.

the importation of extraneous cultural influences into the
home by the children of the immigrants.[1]

The enlarged world of the area of second settlement results also in a shift of vocational interests, and increased
organization. Labor leaders who have had experience in
organizing Jewish workers complain of the difficulty of holding organizations of recent immigrants together. This task
apparently becomes easier as the children of the immigrants
are reached, and as the immigrant removes to the area of
second settlement.[2]

The social organization of the area of second settlement
cuts across the lines of family and *Landsmannschaft*. Village
synagogues which were founded in the ghetto are federated
into large congregations in which the distinctions between
Old World local ties reach the vanishing-point. Hand in
hand with the wiping out of the ties of local and familial
solidarity goes also a greater amount of disorganization and
uncontrolled behavior.

As the ghetto becomes depleted and its population begins to center in the area of second settlement there appear
also a number of conservative influences. The new area
becomes predominantly Jewish, although it is not the Jewishness of the same intensity as that of the ghetto itself. Its
institutions and personalities have undergone a change, but
not sufficient to lose their identifying Jewish color. The later
migrants from the ghetto are the least assimilated, and they
impart to the new area many of the outward characteristics
of the ghetto itself.

In their attempt to flee from the ghetto, the partially

[1] "Culture Conflicts in the Immigrant Family," manuscript.

[2] See William M. Leiserson, *Adjusting the Immigrant to Industry*, New
York, 1924.

assimilated groups have found that the ghetto has followed them to their new quarters. This is as true of Lawndale as it is of the Northwest Side in the region of Division
Street and Humboldt Park. Within fifteen years these areas
have become overwhelmingly Jewish, and have reproduced
—though in a modified form—the general outlines of the
ghetto atmosphere.

Long before this transition is completed, however, a new
exodus has begun. The plans of those who fled from the
ghetto in order to obtain status as human beings—as persons rather than as Jews—have been frustrated by the similar plans of others. Unwittingly the deserters from the
ghetto have become the founders of a new ghetto. Scarcely
does this consciousness begin to dawn upon them when the
flight is resumed, this time to a new frontier lying several
miles from the area of second settlement. The area of third
settlement, in Chicago as elsewhere, is located in the outlying residential sections of the city—in Rogers Park, Ravenswood, Albany Park, the North Shore, and the South Shore,
and finally the suburban regions.

One of the outstanding characteristics of the local areas
in which the Jewish population of the city is to be found is
their separateness and discontinuity from one another. The
ghetto has changed very little in its main geographical outlines since it was first settled by the Jews. Its invisible walls
have been pushed out and dented in here and there. The
frontier of the Jewish settlements, however, is never to be
found in an area along the borders of, and contiguous to, the
ghetto, but rather in isolated settlements some distance
removed from the ghetto proper and from each other. The
movement of the Jews has been in jumps and spurts, not in
continuous lines. This is one of the most striking indications

of the fundamental motive of local migrations: flight from the familiar, escape into anonymity. The Jew stays in a given area apparently just long enough to become conscious of his status as a Jew. Scarcely does he get a glimpse of the freer world that looms in the distance when he becomes irritated by the presence of his fellow-Jews, more Jewish than himself, and restless because his major wishes are left unsatisfied.

The zones of settlement of the Jews correspond roughly to the various generations of immigrants. Those who came earliest are now farthest removed from the original ghetto. They are also farthest along in the process of assimilation and in the departure from Old World customs and orthodox ritual. In the frontier regions the Jew plunges into the political and social life of the community with such zest and enthusiasm that he soon makes himself conspicuous as a Jew by his very attempt not to appear strange, and to be a real member of the community.

In the ghetto the synagogue and the religious life of the community is predominantly orthodox; in the area of second settlement it becomes "conservative"; and on the frontier it is "reformed." But the change is accomplished neither suddenly nor completely. The ghetto is never quite outlived, especially in the case of the older generation, who, in their own lifetimes, cannot quite accustom themselves to the new ways of life. And then there is the problem of the children. The parents may not have completely forgotten that they were Jews, and may have made their compromises; but the children seem generally to carry the de-Judaization a step farther than their parents—who in their day considered themselves quite rebellious—are willing to tolerate. The sentiments that have held the group together in the past still assert themselves when the continuity of the group is threatened.

Rabbi Saul Silber sounded the keynote of pessimism at the banquet which was held by the Anshe Sholom Congregation in celebration of its fifty-fifth anniversary: "What will become of our children?" said he, among other things. "Do we want them to grow up pinochle players and poker sharks, or do we want them to grow up men and women who have an understanding of the problems of life, who know the history of their ancestors, who are proud Jews, and who will be a credit to us? Our children are running away from us because we have nothing to hold them with, to make them worthy of their Jewish heritage. Orthodox Judaism is on the decline and will soon disappear entirely unless we do our duty toward maintaining its traditions. We have fine boys and girls who grow up in fine Jewish homes ignorant of the simplest rudiments of Judaism because we do not give them the opportunity to learn, to know. Let us build houses of worship, social centers and Hebrew schools, and let us provide the means for the coming generation to learn and to know; there can not be a better or more profitable investment."

Well spoken, Rabbi Silber. It is unfortunate that the Jewish population has the moving spirit and neighborhoods change practically overnight. First it was Douglas and Independence Boulevards, then the North Shore district, then Rogers Park; now it is Wilmette, Winnetka, Glencoe, etc. These newly rich want to be "swell," and to be "swell" is to run away from Jews and Judaism—that's the modern curse.[1]

The latest avenue of escape from the ghetto is represented by the rapid influx of Jews into the apartment and residential hotels of the city, particularly of Hyde Park and the North Shore. So popular have these hotels become with the Jewish population that a "Jewish Hotel Row," as it is called by real estate men of the district, is rapidly springing up. Many of these hotels, while not advertising Kosher food, are nevertheless catering to the traditional tastes of the

[1] *Chicago Chronicle*, January 16, 1925.

Jews. The middle-class business men among the Jews moved into these hotels originally, not merely because their wives wanted to be free from household duties, nor merely because they had reached a station in life where they could afford the luxuries of hotel life, but rather because they wished to be taken for successful business or professional men—not merely successful Jews.

The hotels offered anonymity; they offered freedom from ritual and the close supervision of the intimate community. Here one could be one's self, and, if one spent a little occasionally on parties, dinners, and entertainment, and if one "Americanized" one's name and put up a good front by playing golf and being a good sport, one could get to know the best people, and break into gentile society. There was no bar to keep the Jews out at first. A few Jewish residents had lived there for years, and were apparently inoffensive, if not desirable, guests. But when the flood set in, the hotels began to lose their permanent gentile guests. In one hotel the manager joined the Ku Klux Klan. As soon as this fact became known, some Jews moved out, but finally a Jewish corporation bought the hotel and changed the management.[1] Not only did most of the Gentiles leave these hotels when the Jewish invasion set in, shortly after the war, but the older settlers among the Jews as well moved to new quarters.

There is a striking difference between the social stratification of the Jewish community in Chicago and that of New York. In New York City, where the earliest Jewish settlers, who are known in the community as the Jewish Mayflower stock, consisted of Spanish-Portuguese Jews, that group has always considered itself the élite and had led

[1] "Jewish Hotel Row," manuscript.

a separatist existence. The German Jews came almost two centuries later, and occupied a sort of intermediate position between the aristocratic Sephardim and the Russian-Polish group, which came toward the end of the nineteenth century. The economic position of these various groups has followed the same rank, although the Germans have to a large extent outstripped their predecessors in wealth.

In Chicago, on the other hand, the first Jewish settlers were Germans. The Spanish-Portuguese element has come only very recently, and from Turkey and Palestine rather than from Spain. The Spanish Jews in Chicago are, moreover, not of the same cultural and economic stratum as the early American Jewish settlers. They, too, have lived a secluded existence, but largely because of language differences and prejudices on the part of the German and Russian Jews. In Chicago the German Jews have been the undisputed aristocrats, at least until the World War and the Russian revolution. These two events have somewhat shaken the sway of the Germans and given a feeling of self-confidence and personal expansion to the Russian Jews.

Hyde Park was until recently a stronghold of the German Jews, but the business successes and growth in numbers of the Russian-Jewish population in recent years has rapidly altered the complexion of the area. The membership lists of some of the Reform congregations which a few years ago were composed solidly of German Jews indicate that the Russian Jews are in larger numbers giving up orthodoxy as they change their residence.[1] Even the aristocratic German-Jewish clubs are beginning to open their doors to the more successful and "desirable" members of the Russian group.

The outposts of the Jewish community at the present

[1] "A Study of Membership in Jewish Congregations," manuscript.

time are to be sought in the fashionable suburbs of the North Shore: Kenilworth, Winnetka, Glencoe, and Highland Park. The settlement in one of these suburbs of one of the leading German Jews of the city has immensely stimulated the purchase of suburban estates by a host of Jews who have found Hyde Park undesirable because of their Russian-Jewish neighbors, or who have accumulated fortunes within a relatively short time and now wish to add status to their wealth. The realization that wealth alone does not bring a superior social position has come as a sudden and sad realization to many.

It is almost impossible to gather evidence on the extent to which conversion to Christianity and intermarriage with Christians is going on under the changed circumstances brought about by the disintegration of the ghetto. Official records do not give the necessary information, and in the nature of the case such matters are not given publicity by the parties concerned. Such inquiries as have been made indicate that there is probably little conversion to the established Christian denominations. Intermarriage is on the increase, of course, and the precedents of the early Chicago Jews, in accordance with which persons outside of their faith had to be converted to Judaism upon marrying into the group, are no longer insisted upon. There is, moreover, a strong drift on the part of the Jews in this city and others to the Christian Science churches, to Unitarianism, to Ethical Culture, and Rationalism, and a host of other sects. The middle-class Jew leans in the direction of Christian Science, which, as a famous local rabbi put it, "serves the functions of church and drug store combined, and is a good business proposition." These sects are more attractive to the Jew because the process of transition is not so shocking as conversion from Judaism to Catholicism or Protestantism. To many, Unitarianism and Ethical Culture is but a step removed from Reform Judaism. Since Christian Science has proved itself so popular among the Jews, a rival movement known as "Jewish Science" capitalizing some of the features of Christian Science but without the stigma of "Christian" in its name, has been organized and seems to be gaining adherents in New York and Los Angeles.

As long as he remains in the ghetto the Jew seldom becomes conscious of his inferior status. He emerges from the ghetto and finds himself surrounded by a freer but a less comfortable and less homely and familiar world. He flees from his people in order to escape from the bonds by which, whether he wills it or not, he is tied to his group. In the process he changes his character. But the identical desires on the part of many of his co-religionists lead them to adopt the same course that he has taken, and in the end he must either keep on moving or else find the very objective toward which he is moving disappear on the horizon.

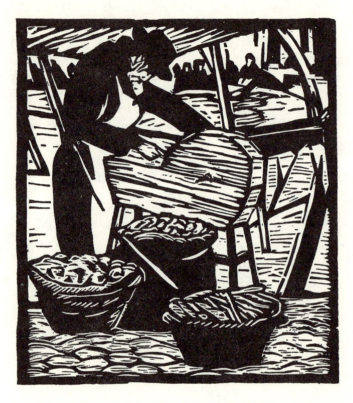

Horseradish Grinder

CHAPTER XIII
THE RETURN TO THE GHETTO
CONFLICT AND SELF-CONSCIOUSNESS

The path that leads out of the ghetto is neither straight nor unobstructed. No sooner does the Jew venture forth from the narrow ghetto streets into the broad cosmopolitan life of the outer world than he encounters external obstacles and experiences inner conflicts. The transition from one culture to another, and from one personality to another, is a process that requires not only time but demands the co-operation of both groups.

The emancipation of the Jews has not taken place without internal struggle and external conflict. Jewry itself has been swept repeatedly by cross-currents of sentiment. When the forward, outward movement of the race has been too rapid, it has invariably provoked a racial reaction in the outer gentile world, and Jewish life has been thrown back upon itself. What, then, happens is that the Jewish community contracts and withdraws into itself. Shadows of the old ghetto walls arise. Jewry returns to the sources of its inspiration and its strength, and becomes conscious of itself as a people set apart, a chosen people, a people with a destiny and a mission.[1]

The following case is typical of the varied turns in the life history of the thousands of Jews of our modern world whose life begins in the ghetto, and, after moving in a circle, finally ends somewhere not far from its starting-point:

During my long residence in New York I have observed the following changes in one man: He arrived a bearded talmudical scholar in 1810. Rabbi Glockman was then less than thirty years old. He had a wife and four children, two sons and two daughters. The oldest was

[1] Robert E. Park, "Behind Our Masks," *Survey Graphic* (May, 1926), p. 136.

twelve years old, which meant that the father had married at eighteen. A year later Rabbi Glockman was still teaching Hebrew in a little afterschool *Cheder* where the Jewish children were sent by their parents so as not to forget that they were Jews. The school was on Division Street, way down on the East Side. Two years later, with beard a little trimmed, Mr. Glockman owned a Kosher delicatessen store on Second Avenue near Tenth Street. The place closed on Friday evening and remained closed till Saturday after prayers. Mr. Glockman was the president of a congregation. Four years later Mr. Glockman was the partner in a shirt-waist factory where they worked on the Sabbath. The beard was completely gone. They lived in the Bronx. Six years later Mr. Glockman smoked on the Sabbath, ate "unclean" food, and was denounced in a strike as the worst exploiter. He employed only Italian labor, and had changed his name to Bell, George Bell, and had moved from the Bronx to Morristown, because there were no Jews there. Eight years later his daughter had married a Gentile. But then the railroad strike broke out. The great Morristown plan, by which the wealthiest commuters manned the trains, entered into vogue. Mr. Bell came to the station every morning with his overalls under his arms, ready to take his place as a scab—to help the country. But Mr. T. and Mr. D. and Mr. F., who were at the head, would not have the Jew with them in the cab. He had to ride as a passenger. They would not even give him the privilege of acting as conductor. Today Mr. Bell is again Solomon Glockman. He lives in Harlem, in the heart of the Jewish district, is a member of the congregation, and a fanatical Zionist. Even the beard was allowed to grow back, a little trimmed, to its full length. Until the daughter divorced her husband and married a Jew she was not allowed to enter her parents' home.[1]

The rebuffs administered by prejudice and exclusion serve to make the Jew keenly conscious of his separateness. He finds that the outer world will not receive him as an individual, but insists upon attaching the obnoxious label "Jew" to him and to his children, not taking cognizance of the fact that he

[1] Konrad Bercovici, "The Greatest Jewish City in the World," *Nation* (September 12, 1923), p. 259.

feels himself no more a part of his people than they consider him a part of themselves. He stands on the map of two
worlds, not at home in either. His self is divided between
the world that he has deserted and the world that will have
none of him.

Among those Jews who, because they have lived among us all longer, have departed farthest from the ancient heritage and penetrated
deepest into the life of the outer gentile world, these recurring outbursts
of racial prejudice and the resulting revulsions of Jewish life inevitably
provoke profound moral disturbances. It is not easy—in the long run
it is impossible—for those who have once gone out ever to return,
even though the ghetto walls are no longer visible. The result is,
however, that they are obsessed with a sense of moral isolation; they
feel themselves not quite at home either in the gentile or the Jewish
world. Life goes on outwardly as it did before, but they are possessed
by insatiable restlessness, and a "secret anguish" gnaws at the core
of their existence.[1]

Having been successful in business or in his profession,
the Jew who was cradled in the ghetto and has tasted some of
the fruits of the gentile world in free association with his
more intimate circle of associates, with fellow-students in
the university, or with the members of his professional
group, at first seems to find the stories of prejudice and exclusion either exaggerated or at least not applicable to himself. His personality expands, and he relaxes somewhat in
his studied manners and courtesies, just to be natural and
act the part of one who is at home and feels at home. All the
time, however, he is conscious of a bit of formality, sometimes overcordiality, which puts him on his guard. Stories
of the prejudice and rebuffs that others of his faith have
suffered reach him. Secretly he hopes that he will be able to
put an end to all these unfounded rumors and will be able to

---

[1] Robert E. Park, *op. cit.*, p. 136.

return to his people to tell them that prejudice against the Jew is either a fiction or a justified reaction on the part of the Gentiles to the coarseness, the aggressiveness, and lack of tact of the Jews themselves. And sometimes he succeeds. But more often his hopes are shattered before he has even entered halfway into the outer world.

I graduated with the highest honors from the medical school. Of course in my college career I felt somewhat out of the run of things because there were certain fraternities that some friends of mine belonged to that never asked a Jew to join. But I took that gracefully. I said to myself, "They have a long tradition against admitting Jews, but as individuals they are quite friendly to me, and I'm sure they would ask me to join if it weren't for the rules, for which they are not to blame."

Of course I never hid the fact that I was a Jew, although I may say that my appearance would never betray my race. I said to myself, as I looked at all of the ghetto boys in school: "I don't blame them for being prejudiced. Look at them, with their outlandish ways, their mannerisms, their unmitigated nerve and forwardness. Who wouldn't be ashamed to be a Jew? Under circumstances like that, who blames the fraternities for not taking them in? They can't be just an ordinary member of anything. They've got to run the thing or ruin it."

Secretly I sympathized with the feeling against the Jews, and I decided that as for myself, while I would never renounce my people, I would try to make myself worthy of the friendship of Gentiles. I sometimes argued with these Russian Jews (I was German myself, American-born), and told them that if they didn't make themselves so conspicuous and obnoxious the rest of the Jews would stand a chance. But they told me that I would find out soon enough that there were no exceptions, that to the Gentiles a Jew was a Jew whether he had blond hair or dark hair, and that they could smell them a mile away.

I got into my profession and worked in an office where there was one prominent Jewish specialist who was respected by all of his colleagues. There was a model Jew—quiet, dignified, inconspicuous. I would emulate him. Once a gentile friend in the profession asked me whether I didn't want to join a club he belonged to. I didn't know much about it, but I liked him and wanted to be a good sport. I said I would join. A couple of weeks later he met me rather shamefacedly and said, "You know I'm sorry, old pal, they found out you were a Jew and there is a rule against admitting Jews. It's a disgusting arrangement. I've decided to resign my membership." I calmed him and told him not to go to the trouble, that if I had known it would cause him any trouble I would have told him so to begin with, but I didn't know that they excluded Jews. It didn't interfere with my friendship with him, but it caused me a lot of mental anguish.

I brooded over the thing, and concluded that you simply couldn't escape it. There are only two ways out: One is to stand up and fight back like a man, and I didn't have the courage to do that single-handed, and didn't like to join the kind of bunch that is doing the fighting, because I think they make the thing worse than it is. The other is to go right on brooding over your lot, and join the B'nai Brith and become a Zionist and join the Jewish clubs and the temple, and let the world take its course. I say I didn't have the courage for the first, and had no inclination for the latter, so here I am—nobody, a dual personality—a man with two souls, a man without a country.[1]

The difficulty is that the Jew, as long as he remains in the ghetto, is of a separate caste, living in a world that is narrow, but warm with the glow of familiar life, full of sentiment, and with opportunity for self-expression within the limits of the group. But when he emerges from the ghetto he becomes human, which means he has contacts with the outer world, encounters friction and hostility, as well as familiarity and friendship. But sensitive as he generally is even to the slightest gestures of those of whom he is not yet a part, he has difficulty in acting without restraint and with poise. He shrinks from conflict, and is likely to attribute his failures and rebuffs exclusively to the fact that he is a Jew. Like Lewisohn,[2] he tends to return to the flock and become an

[1] "The Autobiography of a Jewish College Man," manuscript.

[2] See Ludwig Lewisohn, *Up Stream*, which is the story of a sensitive, intellectual German-Jewish immigrant who finds himself repelled by the

ardent "Jew" and sometimes even a rabid advocate of orthodoxy and Zionism as the only fitting answer to a world
that excludes him and insults him.

The social distance between Jew and Gentile manifests
itself, not only in exclusion of the Jew from the social life
of the Christians, exclusion from clubs and fraternities, but
also exclusion from vocational pursuits, such as trade
unions, and exclusion from certain residential areas. Not
infrequently one finds ads in the newspapers with the post-
script, "Only Gentiles need apply." For a time the carpen-
ters and cigar-makers' unions of Chicago would not admit
Jews; and when a strike came, rather than risk the danger of
Jewish strikebreakers, the unions organized the Jews into
separate locals.   The Hebrew Trade Union Council of
Chicago was until recently a going concern. The Jew has
been in a class with women and with Negroes. In recent
years this exclusion has of course been overcome, especially
since the president of the American Federation of Labor was
himself a Jew. A recent newspaper advertisement reads:
"A summer paradise. Gentiles! Buy your summer home-
sites now on the north shore of Crystal Lake."[1] The result is
the following:

An encouraging sign of the social life of the Jewish Community in
the middle-western states is the enterprise of the Roosevelt Hills
Syndicate. Mr. A. S. De Kofsky, president of the syndicate, is well
known as a builder of a number of modern apartment buildings in the
West Side, and as an enterprising real estate dealer. He saw the need
of organizing a summer resort colony on an extensive basis, and se-
cured a stretch of fine land between South Haven and Benton Harbor,

---

narrow ghetto, and seeks free expression in the world of letters. Handicapped
there, he returns to the fold. See his *Israel*, and his "The Island Within,"
for the successive stages of the evolution of a pattern of life.

[1] *Chicago Daily News*, May 18, 1925.

Michigan, with an extensive lake frontage. The Roosevelt Hills Syndicate, located in the Roosevelt Building, 179 West Washington Street, has subdivided this land, and offered sites for summer homes to the Jewish public. . . . .[1]

Where it is merely a question of buying one's way, the Jews have no difficulty; but the effort to break down prejudice in this fashion soon is found to defeat itself, for instead of establishing contact with the Gentiles, the Jews find that they are merely re-establishing contact with fellow-Jews from whom they were fleeing in the first instance.

Many years ago Nathan Straus went to a Lakewood hotel to pass a few weeks at that rather exclusive winter resort. The manager told him, "No Jews here." So he built a hotel next to it for Jews only. The result was that in a few years hundreds of little and big "Kosher" hotels swamped the place. What happened to the "No Jew" place is history. The natives have not yet regretted the change. Last Christmas there was a Jewish flag on top of the community's Christmas tree on Main Street.[2]

THE HOME-COMING

It takes an extreme courage to "face the music" of racial hostility as an individual. More often the tendency is to return to one's own people, to the small but human and sympathetic group of the family and the *Landsmannschaft*, where one is appreciated and understood. The applause is not so loud, but it is more genuine. That is why a number of large and sumptuously furnished synagogues on Douglas Boulevard are considered merely as branches of the dilapidated shacks in the ghetto. The older folks find these new buildings with their strange ceremonies cold and uninviting, and on Sabbath and the holidays they return to pray in the familiar, though humble, structures where they find their cousins and *Landsleute*.

[1] *Chicago Chronicle*, January 16, 1925.   [2] Bercovici, *loc. cit.*

Life in the fashionable hotels is boredom to most of their inhabitants who have come from the ghetto or even from *Deutschland*. The patent leather slippers fit a little too tightly and the tuxedo suit is a little too snug; and most of all, there is nothing to do.

Wonder how many of the North Shore Ma Jongg Brigade and Bridge Regiment are members of a literary group or study circle? How many of these overfed, bejeweled, loud-voiced mink-coated women belong to the Council of Jewish Women, or the Hadassah? What interest in life have these *noveau riche* besides cards and parties and *rechilos?*[1]

What has held the Jewish community together in spite of all these disintegrating forces is, not only the return of disappointed Jews who have sought to get out, and, failing, have returned to become apostles of nationalism and racial consciousness, but also the fact that the Jewish community is treated as a community by the world at large. The treatment which the Jews receive at the hands of the press and the general public imposes collective responsibility from without. The New York Jewish Community (Kehillah) owes its formal organization, at least, to such an external stimulus:

Beginning with the mass immigration of Eastern European Jews, one generation ago, the problem of organizing the Jewish community in New York City became more acute from year to year. But the formative forces making for such an organization were continually gaining strength, and it required some external impetus to bring these forces into play and to precipitate the formation of a Kehillah, or Jewish Community, in this city. This external impetus was supplied by the Bingham incident, in the fall of the year 1908. General Bingham, who was then Police Commissioner of New York, made a statement that the Jews contributed 50 per cent of the criminals of New York City. This statement was afterwards retracted as the result of many

[1] *Chicago Chronicle*, February 6, 1925.

meetings held by Jewish organizations, which protested vehemently against this unfounded accusation. While probably undue importance was attached to this incident at the time, it is certain that it sufficed to arouse the community consciousness to a degree where the organization of the Kehillah became feasible.[1]

In Chicago the Jewish community is only in an embryonic stage of formal organization. There is a Kehillah, but it includes only the orthodox synagogues. But on the other hand, the centralization of fund raising and communal institutions has brought about a degree of unity in recent years which eclipses the solidarity of the Jewish community in any other large city of the country. Until recently the German Jews, i.e., the reform element, and the Russian Jews, or orthodox element, each had its separate set of communal institutions. Consolidation for any length of time of the more important communal enterprises invariably was frustrated by the internal dissensions of the factions. Again under the impetus of external pressure the group was welded into a solid mass.

Nothing probably has done more in this direction than the revival of anti-Semitism. The attacks of Henry Ford and the organization of the modern Ku Klux Klan have mobilized the Jewish community into numerous organs for combat. The immigration legislation has called into existence national and local organizations for political action. And the cataclysmic changes in the economic condition of Eastern-European Jewry has produced international Jewish relief organizations which collect millions of dollars annually. Finally, the revival of anti-Semitism on a world-wide scale, with the heightened social consciousness of the Jews, has

[1] Harry Sackler, "The Kehillah of New York: A Brief History," *Jewish Communal Register of New York City*, New York, 1918.

turned the utopian Zionism of the nineteenth century into an active nationalistic movement with practical objectives and organized political action. The alarming rate of intermarriage has turned the Jewish community inward and caused it to scan its social structure with a more critical eye. The unbounded faith in nostrums so characteristic of the Jew is shown by the promptness with which he turned to a reconstruction of what he considered the weak spots in this structure. The slogan has been, "For God's sake let us do something!" A recent editorial reads:

The Jewish community of Berlin, Germany, has recently published some interesting statistics. In the year 1922 there were registered in that great city 1,422 Jewish marriages, out of which 781 (more than half) represented intermarriages. Leaders of Berlin Jewry are naturally agitated over these figures, and they are now looking for ways and means whereby the tide of intermarriage in that city could be stemmed.

The causes of this startling phenomenon are not hard to find. German Jewry has for the past half-century busied itself with combating anti-Semitism. In recent years we have been hearing a great deal about a variety of cultural Jewish work of a very high order which has been done in Germany in general, and in Berlin in particular. All this, however, has been carried on primarily by the goodly number of East European Jews who in the last few years moved to Germany, and by the German Zionists. These two elements, however, constitute only a minority. The majority of native-born German Jews who are at all interested in Jewish questions have been concerned about anti-Semitism more than anything else. Of course, since the tide of anti-Semitism is strong in Germany, the Jews of that country naturally had to fight it. But then German Jewry committed a serious error by devoting its best energies toward this negative activity. German Jewry should have realized that propaganda against anti-Semitism does not give its youth anything constructive, and it cannot therefore keep them within the Jewish fold. What the Jewish youth needs is knowledge and inspiration, and this German Jewry has failed to give them. There are, of course, a number of other reasons for the increase of intermarriage among German Jewry, but we maintain that the strongest reason is to be found in the absence of a vigorous religious life among our people of that country. When Jewish young men or women marry out of their race, it simply shows that there is nothing in Judaism which they love or care for.

Let American Jewry study these facts and learn a much-needed lesson. The Jews of this country are seriously divided on religious questions. All of us, however, are agreed in our opposition to inter-marriage. At present it is no secret to anybody that the number of intermarriages in this country is quite large, and that it is constantly on the increase. This number will undoubtedly grow and multiply if we don't wake up to the seriousness of the situation. The leaders of our communities believe that our greatest problem is charity and re-lief; but while we do not wish to minimize the importance of these activities, we know that the spirit of charity alone is not going to keep our youth interested in Judaism. The panacea for Jewish ailments is Torah v'avodah, study, and practice. If the Chicago Jewish com-munity is not to repeat the unpleasant experience of Berlin, we must impart to our youth Jewish knowledge, and we must train them in the ways of Jewish life.[1]

Appeals similar to the foregoing have frequently been made in the local community. The result has been a revival of interest in "Jewish education," the building of additional Hebrew schools of a modern type, conducted along the lines of the latest pedagogical principles. The support for these schools has come not only nor even mainly from the ortho-dox Jews. Even the Reform Jewish section has taken an interest in the revival of religious learning; if not for their own children, then at least for the children of the ghetto.

Apparently there is no limit to the extent to which pres-sure from the outside is able to solidify a group. The height-ened group-consciousness of post-war days is seen even in the consolidation of the irreconcilables in the community:

[1] *Sentinel*, January 16, 1925.

Merging our forces: Last week we ventured to express the prediction that the future type of American Judaism will consist of a compromise between reform and conservatism. We were therefore happy to observe that our views are being corroborated by careful students of the trend of American Jewish life. The *Jewish Morning Journal*, which is a large and influential Yiddish daily of New York City, in discussing the resolution passed by the convention of the Union of American Hebrew Congregations to call a conference of all the Jewish religious bodies of the United States for the purpose of advancing Judaism, made the following comment:

"The boundary lines between reform and conservative Jews are not being effaced by resolutions, but by the forces of life. But the resolutions are symptomatic of the changing conditions. The tendency is undoubtedly toward the right, the majority of Jews leaning towards orthodoxy, even if they are not very pious themselves. And yet it is becoming more and more difficult to distinguish between Polish and Lithuanian Jews who graduate from the Hebrew Union College (a reformed seminary) and their *landsleit* who are educated at the New York Jewish Theological Seminary. A federation of the United Synagogue, which represents orthodoxy, and the Union of American Hebrew Congregations, which represents reform Judiasm, is inevitable and will come about sooner or later."

We simply wish to add that the *Jewish Morning Journal* has always been a conservative newspaper, championing orthodoxy, and vehemently opposing reform. That the above words should emanate from so unexpected a source is truly a sign of the times.[1]

Between 1914 and 1924 the American Jews raised the stupendous sum of sixty-three million dollars for the relief of the Jewish war-sufferers. This sum came from 900,000 contributors. Among the most active of the "drivers" were Jews who had hitherto taken little interest in the Jewish community. But

. . . . The touch of common danger made all kin. In the pools of war-blood all Jewish hyphens have been washed away. Jews today

[1] *Ibid.*, February 6, 1925.

are closer together than ever before. Louis Marshall and Judge
Horace Stern are espousing a Jewish agency for Palestine (formerly
they were anti-Zionists). Samuel Untermeyer is pleading the cause of
Zionism. These examples could be repeated a thousandfold.

We are no longer orthodox and reform, conservative and radical—
all are becoming united, bound together by that ancient formula,
"I am a Jew!" And for this we owe our brethren across the sea an
eternal obligation which outweighs our help to them, as fidelity to
faith casts the scales of Israel against even the gold of unselfish charity.[1]

In these campaigns the Chicago community stood second
only to New York in the size of its contributions. The extent
to which the local Jewish community has grown and has
become capable of collective action is decisively demon-
strated by its local fund-raising campaigns for communal
activities. In 1923 the sum of $2,500,000 was raised through
official channels in Chicago. In 1925 a "drive" for $4,000,000
was started under the slogan "Are You a Jew?" which was
oversubscribed. The chairman of this campaign expressed
himself as follows:

The United Drive for $4,000,000, of which I have been made
chairman, has taken as its slogan this query, "Are You a Jew?"
Many of you, understanding the question in its true significance,
answered it in the spirit of those who asked. . . . . Of those who could
not so accept it, there are three classes. First, there is the Jew who is
wise—wise not in the ways of sacrifice nor in the ways of service, but
wise in the ways of the world. His are the little wisdoms of the time-
server and the menial. He hungers after the aristocracies of wealth
and social place. But despite every guile and every circumvention to
which that hunger goads him, the doors of all snobbery are forever
slammed in his face. He shall not enter them though he deny his father
and cast off his mother. Yet for him there is a hope of salvation. Let
him remember that, though he has striven in vain for the prizes to be
won in Vanity Fair, he may still make for himself a place in the only

[1] Henry H. Rosenfelt, *This Thing of Giving* (New York, 1924), p. 325.

aristocracy Jews can ever know. I mean the Aristocracy of Souls. There he will be rated by his impulses, not by his vocation. There he will be judged by what he gives, not by what he has. There he will be ranked as noble or ignoble by the nobility of his own soul, not by the blood that flows in his veins.

And second, there is the Jew who is frightened and ashamed. Ashamed of what? And why afraid? Is he not in America, in our Blessed Land of Promise, where he is assured equality and the end of all oppression? Then why does he speak of his Judaism in whispers, and cower if he thinks himself overheard? Because, though his body is safe, his soul is still dark with the shadow of the pogrom. Because though his speech and his manners are American, his heart is still heavy with the dread of persecution. Because some inner sense of shame has made him shameful. Because some inner servility bids him accept exile as his due, and the ghetto as his rightful dwelling place.

Through pretense and through denial he seeks escape. But from what? From the shame in his own heart, there is no escape. From his obligation as a Jew, to Jews, there is no escape. There is no escape from his ancestry, there is no refuge from himself. His kinship with his people is deeper than he knows, deeper far than he dares acknowledge. He is shackled forever to the past from which he comes. Let him then learn that his personal freedom is forever bound up with the freedom of all Jewry. Let him learn that, as the shame and the fear of the Jew in Russia have become his fear and his shame, so is the opportunity of the Jew in Russia his opportunity. Let him be imbued with the simple courage of the Jew who can accept, without fear and without shame, the fact of his Jewishness, as without fear and without shame that same Jew accepts the fact of his Americanism.

And third, there remain those who, falling into neither of these categories, were nevertheless troubled by the publication of the slogan. These are my personal friends—generous men, men of warm hearts and wide experience, in the best sense of good Jews, who have come to me with the frank disagreement which is the privilege of intimates. . . . . Their love for me is as staunch as their loyalty to our cause, but they regret what they describe as my want of dignity. . . . . What they call want of dignity, I call reverence. What they think unseemly, to me is sacred. I wish, no more than they, to cry our ancestry in the market place, nor to flaunt our faith where it is irrelevant. But in this drive, what we *are* matters—it cannot be forgotten or hushed over. This is a drive for Jews to carry the burden of Jews. It matters terribly that we should know—that we should ask, one of the other, "Are you a Jew?"[1]

As the chairman of this drive put it, "there is no escape," for the whole community combined to make escape impossible.

Here is the essence of the recent membership campaign of the Jewish Charities of Chicago, a campaign so far-reaching in its inception, so thorough in its execution, so amazing in its results, that it challenges every non-Jewish citizen of Chicago to stop, look, and listen; and while listening, respectfully to remove his hat. At the beginning of 1924, this central organization of twenty-six affiliated Jewish Charities, with regular subscriptions amounting to somewhat over $1,090,000, faced a deficit of $200,000.00 for the fiscal year.

On November 11 of that year, at the close of a four weeks' membership campaign, 9,000 new names had been added to the list of regular subscribers, making a total membership of 21,000; and the extraordinary momentum of the drive is still bringing in new subscriptions, daily, in substantial numbers.

Meeting of the deficit was the smallest part of this achievement. Deficits have been met before. This one could easily have been wiped out by laying the figures before a few loyal and generous subscribers. The heart of the business is in those 9,000 new memberships, averaging $18 each; in the astonishing fact that practically every Jew in Chicago capable of contributing ten dollars or more to charity was given the opportunity—perhaps several opportunities—to subscribe.

"You are not begging. You are offering a privilege," reads the team-workers' manual; and from the beginning to the end of the solicitation this tone was consistently held.

The inner workings of such an undertaking have a vital significance. It will interest you to know that for five years before this census taking an unofficial clipping bureau had blue-penciled and noted the Jewish names mentioned by Chicago newspapers in connection with

---

[1] Jacob M. Loeb, *Are You a Jew?* Address delivered at Sinai Temple, November 1, 1925, published in pamphlet form.

real estate transfers, weddings, parties, robberies of valuable jewels or fur—even in the "Lost and Found" columns. Such prospects were carefully cleared against the subscribers' list of the Jewish Charities, and divided among the volunteer solicitors who took the census.[1]

Then followed personal calls, often in committees; and when these failed to bring the desired subscription the culprit was called upon by some important member of the community whose personal solicitation was considered sufficient pressure. There were rallies and dinners at which opportunity was given for those who had already contributed to win added recognition by increasing their subscription in the presence of the most distinguished members of the community. If the ability to act corporately be the test of a community, then the Jews of Chicago are well on the way to becoming a community.

There are at the present time approximately 300,000 Jews in the city.[2] Of these, 159,518 gave Yiddish or Hebrew

[1] "Taking the Census," *Social Service*, January, 1925.

[2] The exact number of Jews in Chicago has never been determined. In 1902 the Jewish population was estimated by the *Jewish Encyclopedia* as 80,000. A study made by the *Chicago Tribune*, based upon the 1910 census, indicated a population of 134,834. The next figures are those taken from the school census of 1914, which showed 166,134 foreign-born Russians and native-born of Russian fathers. At least 90 per cent of these, or approximately 150,000, may be reasonably estimated to be Jewish, of Russian birth or parentage. The *Jewish Yearbook* estimated the total Jewish population of Chicago in 1918 to be 225,000, and in 1922 the school records indicated a total Jewish population in the city of 285,000. The distribution of this population is as follows (from "Jewish Social and Recreational Needs of the Jewish Community of Chicago," manuscript):

Lawndale	99,000	Irving Park (Albany Park)	4,500
Northwest	77,000	Englewood	4,000
West Side	73,000	Rogers Park	3,000
South Side	30,000	North Side	6,500

Incomplete tabulations of the 1920 census indicate a larger Jewish population on the South Side and the North Side than here given, but a considerably smaller number on the near West Side.

as their mother-tongue in the United States Census of 1920. This indicates that substantially more than one-half, and probably three-fourths, of the Chicago Jews are Russian or Eastern Jews. The rate of influx of these Jews has probably been somewhat reduced, however, by changed immigration laws.

While the ghetto has been emptying, there have been few new recruits to fill the vacancies. In the past it was the influx of a constant stream of orthodox Jews that was relied upon to hold the community together and to perpetuate the faith. Today, however, this force can no longer be depended upon. The revival of race prejudice against the Jew has served as a substitute. It has immensely stimulated group-consciousness and strengthened solidarity. It has turned a great number of Jews who were in the advanced stages of assimilation back to the tribal fold. It has given impetus to the Jewish nationalistic movement and to orthodoxy.

Prejudice from without has revived the ghetto wall, less visible, perhaps, than before, but not less real. The rise and decline of the ghetto seems to be a cyclical movement. As the Jew emerges from the ghetto and takes on the character of humanity in the outside world, the ghetto declines. But as this freedom is restricted, generally as a result of too massed or hasty an advance, distances between Jews and non-Jews arise; and the retreat to the ghetto sets in. The very existence of the ghetto tends to hold the larger Jewish community together. Jews like Lewisohn and Philipson rightly see in the persistence of the modern ghetto the core of the "Jewish problem":

The modern ghettos, the Jewish quarters in the large cities of the world . . . . are another direct result of the officially instituted ghetto of the Middle Ages. The poverty-stricken huddled together in these districts, because here they find companionship and sympathy, and their social instinct is satisfied. But at least they are not forced to stay there, and as soon as they desire, they can remove thence. If such a thing as a Jewish question in any but the religious signification of the term can be spoken of in this country, it is in reference to these Jewish quarters in New York and other large cities, and their inhabitants. How to break these up and disperse their denizens over the surface of this broad, fair land, and make them self-supporting, self-respecting citizens, is the great problem now pressing for solution. . . . . These voluntary ghettos are a constant menace, for they arouse the worst passions of non-Jewish demagogues, and the Jews are referred to as a class, and discriminated against as a separate body. . . . . These last visible vestiges of ghetto existence must be wiped out. They are fraught with menace. . . . . Away with these ghettos, too. The law cannot order their removal as it did with the officially instituted ghetto. Voluntary effort alone will accomplish it. In the words of the old prayer, "May we see it done quickly in our days."[1]

While the Jews see the modern ghetto as a menace to their status as persons and as citizens, the inhabitants of the ghetto itself are immune to the conflicts that disturb the peace of mind of the rest of Jewry. The "Jewish problem" is a problem of a divided consciousness that is experienced by the partly assimilated Jews on the frontier of the gentile world, not by the inhabitants of the ghetto itself, who cling to the warmth of the familial and tribal hearth.

The modern invisible ghetto wall is no less real than the old, because it is based on the sentiments and prejudices of human beings who are products of distinct cultures, and upon the most fundamental traits of human nature that govern our approach to the familiar and our withdrawal from the strange. The Jews as individuals do not always find the way to assimilation blocked. They make friends as well as enemies. It is not altogether obvious, however, that

[1] David Philipson, *op. cit.*, pp. 217–19.

the contacts between cultural groups inevitably produce harmony as well as friction, and that the one cannot be promoted nor the other prevented by any ready-made administrative devices. Interaction is life, and life is a growth which defies attempts at direction and control by methods, however rational they may be, that do not take account of this dynamic process. In the struggle to obtain status, personality comes into being. The Jew, like every human being, owes his unique character to this struggle.

CHAPTER XIV

THE SOCIOLOGICAL SIGNIFICANCE OF
THE GHETTO

NON-JEWISH GHETTOS

The ghetto is a chapter in the history of the Jews and of Western civilization worth the telling for its own sake. But the ghetto has a much wider significance which makes it of interest to the student of human nature and society. What we find in the ghetto is essentially the same phenomenon that we see in the social life of other minority groups who live side by side with one another, or, as often is the case, live side by side without one another. Whether it be the treatment of the Czechs in the Austrian Empire of the Hapsburgs, or Fiume in the Italian Irredenta, or the British in India, or the whites in the cities of China, or the Chinese in San Francisco, fundamentally the problem is the same, because the human nature aspects of the situations are akin to those of the ghetto.

The relations between the two groups in such instances are usually relations of externality. Problems are settled by rules and laws, not by personal contact and intimate discussion. It is because the contacts between the larger and the smaller, between the dominant and the subordinate groups, are confined to mere externals that they are able to live so close to each other at all. In such cases human groups manage to live side by side, much like plants and animals, in what is known as symbiosis. The economy that arises persists without consciousness being at all involved. But among human beings consciousness and feelings will arise, and two groups can occupy a given area without losing their separate identity because each side is permitted to live its own inner life, and each somehow fears the other or idealizes the other. This relationship has been properly described as accommodation, to distinguish it from the assimilation that takes place when two people succeed in getting under each other's skins, so to speak, and come to share each other's inner life and thus become one.

The Jews drift into the ghetto, as has already been pointed out, for the same reasons that the Italians live in Little Sicily, the Negroes in the black belt, and the Chinese in Chinatowns. The various areas that compose the urban community attract the type of population whose economic status and cultural tradition is more nearly adapted to the physical and social characteristics to be found in each. As each new increment is added to the population it does not at random locate itself just anywhere, but it brings about a resifting of the whole mass of human beings, resulting finally in the anchoring of each to a milieu that, if not most desirable, is at any rate least undesirable.

What is important in this connection is, not where each shall locate, however, but the fact that each seems to find its own separate location without the apparent design of any one. Once in the area, each group tends to reproduce the culture to which it was accustomed in its old habitat as nearly as the new conditions will permit. It is this tendency which is responsible for the abrupt transition in local atmosphere as we sometimes pass from one street to another in the patchwork of little ghettos that constitutes the great immigrant quarters of our large cities.

Unlike the ghettos of old, these new ghettos do not need a wall or gates to keep the various species of man apart.

Each seeks his own habitat much like the plants and animals in the world of nature; each has its own kind of food, of family life, and of amusement.

The physical distance that separates these immigrant areas from that of the natives is at the same time a measure of the social distance between them and a means by which this social distance can be maintained. This does not so much imply mutual hostility as it implies and makes possible mutual tolerance. These segregated areas make it possible for the immigrants to avoid the ancient dictum, "When in Rome, do as the Romans do," and permits them to be themselves. But the price that is paid for this freedom and relaxation is the loss of intimate contact with the other group. Here and there an individual bridges the gulf and does fraternize with the stranger, but he does so at the risk of excommunication from his own group, without the assurance of a welcome reception in the other. And yet it is the occasional adventurer into the camp of the enemy or the stranger who is finally the agent bringing about the fusion of the two.

THE GHETTO AND THE SEGREGATED AREA

The ghetto illustrates another phenomenon in local community life, a phenomenon which underlies also the segregation of vice areas, of bright light centers, of bohemias and hobohemias in modern cities. If we compare the medieval town with the modern urban community we find that the two structures have something fundamental in common, namely, the segregation of the population into distinct classes and vocational groups. This process is essentially a process of competition. Basically it is akin to the competitive co-operation that underlies the plant community. It differs from the plant community in that human beings are more mobile, and through locomotion can seek those areas in which they can most satisfactorily gratify their fundamental interests and wishes.

Just as there was a natural ghetto, a voluntary ghetto, before the ghetto was decreed by law, so vice areas existed before police regulations drove the prostitutes into restricted zones, and just so business centers arose before city planners and zoning ordinances took cognizance of these specializations in the urban economy. And as the ghetto persists long after it has been abolished by law, so the red light district goes on long after a righteously indignant populace assuages its conscience with the conviction that vice has been driven out of town.

This specialization of interests and cultural types is at bottom a phase of the elementary process of the division of labor. Each area in the city is suited for some one function better than for any other. Land values, rentals, accessibility, and the attitude of its inhabitants and owners determine, in the last analysis, what type of area it shall become. The more fundamental of these factors is probably that of economic values, for the sentiments of the people tend ultimately to bow before this criterion which is the expression of the competitive process. Ultimately a city plan or any artificial regulation will be successful only to the extent to which it takes account of these factors and to the extent to which it reckons with the fact that these areas are the product of growth rather than of deliberate design.

Not only does each of these areas have its own external

characteristics in the form of buildings, institutions, and general appearance, but each also has its own moral code. A population seeks an area in which it is tolerated and in which the wishes of its members can be gratified with the least amount of interference. The Bohemian drifts to the Latin Quarter because there he can be himself, express himself with the minimum of restraint. The hobo seeks the main stem, not only because its institutions and standards of living are suited to his personal requirements, but also because here he finds himself and makes his home. The immigrant drifts to the slum without even being aware of the fact that he lives in a slum.

The ghetto furthermore demonstrates the extent to which a local culture is a matter of geographical location. The anthropologists have made us familiar with the concept of the culture area by which they refer to the distribution in space of more or less integrated complexes of material or immaterial cultural traits. The persistence of traditional Jewish life seems to depend upon the favorable soil of the ghetto, upon exclusion from the disintegrating and corroding influences of other cultural areas. Once the individual is removed from the soil to which he and his institutions have been attached, he is exposed to the possibility of losing his character and disappearing as a distinct type. His institutions, too, can ill afford the strain that comes with migration to another locality. That is why the synagogue in the ghetto retains its importance in Jewish communal life which it promptly loses as soon as it migrates to *Deutschland*. Each of these areas has its own distinct types of dominant personalities which change as the local life of the group undergoes transformation. Where the Jew lives is as good an index as any other as to the kind of Jew he is.

THE GHETTO AS A SOCIAL PHENOMENON

If we knew the full life-history of a single individual in his social setting, we would probably know most of what is worth knowing about social life and human nature. If we knew the full story of the ghetto we would have a laboratory specimen for the sociologist that embodies all the concepts and the processes of his professional vocabulary. The institution of the ghetto is not only the record of a historical people; it is a manifestation of human nature and a specific social order.

The ghetto has been viewed in this study primarily as an effect of isolation. The isolation of the Jews has not been merely of a physical sort, but it has been pre-eminently of a less tangible and less visible character. It has been the type of isolation produced by absence of intercommunication through difference in language, customs, sentiments, traditions, and social forms. The ghetto as we have viewed it is not so much a physical fact as it is a state of mind. The isolation of the Jew has been akin to the type of isolation of the person who feels lonely though in the midst of a crowd.

There was a time when students of human nature assumed "that strikingly different customs have been produced by peoples with differing instincts, or with instincts of different degrees of strength or intensity."[1] The Jews, it has been argued by some, are living a separate secluded existence because they are haughty and clannish, and not a sociable people. They lack in the instinct of gregariousness. Fortunately, in the case of the Jews we have a long written history, which leads us to believe that there was a time, at least, when they were not clannish, when they were a people

[1] Ellsworth Faris, "The Nature of Human Nature," *Proceedings of the American Sociological Society*, XXXII, 25.

of many contacts. The attempt that so many Jews of today are making to break into the gentile world seems to be another instance to the contrary. It is probably more correct to say that the Jews became exclusive because at a certain period of their history they were excluded. Another answer would be that they were separate because they had a different cultural life from that of their neighbors.

If students of human nature have learned to be cautious about any one thing more than another in recent years, it is to be cautious about attributing the character of a people and of an individual to human nature without a scrutiny of the historical experiences of the group or the individual. It may be a platitude to say that the Jews are what their history has made them, but it is a platitude worth reiterating.

The Jews owe their survival as a separate and distinct ethnic group to their social isolation. The continuity of their particular social life and their survival as a social type depends primarily upon the continuance of this isolation, just as the distinct character of any people depends upon its exclusion from contacts with other peoples. What made the career of the Jews in European ghettos so adventurous and stormy was not the fact that they were so different from the rest of the population, but that they were so much alike. "Where racial characteristics are marked, and where the social distances that separate the races are great, it sometimes happens that the individual is not discovered at all. Under these circumstances, as Shaler points out, the stranger remains strange, a representative of his race, but not a neighbor."[1] As the Jew leaves the ghetto his type undergoes profound transformation. He changes, not merely his dress, his facial expression, and his bearing, but he generally complete-

[1] Robert E. Park, *ibid.*, p. 136.

ly transforms his consciousness: "In the vast tide of cosmopolitan life the Jewish racial type does not so much disappear as become invisible. When he is no longer seen, anti-Semitism declines. For race prejudice is a function of visibility. The races of high visibility, to speak in naval parlance, are the natural and inevitable objects of race prejudice."[1]

In quite another way the ghetto is able to throw light on a subtle feature of isolation. The ghetto is a cultural community that expresses a common heritage, a store of common traditions and sentiments. The attitudes and sentiments in the consciousness of the Jew, and the institutions and practices in which they find their external expression, have been centered around the religious life of that people. The Jewish culture, to speak in anthropological terms, represents a synagogue complex. The Jewish community of today, like that of the medieval ghetto period, has much in common with the modern sect. "Free intercourse of opposing parties is always a menace to their morale..... The solidarity of the group, like the integrity of the individual, implies a measure at least of isolation from other groups and persons as a necessary condition of its existence."[2] Within the sect, as the ghetto clearly shows, life becomes increasingly a matter of form. Finally the form has to be preserved at all costs, though its content has long ago evaporated.

When the ghetto walls do finally crumble, at least sufficiently to permit the escape of some of the inmates, those that get a taste of the life in the freer world outside and are lured by its color are likely to be torn by the conflicting

[1] *Ibid.*

[2] Park and Burgess, *Introduction to the Science of Sociology* (Chicago, 1924), p. 229.

feeling that comes to hybrids generally, physical as well as social. On the one hand there is the strange and fascinating world of man; on the other, the restricted sectarianism of a little group into which he happened to be born, of neither of which he is fully a member. He oscillates between the two until a decisive incident either throws him headlong into the activities of the outer world, where he forgets his personality and metamorphoses into a new being, or else a rebuff sends him bounding into his old familiar primary group, where life, though puny in scale, is rich and deep and warm.

This same problem is not only encountered by the individuals in their own lifetimes, but it is the problem of succeeding generations in any immigrant group. This accounts for the fact that the immigrant himself scarcely ever is fully assimilated into the new group in his own lifetime, and at the same time is seldom a criminal, but that his children do become assimilated and are at the same time giving rise to problems of disorganization and crime. The ghetto shows that what matters most in social life is not so much the "hard" facts of material existence and external forms as the subtle sentiments, the dreams and the ideals of a people.

What makes the Jewish community—composed, as it is in our metropolitan centers in America, of so many heterogeneous elements—a community is its ability to act corporately. It has a common set of attitudes and values based upon common traditions, similar experiences, and common problems. In spite of its geographical separateness it is welded into a community because of conflict and pressure from without and collective action within. The Jewish community is a cultural community. It is as near an approach to communal life as the modern city has to offer.

The anomalous status of the Jew is based upon the

solidarity of his communal life and his amazing ability to act collectively. It is his historical isolation—it is the ghetto, voluntary or compulsory, medieval or modern, which not only accounts for his character, but for the fantastic conception that others have of him. The history of the Jews and the history of the ghetto are in essence a history of migrations. In the course of these migrations the Jews have developed connections which have crystallized into what seems to be an international organization. As a result the Jew appears to be not merely ubiquitous but something of a mystery. If, therefore, we have not found a solution to the so-called "Jewish problem," is it not possible that in dealing with the ghetto as a natural phenomenon, without offering an apology and without presenting a program, we have made that problem more intelligible?

INDEX OF AUTHORS

SUBJECT INDEX